Israeli Strategies in the Middle East

Ehud Eilam

Israeli Strategies in the Middle East

The Case of Iran

Ehud Eilam
Clinton, MA, USA

ISBN 978-3-030-95601-1   ISBN 978-3-030-95602-8   (eBook)
https://doi.org/10.1007/978-3-030-95602-8

This Palgrave Macmillan imprint is published by the registered company Springer Nature
Switzerland AG
The registered company address is: Gewerbestrasse 11, 6330 Cham, Switzerland

PREFACE

Israel was established in 1948. Its national security policy was focused on the Arab–Israeli conflict.[1] In the last two decades there has been a clear change in Israel's priorities, since Iran and its proxies became Israel's main enemy.

This book analyzes key national security aspects of the Israeli perspective on Iran and its proxies. It examines how Israel, with US assistance, can handle major national security challenges: Iran's nuclear program and Iran's protégés such as Hezbollah.

Iran and Israel were allies, until 1979. Since then Iran sees Israel as its arch enemy. Iranian leaders, including Iran's supreme leader, Ali Khamenei, have been consistent over the years in expressing both their hatred toward Israel and their desire to destroy it. Israel is therefore very worried about the possibility that Iran produces nuclear weapons. Many Arab states, mostly Gulf Arab states, are also very concerned about Iran, due to its regional ambitions. This triangle between Iran, Israel, and some Arab states has various aspects such as willingness by Israel to accept the

---

[1] David Ben Gurion, Uniqueness and Destiny (Tel Aviv: Ministry Of Defense, 1972); Avner Yaniv, Politics and Strategy in Israel (Tel Aviv: Sifriat Poalim, 1994); Israel Tal, National Security (Tel Aviv: Dvir, 1996); Michael L. Handel, Israel's Political-Military Doctrine (Cambridge: Harvard University Press, 1973). Avi Shlaim, The Iron Wall, (Tel Aviv: Ydiot Ahronot 2005). Yossi Alpher, Periphery—Israel's Search for Middle East Allies, (Rowman & Littlefield Publishers, 2015). Kenneth M. Pollack, Arabs at War (University of Nebraska Press, 2004).

sale of advanced US weapon systems to Gulf Arab states. It could be part of a cooperation between Israel and Gulf Arab states against Iran, including if Israel strikes Iran's nuclear sites.

Iran has allies, NSAs (Non-State Actors) such as Hezbollah and Hamas and states such as Syria and Russia. Hezbollah proved its loyalty to Iran, when Hezbollah sent its fighters to assist the Assad regime, during the Syrian civil war. In contrast Hamas refused to do the same, which caused a rift between Hamas and its Iranian patron.

Since 2012 Israel had exploited Assad's low point, due to the Syrian civil war, to launch hundreds of air sorties inside Syria. Those bombardments had destroyed advanced weapons, before they reached Hezbollah in Lebanon. In recent years Israel also attacked Iranian targets in Syria, in an effort to stop Iran from building a base there. Israel had a certain success, but it needs to have an exit strategy from this campaign.

Following the official Russian intervention in Syria, an arrangement was made between Russia and Israel, to allow the latter to continue to bomb Iranian objectives inside Syria. Russia and Iran fought side by side to assist their ally, Assad. However, Russia and Iran have their disputes such as which one will be the dominant force in Syria. Israel can try to turn Russia against Iran.

Hezbollah and Israel fought each other in the 2006 war that ended in a draw. Since then the two sides have been preparing for another war. In such a war Hezbollah might launch tens of thousands of missiles into Israel. The latter will respond by conducting a massive air, land, and sea offensive in Lebanon, aimed at destroying Hezbollah's arsenal, not on seizing any territory. It would be quite a challenge for Israel. However, Israel's biggest concern, has been the process that could lead to the production of an Iranian nuclear weapon. A lot of Israel's attention has been devoted to ways of stopping this process. The IDF (Israel Defense Forces) has been planning to bomb Iran's nuclear sites, mostly by using the IAF (Israeli Air Force).

The United States is quite worried that Iran will produce nuclear weapons. Yet both the Obama and the Trump administrations did not strike Iran's nuclear sites, out of concern it might entangle the United States in another war in the Middle East. The United States could help Israel to prepare for an attack against Iran, but the United States opposes an Israeli strike in Iran, due to its possible ramifications.

On July 14, 2015 an agreement was signed between Iran and the United States and other powers, the JCPOA (The Joint Comprehensive

Plan of Action). It limits Iran's nuclear capabilities. However, in recent years Iran breached the JCPOA. If Iran produces nuclear weapons, Israel and its American patron could try to contain Iran, but they might have different approaches about it.

There is an emphasis in the book about the relevance of past lessons. Some have to do with relations between foreign powers, such as the Cold War between the United States and the Soviet Union, aspects of which could be relevant to Israel, if Iran obtains nuclear weapons.

This book does not provide a main thesis or a theoretical framework. It also does not focus on Iran's point of view. The book provides an in-depth discussion of key national security aspects of the Israeli approach toward Iran and its allies and protégés, in the last decade. The emphasis is on military issues, strategic and operational ones, not on political, economic, and social aspects.

There are very few books that examine the Israeli position on Iran in the last decade, ones that focus on security aspects.[2] Other books only partly deal with this subject.[3] This book seeks to contribute to the discussion on this important subject. The text includes hundreds of endnotes supporting my ideas. The information and references to books, articles, etc., are always incorporated into the text itself, in a way that does not disrupt the flow of reading. The only purpose of the endnote is to reveal the details of the source.

Both my theses for my M.A. and Ph.D. degrees examine Israel's national strategy and military doctrine. I have been involved, academically and practically, with the study of those subjects for more than twenty years. Among other professional activities, I worked for a few years for Israel's Ministry of Defense, as a private contractor in my field of expertise. This book is a completely personal project, and it is not a part of any research I did for the Israeli Ministry of Defense. The book expresses my personal observations, not necessarily representing the opinions of others.

[2] Yoaz Hendel and Yaakov Katz, Israel vs. Iran: the Shadow War (Dulles: Virginia Potomac Books, 2012).

[3] Charles D. Freilich, Israeli National Security, (Oxford University Press, 2018). Trita Parsi, Losing an Enemy, (Yale university press: New Haven, 2017). Michael Oren, Ally, (Random house: New York, 2016).

I have worked on this study in Israel as well as in the United States, where I now reside.

Clinton, MA, USA   Ehud Eilam

CONTENTS

1   Introduction   1

2   Israeli National Security Concerns About Iran   11

3   Could There Be an Israeli–Arab Cooperation Against
    Iran?   33

4   Iran, Hezbollah, and the Palestinians   59

5   How the IDF Prepares to Confront Hezbollah   79

6   Iran and Israel Fight Over Syria   97

7   Israel and the Russian Presence in Syria   125

8   The Relations Between the United States, Israel,
    and Iran   137

9   How the United States Can Help Israel to Bomb
    Iran's Nuclear Sites   169

10 Historical Perspective of the Iranian Challenge   189

11 Conclusion   209

Appendix: North Korea Compared with Iran
          and Hezbollah   215

Glossary   219

Bibliography 221

Index 227

LIST OF MAPS

Map 1.1   Map No. 4102 Rev. 5, November 2011, UNITED
NATIONS https://www.un.org/geospatial/content/
middle-east   xii

Map 2.1   Islamic Republic of Iran, Map No. 3891 Rev. 1, January
2004, UNITED NATIONS https://www.un.org/
geospatial/content/iran-islamic-republic   11

Map 4.1   Lebanon, Map No. 4282, January 2010, UNITED
NATIONS https://www.un.org/geospatial/content/
lebanon   64

Map 6.1   Syria, Map No. 4204 Rev. 3, 1 April 2012, UNITED
NATIONS https://www.un.org/geospatial/content/
syrian-arab-republic   96

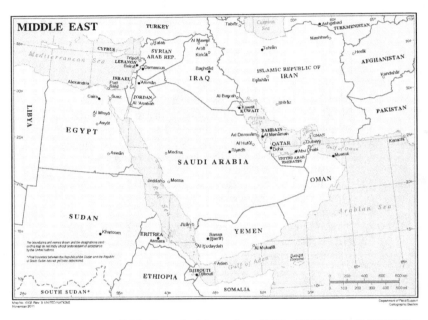

Map 1.1 Map No. 4102 Rev. 5, November 2011, UNITED NATIONS
https://www.un.org/geospatial/content/middle-east

CHAPTER 1

Introduction

This book examines key national security aspects of the Israeli perspective on Iran and its proxies, in the last decade, and the implications on Arab states and the United States. The book explains Israeli concerns in regard to Iran and its allies: Assad, Hezbollah, and Hamas. The book also analyzes how Israel and Gulf Arab states and the United States can work together against Iran (Map 1.1).

CHAPTER 2—ISRAELI NATIONAL SECURITY CONCERNS ABOUT IRAN

In 1979 while Egypt signed a peace treaty with Israel, the new Iranian regime reversed its former ruler's policy and became an enemy of Israel. Iran has not sent its forces to fight Israel, but Iran has been running a proxy war, by supporting Arab groups that collide with Israel.

Gulf Arab states as well as other Arab countries have been openly supporting negotiations with Israel, whereas the Iranian regime strongly opposes this policy, seemingly for the good of the Arabs. The Iranian regime wants to destroy Israel. The latter could tolerate the Iranian regime for lack of a better option. Israel certainly has not been seeking to annihilate Iran as a state, following this the same strategy Israel has been having with hostile Arab rules since 1948.

© The Author(s), under exclusive license to Springer Nature Switzerland AG 2022
E. Eilam, *Israeli Strategies in the Middle East*,
https://doi.org/10.1007/978-3-030-95602-8_1

Iran sees itself as a former and future empire, while Israel has always been a tiny state. The balance of power in terms of the size of population, land, and natural resources, is completely in favor of Iran. Yet, Israel does have nuclear weapons, according to non-Israeli sources.[1] From Iran's perspective if such a small state like Israel has nuclear weapons, clearly Iran must have it too. If Iran produces nuclear weapons, it might not nuke Israel, but forcing it to make concessions that will weaken and perhaps ultimately destroy Israel.

Israel destroyed Iraq's nuclear reactor in 1981. In 2007 Israel annihilated Syria's nuclear reactor. If Israel had bombed Iranian nuclear sites, it would have hoped for the same result in Iran, as in Iraq after 1981 and Syria after 2007, i.e., no rebuilding or proceeding with the nuclear program up to a degree of producing a Bomb. This expectation would be based on the assumption that in the case of Iran there would be outside intervention, such as a Western attack, or internal upheavals such as a mutiny. Either way as in 1981 and 2007, Israel has to bomb in Iran before any collateral damage happening, due to the destruction of an active nuclear reactor. Israel might also try to kill a part of the manpower in the Iranian nuclear sites, which might delay the Iranian nuclear program even more than destroying the infrastructure.

As long as the Arab–Israeli conflict is not over, Israel would not agree to give up its nuclear weapons, as part of a similar deal with Iran. If Iran has nuclear weapons there might be many negative ramifications for Israel, yet the latter could adjust as it has been doing for more than 100 years of struggle against Arabs.

Chapter 3—Could There Be an Israeli–Arab Cooperation Against Iran?

Arab states have been tolerating Israel holding nuclear weapons, without trying to get their own nuclear weapons. However, if Iran has it too, some Arab states such as Saudi Arabia might try to gain nuclear weapons. Arabs might also wish Israel and Iran collide so that two non-Arab states—perceived as threatening to Arabs—are mutually destroyed.

Arab Gulf states, mostly Saudi Arabia and the UAE (United Arab Emirates) might try to prevent Iran from producing nuclear weapons, by allowing Israeli aircraft to cross their countries to attack Iran's nuclear sites. In 1981 and 2007 Israel saved Gulf Arab states the need to deal with Iraq or Syria possessing a nuclear weapon. Israel might have done it again, this time with Iran. The latter might have retaliated against Israel, and Arab Gulf states as well, but the ramifications of retribution against Iran's oil and gas industries might limit its response.

Israel is worried about selling Gulf Arab states advanced weapon systems such as providing the F-35 to the UAE, but there are several factors that can calm Israel. Even if the UAE does not have ties with Israel it is unlikely the UAE will fight Israel. There are also military constraints that can make it difficult for the UAE to strike Israel. Arming the latter could also assist Israel as part of confronting Iran.

Iraq is under strong Iranian influence, but many Iraqis oppose it. Furthermore, some Iraqis, such as Kurds, want to have ties with Israel. Jordan seeks to stay out of an Israeli–Iranian conflict, but Jordan might allow, unofficially, Israeli aircraft to cross the kingdom on their way to Iran. Egypt and Israel cooperate with each other in the security level, such as against ISIS. Egypt can also be a key player, in establishing an anti-Iranian bloc, based on Israel and Arab states.

Chapter 4—Iran, Hezbollah, and the Palestinians

Iran has an alliance with two NSAs bordering Israel–Hamas in the Gaza Strip, in the south of Israel, and the Hezbollah in the north of Israel, in Lebanon. Those protégés fought Israel several times, although it was not always because of Iran. Furthermore the Syrian civil war caused a rift between Iran and the Hamas. For a certain period it left Iran with its Lebanese protégé, but Hezbollah is more powerful and closer to Iran than Hamas and therefore more important to its Iranian patron. Hezbollah has its own challenges such as recovering from its costly involvement in the Syrian civil war and handling the deep economic crisis in Lebanon.

Israel and the PA (Palestinian authority) seek to restrain Hamas in the West Bank. Israel would not allow the pro-Iranian Hamas to take over the West Bank, if the PA collapses. Israel accepts, for lack of a better choice, Hamas rule in the Gaza Strip, in spite of all the clashes they had.

Chapter 5—How the IDF Prepares to Confront Hezbollah

The IDF was used to run high intensity wars, in the years 1948–1982. Since the mid-1980s the IDF had to get ready for such a war against its main enemy, the Syrian military. The latter, following the Syrian civil war, experienced a sharp decline and it is no longer a major threat to Israel. In the same time pro-Iranian NSAs mostly Hezbollah, became stronger.

The IDF outnumbers Hezbollah in the amount of troops and weapon systems. The IDF seeks to gain decisive victory, relying mostly on the IAF to produce massive and accurate firepower. Yet, the IDF needs its ground units too, to be part of the offensive. Its air defense will try to intercept as many rockets as possible. The IDF's new multi-year plan, "Momentum" for 2020–2024 will be the foundation of its buildup, using new technology for training and combat.

The IDF will have to run urban warfare, including underground, inside tunnels. The IDF has been training for that in various ways. Its troops must be familiar with the terrain of Lebanon, so they exercise in similar areas, in the north of Israel. Cooperation between the corps such as infantry and armor is another important factor the IDF has been working on, as part of the preparations to fight Hezbollah. The IDF will also rely on its advanced C4I (Command, Control, Communications, Computers, and Intelligence) network.

CHAPTER 6—IRAN AND ISRAEL FIGHT OVER SYRIA

Syria has been an enemy of Israel since 1948. The alliance between Iran and Syria, which goes back to the early 1980s, made the Assad regime part of the Iranian–Israeli conflict. Yet, it was the Syrian civil war that started in 2010 that actually created a new battlefield between Israel and Iran. The chaos in Syria, following the civil war there, gave Israel an opportunity, although not one without risks, to reduce the amount of advanced weapons that were sent from Syria to Hezbollah. Since 2012 the IAF had bombed inside Syria weapons such as long-range and antiaircraft missiles. Israel also tries to prevent and at least to slow down the establishment of an Iranian base in Syria. The fight over Syria plays a significant part of Israel's "campaign between the wars."

Iran helped to save the Assad regime, but Assad might have not intervened in a clash between Israel and Iran, wishing to avoid a massive Israeli retaliation. The IDF might have threatened the survival of the Syrian regime, a constraint that Iran might have understood, and perhaps would have not wanted to risk losing Assad after all its investment in him. All that could have led to a compromise about reducing the scale of Assad's contribution to Iran's war against Israel.

Iran wants to get back at least some of the tens of billions of dollars Iran invested in Syria. It might not be easy for Assad to pay back its debt, since Syria is almost a failed state. Iran can hope to gain from the reconstruction of Syria, but many states and companies don't want to invest in Syria, due to their hostility toward Assad, lack of stability in Syria and fear of US sanctions. Nevertheless, Iran continues to pour money into Syria, at the expense of the Iranian people, which causes resentment in Iran. It might be one of the factors that would eventually bring down the Iranian regime. In that sense Israel can benefit from letting Iran allocate resources to Syria.

CHAPTER 7—ISRAEL AND THE RUSSIAN PRESENCE IN SYRIA

Russia, Iran, and Hezbollah formed a coalition in Syria during the civil war there, which kept Assad in power. While Hezbollah and its Iranian patron are against Israel Russia has reasonably good relations with Israel. The two states have reached an understanding about the Israeli strikes inside Syria. During one of the Israeli air bombardments, on September 18, 2018, the Syrian air defense shot down a Russian reconnaissance plane, killing 14 Russian crew members who were on board. It created a crisis between Israel and Russia. They managed to keep their coordination, but the Russian presence has been a serious constraint for Israel, in attacking targets inside Syria. The Israeli nightmare has been a clash between Israel and Russia, which would serve Iran. The Israeli hope is to mobilize Russia to reduce and maybe even to get rid of the Iranian military presence in Syria. Russia and Iran remain partners, they both support Assad, but they do have major disagreements such as on which is the dominant power in Syria. Israel can use it against Iran.

CHAPTER 8—THE RELATIONS BETWEEN THE UNITED STATES, ISRAEL, AND IRAN

The United States and Iran have been foes since 1979. Iran helped insurgents fight against the United States in both Iraq and Afghanistan. Those wars, in two countries close to Iran, were like the first stage of a land campaign in which Iran was striving to prevent an actual invasion into its territory. Another issue that could have led to a war between the United

States and Iran, was the latter's desire to gain nuclear weapons. Iran could have been attacked by the United States for other reasons as well, blocking the straits of Hormuz, for example. During such a confrontation the United States could have bombed Iran's nuclear sites as well. However, from an American perspective, the overall cost of the wars in both Iraq and Afghanistan ruled out an offensive against Iran. The United States did not want to face fighting on a giant front starting from Afghanistan through Iran, and into the Gulf and Iraq, and even all the way to the Levant. Therefore both the Obama and the Trump administrations did not strike Iran's nuclear sites. Instead they used sanctions. The Obama administration also managed to negotiate with Iran about the latter's nuclear program, which led to an agreement that was signed on July 14, 2015.

If Iran has nuclear weapons, the United States might try, along with its allies such as Israel, to contain and wear down Iran by sanctions and an arms race. A coordinated and effective effort might eventually cause Iran to invest so much in its military, at the expense of its economy and society that a revolution breaks out there. But the United States might lead from behind, i.e., let others, including Israel, deal with Iran and its nuclear weapons. This would force Israel to rethink its nuclear policy, and probably declare it has nuclear weapons. Israel might seek to keep Iran away from Israel, while hoping to push Iran to be more involved in the Caucasus and central Asia. Iran might assume there are more chances and fewer risks in such a shift.

CHAPTER 9—HOW THE UNITED STATES CAN HELP ISRAEL TO BOMB IRAN'S NUCLEAR SITES

Israel might have bombed Iran's nuclear sites. The IAF might have run into difficulties in cracking the natural and/or artificial protection of some Iranian nuclear sites. The United States could have given Israel the MOP (Massive Ordnance Penetrator), a huge bomb, and also the B-52 to carry it. Having such impressive capabilities might have deterred Iran from trying to produce nuclear weapons, since Israel can then destroy Iran's nuclear facilities.

During a raid in Iran some of Israel's air crews might have been forced to abandon their aircraft in case of trouble. The Israelis would have tried to avoid parachuting into Iran, or into its allies' countries like Iraq and Syria. In Iraq, the United States would have probably not managed to help much in preventing the local government from turning Israeli air crews to the Iranians. The United States could have helped more in other states, like Jordan and in the Gulf. The biggest test in this matter might have been if Israeli air crews had landed in the Gulf waters, near an American force, with Iranian boats trying to capture them. The American troops would have had to decide whether they could rescue the Israelis, without clashing with the Iranians or risk a crisis which in the worst case could turn into a war between Iran and the United States.

Even if Israel had concluded that the United States might not assist it to attack Iran, Israel had to consider when to notify its American patron about the Israeli raid. Such a consideration had to take into account that upon being informed, the American forces around Iran, in the Gulf, etc., would immediately go into high alert, which in turn would almost certainly warn Iran that an attack on it is imminent.

The United States might have collaborated with Arab Gulf states in an offensive against Iran. Israel would have probably been asked to stay out of it, in order not to undermine the anti-Iranian coalition. If subsequently the pro-Iranian Hezbollah had confronted Israel, Iran might have tried to connect that clash with the war against Iran, assuming Arab states would leave the anti-Iranian coalition, not to seem fighting with Israel against Muslims, including Arabs, i.e., Hezbollah. Arab states like Saudi Arabia oppose Hezbollah, and they would have wanted Israel to destroy this Shiite organization. However, the United States and its Arab allies might have tried to show they distinguish between their fight against Iran and the one between Israel and Hezbollah.

CHAPTER 10—HISTORICAL PERSPECTIVE OF THE IRANIAN CHALLENGE

If Iran produces nuclear weapons, its conflict with Israel may resemble the balance of terror between the United States and the Soviet Union during the Cold War.

Iran, as the Soviet Union was, is much bigger than its foe, i.e., Israel, but Iran's main population centers and industries are vulnerable, and its leadership might not want to pay an unbearable cost for destroying its enemy. Israel has been developing second strike capability, just as the United States did. Israel could launch a nuclear attack by sea, air, and land, but it might be very limited because of Israel's budgets constraints. Israel's weapon systems, carrying nuclear weapons, would also be exposed, due to few harbors and quite a small number of airfields the IDF has.

If Iran deploys nuclear weapons in a state near Israel, such as Lebanon, a dangerous situation may rise, similar to the missile crisis in Cuba in 1962, which almost ended in a nuclear war. Even without such an event, the relatively short distance between Israel and Iran allows them to launch a surprise attack, with missiles or aircraft, as Soviet and American submarines could have done. In the Middle East in particular, because the enemy is so near, Israel and/or Iran might be both attacking and absorbing a hit at a very short notice. It would be a nuclear knife fight. This is why deterrence is so important, as it was between the two superpowers.

A conventional war in Europe between the United States and the Soviet Union, might have bought time for talks, aiming at preventing a nuclear catastrophe, but the battles could have also deteriorated into a mutual exchange of nuclear strikes, due to the threat to Western Europe. A conventional war between Israel and Iran might be used to gain time to reach an understanding that would prevent an escalation to a nuclear showdown, as it were with the superpowers in the Cold War. Furthermore, a conventional war between the IDF and Iranian proxies should not escalate into a nuclear war, because of lack of an existential threat to Israel. Nevertheless, ending a nuclear crisis between Israel and Iran would be more difficult than in the Cold War, since Israel and Iran don't have the measures the United States and the Soviet Union had namely diplomatic ties, a hotline, etc. Israel and Iran might agree on a broker, a state that has relationships with both of them, Russia or India, but this would be a problematic solution.

If the United States had absorbed a Soviet massive nuclear attack, it would have recovered not only because of its size and basic strength, but also because the Soviet Union, having also been hit by a major nuclear offensive, could not have invaded American mainland. Israel is much smaller and weaker than the United States. Although Iran could not invade Israel, Arabs might exploit Israel's low point, if the latter is almost helpless following a nuclear war. Arabs might force Israel to make huge concessions and even try to destroy it.

Iran resembles Israel's former enemy, Egypt, in the 1956 war, when Israel needed Western military assistance, from France and Britain, to protect its rear from Egyptian bombers. In several exercises in the last decade US forces trained with the IDF in defending Israel from missiles, in case of a war against Iran. In addition, in 1956 Israel wished to slow down the Egyptian military buildup, while in recent years Israel has been striving to stop or at least to delay the production of an Iranian nuclear weapon.

The friction between Israel and Iran has a linkage to the 1967 war too. On the eve of that war, many Israelis believed they face a mortal threat from Arab militaries, particularly the Egyptian one. If Iran produces a nuclear weapon, many Israelis will feel the same. In 1967 Israel would have tolerated an Egyptian military presence in Sinai, but not a massive one. Similarly, Israel might accept an Iranian nuclear project if it is not aimed at producing nuclear weapons. As it was with the potential of Egypt's armed forces in 1967, Iran's nuclear capabilities are not completely obvious either. Israel might give Western powers an opportunity to resolve the problem with Iran diplomatically, as it did with Egypt in 1967, but eventually Israel could decide it must strike. Militarily Israel could have gained tactical surprise in Iran, as it did in Egypt in 1967, in spite of it being at a time of great tension, when the other side was on alert.

Iran is not a new version of the Third Reich, although there is a certain resemblance between Iran and the Third Reich. They are both dictatorships that suppress their population, including persecuting and killing gay people. Iran and the Third Reich are also an example for a regional power wishing to take over their neighboring states. As the Third Reich in the 1930s, Iran has been expanding its grip on other countries, without starting an official war and without any of the Western powers willing to stop it, by force if necessary. Furthermore, world powers had to prevent Iran from getting nuclear weapon capability, just as they had to stop the rearming of the Third Reich in the 1930s. In the Second World War the German military was a weapon of mass destruction that killed millions, similar to what Iran could do, if it has nuclear weapons. The Third Reich also wished to avoid an exhausting showdown like the First World War, while Iran would also shy from a highly costly collision like the Iran–Iraq war in the 1980s.

Israel is concerned Iran could jeopardize Israel, the home of more than six million Israeli Jews, a little more than the number of Jews who were annihilated by the Third Reich. Iran has methodically been demonizing Israel because of ideological and political reasons, as the Third Reich did with Jews. The Third Reich took from the Jews their basic rights. Iran opposes Israel's right to exist. The Third Reich first sought to kick out the Jews from its territories and eventually mass murdered them, using gas. Iran too might reach the conclusion it has no choice but to annihilate the Israeli Jews with its unconventional weapons. In Israel today, there are still some Holocaust survivors, and many families related to them, as well as to those who did not survive. They, like other Israelis, have been debating to what extent Iran is a clear and present danger to Israel. As with the Holocaust in the 1930s, when many Jews did not believe in a coming catastrophe, a massive Iranian nuclear attack on Israel might seem unlikely, but it could happen.

NOTE

1. On the Israeli Bomb see: Avner Cohen, *The Last Taboo* (Or Yehuda: Kinneret, Zmora—Bitan, Dvir, 2005). Shlaomo Aronson, *Nuclear Weapons in the Middle East* (Jerusalem: Akademon, 1995).

CHAPTER 2

Israeli National Security Concerns About Iran

Map 2.1 Islamic Republic of Iran, Map No. 3891 Rev. 1, January 2004, UNITED NATIONS https://www.un.org/geospatial/content/iran-islamic-rep ublic

E. Eilam, *Israeli Strategies in the Middle East*, https://doi.org/10.1007/978-3-030-95602-8_2

11

Israel and Iran were partners until 1979. Since then Iran has been considering Israel to be a sworn enemy, which should be destroyed. This goal, and Iran's desire to produce nuclear weapons, has been Israel's most important national security concern in the last decade. If Iran has nuclear weapons Iran's leaders might be driven to prove their commitment to destroy Israel or at least to use Iran's nuclear might to put huge pressure on Israel in order to undermine it. Therefore Israel, as a last resort, might attack Iran's nuclear sites, before the latter obtains nuclear weapons. Another possibility is that Israel would have to accept Iran has nuclear weapons, with the negative consequences of such a reality.

Iran's Approach Toward Israel

From the 1950s to the late 1970s there were productive relationships between Israel and Iran. They had joint projects including military ones.[1] In the 1950s and 1960s the Shah of Iran considered Israel as a state that could help him block the momentum of Gamal Abdel Nasser, the ruler of Egypt.[2] It seems unlikely that Israel and Iran would have fought together in a high intensity war against Egypt and its allies, their common enemies. Yet, a kind of alliance between Iran and Israel might have made it more difficult for Arab states such as Egypt to concentrate efforts against Iran or Israel (Map 2.1).

Iran started to turn in favor of the Arabs after the 1973 war, which revealed Israel's weakness[3] that stood in contrast to Israel's convincing victory in 1967. Iran evaluated Israel according to its achievements in the battlefield, gained against their mutual foe—Arab states such as Egypt. Consequently, the Iranian–Israeli relations might have declined in the 1970s even without the revolution of 1979. There was some cooperation between them even after 1979, but the nature of their relations had clearly changed.[4]

Iran does not support the Arab peace initiative. Iran has been stuck in the famous "Three No's" of the Arab summit in Khartoum in 1967, the refuse to sign peace, talk, or recognize Israel.[5] Meir Litvak claimed that the hate toward Israel became a major component in Iran's foreign policy.[6] Iran's supreme leader, Ali Khamenei, said on November 8, 2014, Israel "has no cure but to be annihilated."[7] Iran's IRGC (Islamic Revolutionary Guard Corps) is the military backbone of the regime. One of its top commanders, Brigadier General Mohsen Kazzemeini, said in early

September 2015 that Iran "would continue enhancing its preparedness until it overthrows Israel."[8]

On September 23, 2016, Mohammad Javad Zarif Iran's Minister of Foreign Affairs, said in regard to Iran's policy toward Israel that "we say it very clearly, publicly and without any qualification that Iran will never use force against any other entity in the world."[9] It was a pale attempt to present Iran as moderate, although the Iranian hostility toward Israel has been very clear. On December 12, 2016, the Iranian Defense Minister Hossein Dehghan threatened to destroy Israel.[10] There are other voices in Iran, more moderate ones, but the regime is clearly against Israel.

On December 13, 2017, the leaders of the member states of the Organization of Islamic Cooperation (OIC), which includes Iran, agreed to reaffirm their commitment to "just and comprehensive -peace based on the two-state solution."[11] Yet, Iran continued to openly support the destruction of Israel, even after Israeli leaders expressed their willingness to accept a Palestinian state.

The tension between Israel and Iran continued in 2018.[12] In November 2019 "calling for the elimination of the state of Israel does not mean the elimination of the Jewish people," Khamenei explained.[13] On May 7, 2021, Khamenei called Israel "not a country, but a terrorist base."[14] Iran has therefore been consistent in its effort to delegitimize Israel's right to exist.

Raz Zimmt explained in August 2021 that the new Iranian President, Ebrahim Raisi, "intends to adopt a tougher line in both internal affairs and foreign policy."[15] It means the conflict between Israel and Iran and its proxies might escalate. Raisi's hard-line aggressive approach might serve Israel, if it urges other states, in the region and outside it, to cooperate with each other against Iran. Inside Iran suppressing might eventually backfire, causing unrest that might undermine the regime.

Avi Primor claimed that Iran strives "for hegemony over the Islamic world."[16] Iran, in other names of course, has been around for thousands of years, sometimes as a vast empire, which included territories now occupied by Israel and Arab states. Therefore Iran assumes it carries much more historical and strategic weight. Arabs also used to be a dominant power in the region, and had in the past conquered what is now Iran, but Jews don't have such a record, even at the peak of their expansion in ancient times. It helps Iran to feel superior to Israel.

Kenneth Pollack mentioned that Iran believes it is superior to nations around it, such as the Turks and Arabs.[17] Iran may conclude it could accomplish what Arabs could not, i.e., beat Israel. The Arab–Israeli conflict has been going on for more than 100 years. During that time there were numerous violent collisions, from minor skirmishes to full-scale wars. After struggling for such a long period, many in both Israel and in the Arab world recognize their mutual failure in forcing their will on the other side. The Iranian–Israeli conflict has been going on for about forty years, as a cold war. It has never deteriorated into a full-blown war, in spite of mutual covert operations and clashes between Israel and pro-Iranian organizations such as Hezbollah and Hamas. (During the last decade and a half Israel got entangled in the 2006 war and in confrontations against the Palestinians in 2008–2009 and in 2014.) All those collisions between Israel and Arabs had mixed results that might have bolstered Iran's assumption that they can gain the upper hand, and encouraged their determination to challenge Israel.

"Iran's economy is characterized by its hydrocarbon, agricultural, and service sectors, as well as a noticeable state presence in the manu-facturing and financial services....Economic activity and government revenues still rely on oil revenues and have, therefore, been volatile." The Covid-19 pandemic "severely affected jobs and income in many labor-intensive activities, including high-contact services and the informal sector....Inflationary pressures also increased in 2020/2021, as the Iranian rial depreciated due to a limited supply of foreign exchange and heightened economic uncertainty... the currency has lost half of its value because of US sanctions placed on accessing reserves abroad."[18] In 2021 "Iran's GDP is $191 billion while Israel's is almost $400b... Israel's current GDP per capita is almost 20 times that of Iran, at $43,000 compared to $2200 in Iran."[19] At the military level, the IDF is known to be as highly effective while Iran's armed forces, both the IRGC and the regular military, are considered to be quite weak militarily.[20]

Nevertheless, the balance of power between Israel and Iran has been clearly in favor of the latter in terms of the size of the territory, amount of population, and natural resources. Israel's territory is around 22,000 sq. km. Iran's territory is almost 1,650,000 sq. km. Israel has almost nine million people. Iran has around 83 million people. Israel has some natural gas, but no oil, while Iran has one of the biggest natural gas and oil reserves in the world. Those huge gaps between Israel and Iran could help Iran to overcome its current weakness, and to present Israel with quite a challenge.

ISRAEL'S PERSPECTIVE

There are many Arab states that—similar to Iran—do not have a border with Israel. The extent of their involvement in the Arab–Israeli conflict differed from one state to another. None of those Arab states was any kind of ally of Israel, as Iran was until 1979, later to become a sworn enemy. Iran did not imitate Arab states far from Israel like Iraq that sent expeditionary forces to fight Israel almost in any high intensity war. However, since 1979 there was only one high intensity war between Arabs and Israel, in 1982, when Iran was occupied with its showdown against Iraq.

Some Arab states that don't have a border with Israel and never signed a peace treaty with Israel, served as brokers between Israel and Arabs. A case in point is Morocco, the troops of which fought inside Syria against the IDF in 1973. Yet Morocco also helped several times to negotiate between Israel and Arabs. In December 2020 it was announced Morocco will normalize its relations with Israel. Iran could have likewise turned from foe to mediator between Israel and Arabs.

Iran is a non-Arab state like Israel, but Muslim like the Arabs, and that could have helped reach a peace agreement, just as Turkey tried to do in 2008 with Syria and Israel. The political and security ties between Israel and Turkey that used to be quite tight have deteriorated in recent years, but are still far from resembling the hostility between Israel and Iran. Turkey also used to be an Israeli partner against Iran. Turkey still sees Iran as a rival, they both compete for regional hegemony. On the other hand Iran and Turkey cooperate with each other in several fields. They have a common enemy, Kurds, who seek to establish a state in Iraq and/or Syria.

Iran has a cold war with other Muslim states like Saudi Arabia. Israel has been an easier target since it is non-Muslim, which serves Iran's ambitions in increasing its influence in the Arab world, and as an excuse to suppress opposition at home. Those reasons have been known tactics of Arab regimes as well, such as the one in Syria. The struggle against Israel is therefore for Iran, as for many Arabs, both an aim and a way to reach other goals, not less important.

Iran and Israel are regional powers having around them what they see as their spheres of influence: only Arab territory as far as Israel goes, while from Iran's point of view non-Arab neighbors too. Israel has concentrated on countries and territories around it, i.e., in the Levant, while Iran has been spreading all over the region, including the Levant. This action causes friction between Israel and Iran, mostly with regard to Lebanon, Syria, and the Gaza Strip.

Iran does not necessarily seek to conquer other states it just wants a pro-Iranian regime there.[21] Iran might tolerate Arab states like Syria, Iraq and Lebanon having Arab rulers as long as they are under Iranian influence. As for Israel, Iran does not seek regime change in Israel, and does not want a pro-Iranian Jewish government, be it what it may. Iran strives to wipe out Israel altogether, and have there an Arab pro-Iranian government.

Israel has no wish to destroy Iran or unfriendly Arab states. As to regime change, Israel could bear an Iranian radical and hostile government, for lack of better option. Israel implemented the same approach toward Arab foes that did not recognize Israel and strove to annihilate it. On the other hand, Israel sometimes sought—in a way like Iran—to have pro-Israeli rulers in Arab states, or at least ones less aggressive toward Israel. The latter hoped in the 1950s and 1960s that one of the results of the wars against Egypt would be the downfall of Nasser, a goal that was never realized. Israel—as Iran—was also willing to use force to keep a friendly Arab regime in power. Israel did it in a certain way in 1970 in Jordan, when it assisted King Hussein to survive a fierce internal fight.[22] In another case, in Lebanon, Israel in 1982 and Iran ever since, have been trying to control that country with their protégés. In 1982 it was part of a plan, based on Israel's allies at the time, Lebanese Christians. That plan eventually failed. Israel did the mistake of relying too much on its Arab partners. The latter wanted Israel to do almost all the work by itself.[23]

Since Israel was established up at least until the 1990s, its top security concern was to handle a massive Arab offensive that in the worst case could put at risk the survival of the state. In recent decades there has been much less probability of a major Arab invasion. Yet, for some Israelis the memories of the Syrian and Egyptian attack in 1973 is still quite strong. Iran has its trauma from an Arab invasion, the Iraqi one in 1980. In spite of the decades that passed from those Arab attacks in both Iran and Israel, it is a significant part of their national experience.

Maj. Gen. Tal Kalman, who heads the IDF's Iran Directorate, emphasized in March 2021 that Israel lacks a synchronized approach toward Iran. Therefore there has been an effort in this matter, which included bodies such as "Mossad, the Foreign Ministry, the Atomic Energy Commission."[24] It was a severe blunder that in 2021 Israel still did not have a well-coordinated strategy, despite its long conflict with Iran.

THE NUCLEAR ASPECT

The Iranian nuclear project that in the 1980s was aimed against Iraq, reached its peak not only when Iraq was no longer a threat to Iran, but ironically when Iraq was a kind of an Iranian protégé. Egypt, another major Arab state that could have challenged Iran, ran into a low point following its huge economic problems. There is no Arab state that poses a threat to Iran let alone one that might invade Iran. The Iranian regime strives to have nuclear weapons for defensive purposes such as to prevent the US attempt to topple it. Yet Iran can also use nuclear weapons as part of its aggressive foreign policy, including against Israel. Many in Iran support the nuclear project. However, the Iranian effort in this matter has a giant cost and it puts Iran in danger.

Iranian Defense Minister Brig. Gen. Hossein Dehqan said in late May 2014 that Iran asks its "nuclear negotiators to focus their utmost efforts on the complete annihilation of the Zionist regime's nuclear, chemical and biological weapons as the biggest danger posed to the region."[25] For Iran it is a certain humiliation that an enemy like Israel possesses nuclear weapons, while Iran does not, considering Iran's overall superiority over Israel, in strategic terms and in the way Iran looks down on Israel. Some Arabs too have been frustrated because of the same factors. Israel does not admit possessing nuclear weapons, although non-Israeli sources, not only Iranian ones, claim Israel has the Bomb.

According to Louis Rene' Beres "Israel, it would seem, may resort to nuclear weapons only as a reprisal, and only in response to over-whelmingly destructive first-strike attacks."[26] Israel certainly never used its nuclear edge to force Arabs to accept its terms. Arab states such as Syria in the 1973 and 1982 wars were willing to confront Israel, assuming correctly that Israel would put at risk its conventional units and would not depend on its nuclear weapons. In spite of Israel's sensitivity to casualties, it sent its troops in harm's way over and over again, rather than threaten its foe, directly or not, with nuclear weapons. For Israel the nuclear option stays as the very last resort. On such a critical issue, however, Iran might not rely on this assumption, and would easily suspect Israel could change its approach. Israel might demand, officially or not, that Iran makes tough concessions in favor of Israel. Obtaining nuclear weapons would give Iran the best guarantee against such an Israeli maneuver.

In 2014 "Egypt, Israel, and Syria have the technology base for manu-facturing chemical weapons. Iran is a self-declared chemical weapons power, but has never declared its inventory. Syria was known to have large stocks of a variety of chemical weapons in 2013, including bombs and chemical warheads for its missiles." In addition "Egypt, Israel, Jordan and Syria each had the technology base to manufacture first and second generation biological weapons, but no reliable data existed to prove any were doing so."[27]

Although Iran has CW (chemical weapons) it might not be enough for Iran.[28] Matthew Kroenig claimed in 2014 that "Iran has in fact made a final decision to build nuclear weapons if at all possible."[29] In early June 2015, a report by the Pentagon claimed that Iran "continues to develop technological capabilities that could also be applicable to nuclear weapons, including ballistic missile development."[30] On July 14, 2015 the JCPOA was signed, which contained and restrained Iran's nuclear program. However, in recent years Iran breached the JCPOA, and came closer to produce nuclear weapons.

COVERT OPERATIONS AND ASSASSINATIONS

In mid-2020 Israel was accused of an explosion that occurred in the Natanz nuclear facility. According to Raz Zimmt this attack caused "a significant delay in Iran's ability to assemble the advanced centrifuges capable of producing enriched uranium."[31] Israel could continue with its covert operations, as the ones it carried out in recent years. In late June 2021 Israel's Prime Minister Naftali Bennett "appeared to hint at Israel's role" in this matter. Israel does it by relying on its highly developed Cyber and intelligence capabilities. It could be used against Iran's nuclear program, and also against other targets, such as Iran's economy.[32]

Gerald Bull was a scientist who planned to build for Iraq a supergun, capable of firing at Israel huge shells, each one weighing two tons. The project failed after Bull was assassinated on March 22, 1990, probably by Israel.[33] In 2010–2012 several Iranian nuclear scientists were assassinated. On November 27, 2020, Mohsen Fakhrizadeh, the mastermind of Iran's nuclear program, was killed.[34] Israel was blamed for all those strikes. While with the Iraqi supergun the entire program collapsed after one assassination, in Iran several assassinations did not end the nuclear program. Therefore this method together with other covert actions, including cyber warfare, might not be enough to stop Iran from producing nuclear weapons. It might leave Israel with no choice but to conduct a large-scale raid.

An Israeli Attack on Iran's Nuclear Sites

In late January 2021 Lieutenant-General Kohavi (Chief of General Staff of the IDF) claimed that he has instructed the IDF "to prepare a number of operational plans, in addition to those already in place," in regard to Iran.[35] Israeli Prime Minister Benjamin Netanyahu warned several times over the years that Israel would not let Iran produce nuclear weapons. On March 5, 2021, Israel's Defense Minister Benny Gantz said that if the international community does not stop Iran Israel "must stand independently, and we must defend ourselves by ourselves."[36] On September 27, 2021, Israeli Prime Minister Naftali Bennett emphasized Israel "will not allow Iran to acquire a nuclear weapon."[37] On October 12, 2021, Israeli Foreign Minister Yair Lapid said Israel "reserves the right" to take action against Iran.[38] There are senior officials in both the Israeli government and in the IDF who hold a more moderate position, with all their deep concern about Iran's nuclear program. Overall eventually there might be a decision in Israel to bomb Iran's nuclear sites, as a last resort.

In October 2021 "Israel has approved a budget of some 5 billion shekels ($1.5 billion)" for making the IDF ready to strike Iran's nuclear sites. The funds would serve "for various types of aircraft, intelligence-gathering drones and unique armaments needed for such an attack."[39] In October 2021 it might take the IAF more than a year to complete its attack plans.[40] Israel took similar steps before, but they were neglected, so in 2021 Israel was required to invest again in the matter, in order to keep its military capabilities up to date. Considering how crucial that task is, the IAF needs to be able to accomplish the mission in its first attempt, which requires proper preparations.

In the times of the Shah Israel assisted Iran's nuclear program. In this sense Israel wants to put an end to what it helped to start. Israel has been striving to prevent Iran from having nuclear weapon capability, if necessary by force, as Israel did with Arab states in 1981 and 2007.[41] In contrast to the Israeli raids in 1981 and 2007 in Iraq and Syria, Iran has nuclear facilities that are well-protected from air strikes because of their artificial and/or natural shield. In Iraq in 1981 and in Syria in 2007 there was one single nuclear reactor. Iran has many nuclear sites and some might be unknown to Israel, in a way it was with the Syrian CW program. For Israel annihilating all and even just the most important Iranian nuclear sites, in one major strike, would have been a tall order. Yet Israel might attack Iran, if the latter tries to produce nuclear weapons.

In Syria in 2007 it was easier as that country is much closer to Israel than Iran, which helped Israel collect intelligence before the raid, destroy its objective, conduct damage assessment, and send off more rounds if necessary. Syria, due to its border with Israel, could have retaliated on a bigger scale than Iran and the Hezbollah combined. In 2007, i.e., before the civil war, the Syrian military could have certainly concentrated more firepower against Israel than the Hezbollah and Iran, if Israel had attacked Iran. However, this worked both ways, since the proximity to Syria allowed the IDF to launch a massive attack in response. At the same time of the raid in Syria, the IDF conducted a vast exercise in the Golan Heights, without calling in reserves, as a cautious move in case of a Syrian attack, and also as a way to deter Assad from retribution, let alone starting a war. It was a huge gamble that paid off.

The IAF would attack Iran with its F-15I and F-16I, which to begin with were assimilated in order to improve the IAF's ability to strike far away from Israel. The spearhead of the raid might be the F-35. Iran has been strengthening its air defense, such as by assimilating the S-300 batteries. It could be suppressed with Israel's F-35, due to the advanced capabilities of this highly sophisticated aircraft.

In 1981, Israel had to bomb the Iraqi reactor before its destruction spread radioactive pollution, causing thousands of casualties.[42] In Iran it seems unlikely that attacking its nuclear sites would cause much ecological damage to the Iranian population.[43] Israel must avoid releasing hazardous material, which could be a kind of a "dirty bomb," in the worst case scenario.

Many Iranians working on the nuclear project are in danger, when they are together in one place. The IDF could storm Iranian nuclear sites, while the employees are inside them. Iranian nuclear facilities are military objectives, as far as Israel is concerned, and the workers there are not just ordinary civilians. Those Iranians have to be aware of the risk they take. Damaged equipment and destroyed nuclear sites can be replaced and rebuilt much faster than training new and skilled work force.

Following the Strike

If Israel had attacked Iran, the latter might have rehabilitated its nuclear sites, but then the IAF might have struck them again. Israel might have done it after a few months or years, according to the progress of the rebuilding in Iran. The IAF had a kind of similar experience in 1969–1970, during the war of attrition against Egypt. Then the IAF had to bomb over and over again in the west bank of the Suez Canal, to slow down the recreating of infrastructure for Egyptian antiaircraft batteries. The IAF eventually failed in stopping the Egyptian deployment. Egypt refused to give up and it also received massive Soviet support, which enabled it to continue to fight.[44]

There are up to 15,000 Jews in Iran,[45] the largest Jewish community in the Middle East, outside Israel. If Israel attacks Iran the local Jews there might be in danger, not only from Israeli bombardments but mostly due to retribution by the Iranian government and/or its people. Iran might blame its Jews for supporting Israel even if it is not true at all, but represents a kind of blood libel. The Iranian government that implemented tough, brutal, and lethal measures against Iranian Muslims, like those who protested in 2019–2020, might not spare its country's Jews. The Iranian rule may avoid a direct action against the Jews, but could incite its population to assault Jews. That would be particularly expected in case Iran absorbs heavy casualties and damages, while failing to make Israel pay a similar price.

After Israel destroyed the Iraqi nuclear reactor in 1981 its assumption was that it would take Iraq three years to repair the damages. Israel did not bomb the Iraqi infrastructure again after 1981. Up to 1988 Iraq was busy in surviving its eight years war with Iran, which made it difficult for Saddam Hussein to focus on Israel, but did not prevent Iraq from investing in its nuclear program. The 1991 war, the efforts of UNSCOM that followed it and the western bombardments in 1998, inflicted a major blow to Iraq's unconventional project. By 2003 Iraq gave up in this matter.[46]

Syria's nuclear reactor was destroyed in 2007. Israel bombed Syria again after that, but only in 2013, and then the targets were not nuclear sites. Until 2011 Syria was not involved in any war and was free to retaliate, but avoided that because of Israeli deterrence. Since 2011 the civil war kept Assad occupied with the rebels who served Israel's interest by preventing Assad from focusing on renewing its nuclear weapon program.

In a way as with disrupting Iraq's nuclear project in the 1990s, Israel got help from others. In Syria's case it was from another enemy of Israel.

Israel might hope that, with or without an Israeli strike, as in Iraq in 1991, Iran too would be entangled in a war with Western powers that would bring the UN to disarm Iran's nuclear program. Another model is the Syrian one, an internal outburst that would postpone the rebuilding of the Iranian nuclear project.

ISRAELI CONCERNS, IN CASE
IRAN HAS NUCLEAR WEAPONS

Israel might eventually not attack Iran or the raid would fail. In such a case Israel might have to accept that Iran has nuclear weapons. Over the years Israel had to deal with various threats such as the wave of suicide bombers all over the country, during the confrontation with the Palestinians in 2000–2005. In spite of all the dangers, Israelis went on with their lives. Iran with a nuclear weapon might be seen by many in Israel as a faraway threat, never to be realized. On the other hand, Iranian nuclear weapons might also be looked at by many in Israel as a clear and present danger, similar to a suicide bomber striking any time any place, only with enormously more effect.

For Arabs the 2006 war proved there is a military option against Israel, i.e., the massive use of rockets against Israeli targets.[47] Those projectiles are a serious national security problem for Israel, albeit a conventional one. An Iranian nuclear weapon would be much more dangerous. Some Israeli objectives would be less exposed, like small and remote towns. But in Israel that has about 22,000 sq. km, places that are completely safe are rare, particularly if Iran has enough nuclear weapons to drop all over Israel. There is an old Israeli phrase "all the country is a front, all the population is in the military." At least the first part of this sentence is rather true, as far as the threat from conventional rockets and missiles goes, and it would also be quite relevant if Iran has nuclear weapons.

In the 1948–1949 war there were about 600,000 Jews in Israel. In the last major Arab–Israeli war, in 1973, there were almost three million Jews in Israel. Now there are almost seven million there. The stakes for Israel got much higher. If Iran has nuclear weapons, Israel would need to upgrade its readiness to an entirely different level, compared with the conventional age, i.e., the wars with the Arabs. Israel would have to make preparations that would demand astronomical budgets, which would be a huge burden on the Israeli economy. Many Jews might also leave Israel, fearing for themselves and their families, looking for a safer country. Tens of thousands have already made sure they possess European passports, issued by countries their families had originally come from, although this was sometimes done for purposes such as facilitating studying in Europe. In a survey by INSS in June 2009, 80% of Israelis claimed that if Iran has nuclear weapons their lives would not change. Only 8% said they would consider leaving their country.[48]

Another problem emanating from an Iranian bomb would be foreign investors and Jewish immigrants possibly steering clear of Israel, which would seem to be a country on the verge of a nuclear war. The combination of those hardships might bring Israel into a severe economic, social, and political crisis. Yet in the past, through every decade, Israel had tough times, and was subject to Arab threats, but overcame them. Militarily, Israel would have to add preparing and studying nuclear warfare to its acquired knowledge about high, hybrid, and low intensity wars against the Arabs.

If both Iran and Israel have nuclear weapons, there might be a conventional war between them. During it there might be a high probability of deterioration to a nuclear war that might occur fast and cause very severe ramifications. Both sides must take it into serious consideration.[49] According to Beres "Excluding an irrational actor—a prospect that falls outside the logic of nuclear deterrence—enemies of Israel would assuredly refrain from nuclear or biological attacks that would presumptively elicit massive counter-value reprisals."[50]

The war between Iraq and Iran in 1980–1988 was very costly,[51] demonstrating to the Iranian regime the risks it faces. It made Iran think about having a nuclear weapon, in order to protect itself.[52] Yet, compared with the war with Iraq in the 1980s, an all-out nuclear war with Israel would be a very different story, one that would devastate Iran. It does not matter that Iran has a lot more people and land than Israel. Iran might remain with most of its population but without most—if not all—its national infrastructure, such as the oil and gas industry. Iran would be a failed state for many years. It might be one of the terrible ramifications of a nuclear war between those two states. Nevertheless, some of Iran's leaders are so fundamentally opposed to Israel's right to existence, they might be willing to take enormous risks and pay a substantial price in order to annihilate it.

A nuclear war between Iran and Israel might happen because of mistakes and miscalculations by one or both sides. Both Iran and Israel deeply suspect the other, let alone if both of them have nuclear weapons. It might lead to an escalation, a very rapid one that might end in a nuclear war. In other cases Iran, even if it tries to avoid a nuclear showdown, might still provoke Israel with its proxies. The latter can also do it on their own, as Hamas did in the past, with or without approval from Iran. Although Iran assisted its protégés during their wars with Israel, Iran did not actually join the fight by attacking Israel from Iran itself, such as by firing long-range missiles. Iran must be much more careful in this matter, if Iran has nuclear weapons. Iran obviously would not want to let Israel understands that Israel has a freedom of action against Iran's proxies. However, Iran must make it clear to its proxies and to Israel too that Iran is not going to risk a nuclear war, in order to assist Iran's protégés. It would help to reduce tension between Israel and Iran and by that to prevent a terrible tragedy.

In another scenario, Israel was always worried that if an Arab leader is about to lose power for reasons such as a war, even one that is not against Israel, like Saddam Hussein in 2003 or Assad in Syria, he might use CW against Israel. Such an Arab leader would seek revenge in the name of Arabs, thus eternalizing himself in the Arab world as a ruler whose last act was to inflict a major blow to Israel. Iranian top leadership might think the same in similar circumstances, in a kind of Iranian Samson option. It could happen in Iran if its regime is toppled after gaining nuclear weapons. Its leadership might assume it has no escape, and would opt for a legacy of hitting Israel with nuclear weapons. The prospect of a similar retaliation from Israel might not deter the leaders of the crumbling Iranian regime, whose end would be coming anyway. It would be a tragic irony if Israel kills not only those responsible for its destruction, but also some of the enemies of the Iranian regime, who might not be as hostile toward Israel.

Iran, by financing organizations like the Hezbollah, Hamas, and Islamic Jihad Iran caused wars that brought death and suffering to Arabs. If there is a nuclear showdown between Iran and Israel, thousands and even tens of thousands of Arabs who live in Israel and near it might be harmed along with Jews. However, since Iran is mostly Shiite and Persian while Palestinians are Arabs and mostly Sunni, Iran might not care too much about Arab–Israelis and Palestinians. Those Arabs would probably feel they are victims of a war that does not concern them, one that rages between two non-Arab states. Iran might see those Arab casualties as acceptable losses, since it considers Israel as a foreign entity in the Middle East, and the price Arabs pay would be part of the cost of the conflict against Israel.

MAKING THE MIDDLE EAST FREE FROM NUCLEAR WEAPONS?

Yigal Allon served as a Maj. Gen. in the IDF in the 1948–1949 war, and became a senior political figure in several governments. In 1960 he claimed that if Israel could have chosen between two situations: both sides in the Middle East possess nuclear weapons or none of them does, his state would have gone with the latter.[53] There were calls to make the Middle East free of weapons of mass destruction (WMD). There were attempts to achieve that, mostly by Arab states and particular Egypt.[54] The latter and Iran that did not possess the Bomb, have been supporting that goal, since Israel is the only state in the Middle East with a nuclear arsenal. Israel has been strongly resisting disarming itself from its nuclear weapons before the Arab–Israeli conflict is over. It will probably continue doing so as long as Iran might produce nuclear weapons. Unfortunately, the chances of the Middle East returning to its early 1960s status, when neither side had nuclear weapons, are very low.

In 1960 Allon was willing to give up Israel's nuclear option, although he was aware that the balance of power was completely in favor of the Arabs. Until 1960 Israel managed to defeat Arabs twice in a high intensity war, in 1948–1949 and in 1956. Yet, there was no guarantee the IDF would once again obtain a victory, essential to the survival of the state. Allon, a former general, probably assumed Israel could win any high intensity war, and thus manage to stop Arabs from conquering Israel, without the threat of nuclear weapons. In the last decade there was a very low probability of an all-out Arab offensive against Israel. Yet, Israel does not want to take a chance, and to give up its nuclear arsenal, particularly since Iran might have nuclear weapons.

Another explanation of Allon's position is that he preferred to take chances in a conventional battlefield and not in a nuclear one. The stakes in a nuclear showdown are obviously much higher. If Iran has nuclear weapons maybe Israel and Iran can limit their fight to the conventional battlefield.

Conclusion

The Iranian regime seeks to destroy Israel, ignoring the Arab failure to accomplish the same goal. Iran is superior to Israel in the size of its land, population, etc. Nevertheless, Iran considers Israel as an obstacle to its regional ambitions, because of Israel's military might, specifically because of Israel's nuclear arsenal. Israel does not seek to annihilate Iran, only to get rid of the Iranian regime.

Israel could bomb Iranian nuclear sites, as it did in Iraq in 1981 and in Syria in 2007, hoping that as in Iraq and Syria it will be enough to stop another of its sworn enemies, in this case it is Iran, from producing a nuclear weapon. Israel, during the raid, might also try to target the manpower of the Iranian nuclear program, as part of delaying the rebuilding of Iran's nuclear project.

If Israel does not attack Iran or its raid would fail, then eventually Iran might possess nuclear weapons. Israel can adjust to this reality, but such a drastic development might have a significant negative impact on Israel.

Notes

1. Ronen Bergman, *Point of No Return* (Or Yehuda: Kinneret, Zmora—Bitan, Dvir, 2007), pp. 30–41.
2. Nadav Safran, *Israel—The Embattled Ally* (Tel Aviv: Schocken, 1979), p. 342.
3. Abner Yaniv, *Politics and Strategy in Israel* (Tel Aviv: Sifriat Poalim, 1994), p. 331.
4. On the years after 1979 see: Dalia Dassa Kaye, Alireza Nader, and Parisa Roshan, *Israel and Iran—A Dangerous Rivalry* (Santa Monica, CA: Rand, 2011), pp. 13–16.
5. On the "Three No's" of the Arab summit in Khartoum see: Moshe Shemesh, *Arab Politics, Palestinian Nationalism and the Six Day War: The Crystallization of Arab Strategy and Nasir's Descent to War, 1957–1967* (Sussex: Academic Press, 2008), pp. 241–242.
6. Meir Litvak, "Iran and Israel—The Roots of Iran's Ideological Hate Toward Israel", The Ben Gurion University, Iyunim Bitkumat Israel: Studies in Zionism,—The Yishuv and the State of Israel (Vol. 14, 2004), pp. 367–392.

7. Marisa Newman, "Iranian Supreme Leader Calls for Israel's 'Annihilation'", *The Times of Israel*, November 9, 2014. http://www.timesofisrael.com/iranian-supreme-leader-calls-for-israels-annihilation/.

8. Times of Israel staff, "Iran Official: We'll Bolster Our Military Until Israel Is Overthrown", *The Times of Israel*, September 2, 2015. http://www.timesofisrael.com/iran-official-well-bolster-our-military-until-israel-is-overthrown/.

9. "A Conversation With Javad Zarif", Council on Foreign Relations, CFR September 23, 2016. http://www.cfr.org/iran/conversation-javad-zarif/p38314.

10. On the Iranian minister of defense see: L. Todd Wodd, "Iran Threatens to Destroy Israel—Again", *The Washington Times*, December 12, 2016. http://www.washingtontimes.com/news/2016/dec/12/iran-threatens-destroy-israel-again/.

11. Member States of the Organization of Islamic Cooperation (OIC), December 13, 2017. https://www.oic-oci.org/doc down/?docID=1699&refID=1073.

12. Bahgat, Gawdat, "The Brewing War Between Iran and Israel: Strategic Implications", *Middle East Policy* (Vol. 25, No. 3, 2018), pp. 67–79.

13. Reuters, November 15, 2019. https://www.reuters.com/art icle/us-israel-iran-khamenei/khamenei-iran-not-calling-for-elimin ation-of-jews-wants-non-sectarian-israel-idUSKBN1XP0WP.

14. France 24, May 7, 2021. https://www.france24.com/en/live-news/20210507-iran-s-khamenei-says-israel-not-a-country-but-a-terrorist-base.

15. Raz Zimmt, "Look Right: Iranian President Raisi Appoints a Government", Institute for National Security Studies (INSS), (the one in Israel), Insight No. 1510, August 18, 2021.

16. Avi Primor, "No Permanent Allies, No Permanent Enemies, Only Permanent Interests': Israeli–Iranian Relations", *Israel Journal of Foreign Affairs* (Vol. 8, No. 1, January 2014), p. 36.

17. Kenneth M. Pollack, *Unthinkable: Iran, the Bomb, and American Strategy* (NY: Simon & Schuster, 2013), p. 10.

18. The world bank, Islamic republic of Iran, March 30, 2021. https://www.worldbank.org/en/country/iran/overview.

19. Seth Frantzman, "Iran Celebrates Israeli 'Budget Waste' in Light of Nuclear Threat", *The Jerusalem Post*, October 25, 2021. Iran

celebrates Israeli 'budget waste' in light of nuclear threat—The Jerusalem Post (jpost.com).

20. Anthony H. Cordesman with the assistance of Grace Hwang, The Changing Security Dynamics of the MENA Region, Center for Strategic International Studies (CSIS), March 22, 2021.

21. Pollack, Unthinkable: Iran, the Bomb…, p. 11.

22. Moshe Zak, *King Hussein Makes Peace* (Ramat Gan: Bar Ilan University Press, 1996), p. 191. Yossi Melman and Meir Javedanfar, *A Hostile Partnership* (Tel Aviv: Yediot Aharonot, 1987), p. 81.

23. On the ties with the Christians in Lebanon see: Zeev Schiff and Ehud Ya'ari, *A War of Deception* (Tel Aviv: Schocken, 1984).

24. Yoav Limor, "Israel Has the Ability to Completely Destroy Iran's Nuclear Program", *Israel Hayom*, March 30, 2021. https://www.israelhayom.com/2021/03/29/israel-has-the-ability-to-completely-destroy-irans-nuclear-program/.

25. Times of Israel staff, "Iran Calls to Destroy Nuclear Capacities of US, Israel", *The Times of Israel*, May 26, 2014. http://www.timesofisrael.com/iran-calls-for-destruction-of-us-israel-nuclear-capacities/.

26. Louis Rene' Beres, "Israel's Uncertain Strategic Future", Parameters (Spring, 2007), p. 41.

27. Aram Nerguizian, "The Struggle for the Levant: Geopolitical Battles and the Quest for Stability", Center for Strategic International Studies (CSIS), September 18, 2014. http://csis.org/publication/struggle-levant-geopolitical-battles-and-quest-stability.

28. On Iran's nuclear ambitions see: Mayumi Fukushima, "Why Iran May Be in No Hurry to Get Nuclear Weapons Even Without a Nuclear Deal", RAND, June 28, 2021. https://www.rand.org/blog/2021/06/why-iran-may-be-in-no-hurry-to-get-nuclear-weapons.html.

29. Matthew Kroenig, *A Time to Attack* (New York: Palgrave Macmillan, 2014), p. 40.

30. Bill Gertz, "Pentagon: Iran Continuing Work on Nuclear Systems", The Free Beacon, June 3, 2015. http://freebeacon.com/national-security/pentagon-iran-continuing-work-on-nuclear-systems/.

31. Raz Zimmt, "Israeli Campaign to Stop Iran's Nuclear Program", *The Iran Primer*, July 15, 2020. https://iranprimer.usip.org/blog/2020/jul/15/israeli-campaign-stop-irans-nuclear-program.

32. On covert operations see: Jodah Ari Gross, "Bennett Appears to Hint at Israeli Involvement in Attack on Iran Nuclear Site", *The Times of Israel*, June 24, 2021. https://www.timesofisrael.com/bennett-appears-to-hint-at-israeli-involvement-in-attack-on-iran-nuclear-site/.

33. Fredrick Forstyb, *At Its Majesty's Secret Service* (London: Greenhill Books, 2006), p. 219. Stephen Hughes, *The Iraqi Threat & Saddam Hussein's Weapons of Mass Destruction* (Canada: On-Demand and Trafford, 2002), p. 371.

34. (No Author), "Mohsen Fakhrizadeh, Iran's Top Nuclear Scientist, Assassinated Near Tehran", *BBC*, November 27, 2020. https://www.bbc.com/news/world-middle-east-55105934.

35. Reuters, January 26, 2021. https://www.reuters.com/article/us-nuclear-iran-israel/israels-top-general-says-its-military-is-refreshing-operational-plans-against-iran-idUSKBN29V2EX.

36. On Gantz see: Alarabiya, March 5, 2021. https://english.alarabiya.net/News/middle-east/2021/03/05/Israel-will-defend-itself-if-world-fails-to-stall-Iran-s-nuclear-plans-Benny-Gantz.

37. Times of Israel staff, "IDF Said to Resume Practicing Potential Strike on Iranian Nuclear Sites", *The Times of Israel*, October 21, 2021. https://www.timesofisrael.com/idf-said-to-resume-practicing-potential-strike-on-iranian-nuclear-sites/.

38. (No Author) "Israel 'Reserves the Right' to Act Against Iran: Yair Lapid", *Aljazeera*, October 13, 2021. https://www.aljazeera.com/news/2021/10/13/israel-reserves-the-right-to-act-against-iran-yair-lapid.

39. Times of Israel staff, "Israel Said to Approve $1.5 Billion Budget for Potential Strike on Iran", *The Times of Israel*, October 18, 2021. https://www.timesofisrael.com/israel-said-to-approve-1-5-billion-budget-for-potential-strike-on-iran/.

40. Jordan Ari Gross, "IAF to Start Training for Strike on Iran Nuke Program in Coming Months", *The Times of Israel*, October 25, 2021. https://www.timesofisrael.com/iaf-to-start-training-for-strike-on-iran-nuke-program-in-coming-months/.

41. On the 1981 raid see: Rodger Claire, *Raid on the Sun: Inside Israel's Secret Campaign That Denied Saddam the Bomb Paperback*

(New York: Crown, 2005). On the 2007 raid see: Yaakov Katz, *Shadow Strike: Inside Israel's Secret Mission to Eliminate Syrian Nuclear Power* (New York: St. Martin's Press, 2017).

42. Shlomo Nakdimon, *First Strike: The Exclusive Story of How Israel Foiled Iraq's Attempt to Get the Bomb* (New York: Pocket Books, 1988).
43. Reuters, August 28, 2012. https://www.reuters.com/article/us-iran-nuclear-environment/big-radiation-risk-unlikely-if-israel-strikes-iran-experts-idUSBRE87R0EX20120828.
44. Yehuda Blanga, "Different Perspectives': The Path That Led to the Cease-Fire Ending the War of Attrition and the Deployment of Missiles at the Suez Canal", *Middle Eastern Studies* (Vol. 48, 2012), pp. 183–204.
    Trevor N. Dupuy, *Elusive Victory* (London: Macdonald and Janes, 1978), p. 441.
    James D. Crabtree, *On Air Defense* (London: Frager, 1994), p. 152. Yaacov Bar-Simon Tov, *The Israeli-Egyptian War of Attrition, 1969–70* (Colombia University Press, 1980).
45. Kim Hjelmgaard, "Iran's Jewish Community Is the Largest in the Mideast Outside Israel—and Feels Safe and Respected", *USA Today*, August 29, 2018. https://www.usatoday.com/in-depth/news/world/inside-iran/2018/08/29/iran-jewish-population-islamic-state/886790002/.
46. Coletta Giovanni, "Politicising Intelligence: What Went Wrong with the UK and US Assessments on Iraqi WMD in 2002", *Journal of Intelligence History* (2018), No. 17, pp. 65–78. IDF—Maarachot (Vol. 450, August 2013), pp. 40–46.
47. Barry Rubin, *The Truth About Syria* (NY: Palgrave Macmillan, 2007), p. 9.
48. On the survey from 2009 see: (INSS), June 14, 2009. http://heb.inss.org.il/index.aspx?id=4354&articleid=770.
49. On a nuclear war see; Anthony H. Cordesman, "Iran, Israel, and Nuclear War", CSIS, November 19, 2007. https://www.csis.org/analysis/iran-israel-and-nuclear-war.
50. Beres, "Israel's Uncertain Strategic…", p. 46.
51. Williamson Murray and Kevin Woods, *The Iran–Iraq War: A Military and Strategic History* (Cambridge University Press, 2014).

52. Ofira Seliktar and Rezaei, Farhad, *Iran, Israel, and the United States: The Politics of Counter-Proliferation Intelligence Hardcover* (Lanham, Maryland: Lexington Books, 2018), p. 25.
53. Yigal Allon, *Curtain of Sand* (Tel Aviv: Hakibbutz Hameuchad, 1960), p. 402.
54. Arms control association, July 17, 2017. https://www.armsco ntrol.org/factsheets/mewmdfz.

CHAPTER 3

Could There Be an Israeli–Arab Cooperation Against Iran?

There are several reasons for the tension between Iran and Gulf Arab states, mostly Saudi Arabia, such as the conflict between Sunnis and Shiites, the friction between Arabs and Persians and also the fight over influence in the Gulf and in Arab countries like Yemen.

Since Israel was established, Israel and Gulf Arab states were not sworn enemies. Gulf Arab states did assist other Arab states and NSAs against Israel, but mostly politically and economically, almost without actually fighting the IDF. Furthermore, Saudi Arabia and the UAE maintained secret ties with Israel for many years. On September 15, 2020, Israel normalized its relations with the UAE and Bahrain. Israel conducts a kind of strategic pincer movement, one north of Iran, in Syria, and the other one south of Iran, in the Gulf. While in Syria there are Israeli bombardments on Iranian targets at the Gulf Israel builds diplomatic, economic, and security ties, which can help against Iran.

Israel could have bombed Iran's nuclear sites, in order to destroy and at least to slow down Iran's nuclear program. Israeli aircraft might be allowed to fly over Arab territory on their way to Iran. If eventually Iran manages to produce nuclear weapons, Arab states such as Saudi Arabia might try to obtain nuclear weapons as well.

The Trump administration, at the end of its term, agreed to sell the F-35, a highly advanced fighter, to the UAE. Israel, which at the time was in the process of normalizing its relations with the UAE, had some

© The Author(s), under exclusive license to Springer Nature Switzerland AG 2022
E. Eilam, *Israeli Strategies in the Middle East*,
https://doi.org/10.1007/978-3-030-95602-8_3

concerns about that. Yet quite quickly Israel basically accepted it, due to the relatively low risk of this arms deal, and since it would help protect the UAE from Iran.

Besides Gulf Arab states there are other Arab states that could be involved in a conflict between Israel and Iran. In Iraq there is strong resentment against the Iranian influence in that country. Jordan wishes to stay out of a conflict between Iran and Israel. Egypt seeks to monitor Israel's nuclear arsenal, but Egypt can also assist Saudi Arabia against Iran.

THE SAUDI APPROACH

Saudi Arabia seeks to contain Iran.[1] Saudi Arabia and other Gulf Arab states have been very worried about Iran, the ambitions of which remind some Arabs of the times they were subjected to another non-Arab power, the ottomans; this is a grim memory for them. This drives them to cooperate with Israel against their common enemy, Iran.

Arab states have been well aware that Israel has nuclear weapons.[2] However, Israel's nuclear arsenal was not exploited to force an Israeli rule on the Arabs, and not even to make Arabs recognize Israel's right to exist. Egypt and Jordan, which signed a peace agreement with Israel, did not do that only because of its nuclear arsenal. Other Arab states, like Syria, that remained Israel's enemy, assumed Israel would not use nuclear weapons to coerce them to accept Israeli terms. In both cases Israel's presumed possession of nuclear weapons did not seem to loom over the situation. This kind of living in denial was an inconvenient compromise the Arabs had to bear. As long as Israel stays with its current nuclear policy Arab states like those in the Gulf might keep their part in an unofficial deal. Israel has been ignoring the fact that it holds nuclear weapons, while Arabs, like Saudi Arabia, have been avoiding the option of getting nuclear weapons. The last decades proved Arabs could tolerate this ongoing and vague nuclear status quo. Yet, Arab states like those in the Gulf might not be sure that Iran would have the same policy as Israel, i.e., leaving the nuclear weapons solely as a last resort.

The Saudi Crown Prince Mohammed bin Salman said in mid-March 2018 that his country would quickly obtain nuclear weapons, if Iran produces nuclear weapons.[3] Saudi Arabia's minister of state for foreign affairs, Adel al-Jubeir, mentioned a similar argument in November 2020.[4] On April 13, 2021, Saudi Arabia expressed its concerns "about Iran's intention to start enriching uranium to 60% purity and said such a move could not be considered part of a peaceful nuclear programme." Saudi Arabia supports an agreement, in regard to Iran's nuclear project, "with stronger parameters of a longer duration."[5] If eventually Iran produces nuclear weapons, Gulf Arab states like Saudi Arabia might get nuclear weapons too, maybe from Pakistan.[6] For Irana Sunni state such as Saudi Arabia with nuclear weapons is more dangerous than the current situation in the Middle East, when only Israel possesses this deadly arsenal.

If Saudi Arabia has nuclear weapons, it would worry Israel. Even if the relations between them would be quite friendly it might change, for the worse, and then Israel would face a very serious threat. For example, Saudi airfields are much closer to Israel than Iranian ones, particularly King Faisal, located about 200 km south-east of Israel. From there a fast Saudi fighter-bomber with a nuclear cargo might surprise Israel. The city of Eilat, with its 60,000 people, would be particularly in danger, since it is the closest Israeli city to Saudi Arabia.

If Iran and Saudi Arabia have nuclear weapons, they would all watch each other carefully, along with Israel. The relative proximity between some of them would contribute to the mutual suspicion. Each one in this nuclear triangle might look for an opportunity to turn its two foes against each other, a win–win situation. Yet if in one scenario Saudi Arabia tries to ignite a nuclear showdown between Israel and Iran, the stakes might be quite high for the Arab Kingdom. Iran might blame Saudi Arabia for allowing Israeli planes to pass Saudi territory on their way to Iran. Therefore, in a nuclear age in the Middle East, each party would have to be careful of provocations that might entangle it in an unnecessary lethal nuclear war.

Bashar al Assad being part of the pro-Iranian camp, places himself as the enemy of both Israel and Arab states such as those in the Gulf. Following the Syrian civil war, Israel was uncertain whether it wants to get rid of Assad or not, while some Arabs states, mostly Saudi Arabia, clearly wished to topple him. Israel did not intervene openly in the civil war in Syria, excluding sorties to prevent both the delivery of advanced weapons to the Hezbollah and the establishing of an Iranian base in Syria. Those strikes harmed Assad's pride more than his ability to suppress the rebels. Several Arab states like Saudi Arabia assisted the rebels by sending weapons and funds to Syria.[7]

During the Syrian civil war the United States, Saudi Arabia, Assad, and Iran were all against ISIS, which ironically put Iran and Saudi Arabia on the same side. Yet, Saudi Arabia also opposed Iran by helping anti-Assad rebels. Even before the civil war in Syria, there was a rift between Assad and Saudi Arabia. It followed the assassination in 2005 of Rafic Hariri, the prime minister of Lebanon who was a close partner of Saudi Arabia. The Assad regime was blamed for being involved in killing him.

The annihilation of the Syrian nuclear reactor in 2007 by Israel probably pleased Arab states like Saudi Arabia. For the latter Assad with nuclear weapons would have been a major change in the balance of power, in favor of two of Saudi's foes: Syria and Iran. This might have pushed Saudi Arabia to go for nuclear weapons, which was another reason for Israel to destroy the Syrian reactor.

UAE and Israel

The agreement between the UAE and Israel in 2020 "may catalyze the consolidation of the US–Israel–UAE alliance and unlock great potential in the region."[8] The UAE and Israel became allies since they share similar political, military, and economic interests. They have common enemies: Iran and its proxies. The UAE is aware that Israel stands as an obstacle to Iran's regional ambitions. If Israel is out of the way, Iran and its proxies will continue to undermine Arab regimes, hoping to replace them with pro-Iranian rulers. The Emiratis know they have to join others in order to avoid such a negative outcome.

The UAE has a reputation of having quite a capable military.[9] However, the UAE can't face Iran alone, so the UAE developed its ties with Israel, which were an open secret for many years, involving national security issues. On September 15, 2020, their relations became official, when they signed a peace accord. It was not a military alliance against Iran, but it was a solid start in building an Arab–Israeli coalition to match the Iranian axis.

Israel and Egypt had a series of wars that cost them dearly, before they ended their conflict in 1979. Since Israel and the UAE don't share a border, they had no territorial disputes, unlike Israel and Egypt. (It took long negotiations to solve those issues between Israel and Egypt.) UAE and Israel actually never fought against each other. The UAE was established only in 1971, i.e., after several wars between Israel and Arab states had already occurred. Furthermore, in wars like the one that happened in 2006, between Israel and Hezbollah, Arab states, including the UAE, sought an Israeli victory over Iran's proxy, Hezbollah. The UAE was not so much on Israel's side, but more against Hezbollah. It was convenient for the UAE, and for many other Sunni—led Arab states, to have Jews confront Shiites. Those are some of the factors that made it easier for Israel and the UAE to end the relatively minor conflict between them.

On September 15, 2020, Israel signed a peace accord not only with the UAE, but also with another Arab state in the Gulf, Bahrain, which was important, but not as much as the agreement with the UAE. The UAE is stronger and bigger than Bahrain. The latter therefore relies heavily on Saudi Arabia. The UAE also does not have a Shiite majority, unlike Bahrain, which make the UAE more stable and less vulnerable to Iranian subversion.

By August 2021 the bilateral trade between Israel and the UAE stood at around $712 million. Israel "is aiming for $3 billion in three years."[10] Israel hopes its accord with the UAE and Bahrain will not only create fertile relations with those two Arab states, but with other Arab states as well. It has to do also with both Egypt and Jordan, following the cold peace with them. Warm relations between Israel and the UAE might bring to an end the ice age: the period of cold peace. Such cooperation would strengthen the relations between Israel and Arab states, which might also help in building a coalition against Iran.

The UAE made peace with the Arab's traditional enemy, Israel, but obviously it was not unprecedented. It occurred after four decades of peace between Israel and Egypt, an accord that was signed in 1979. In the late 1970s, this peace treaty was a bombshell, shocking the Middle East. Egypt, the most powerful and dominant Arab state at the time, the leader of the Arabs in their fight against Israel, accepted Israel's right to exist. Egypt did it alone, without asking for the permission of the Arab league. In 1979 Arab states took actions against Egypt such as kicking it out of the Arab league. Egypt was allowed to return there only 10 years later. In 1994, when Israel signed a peace treaty with Jordan, the latter was not punished by the Arabs. Arab states accepted also the Oslo accords between Israel and the PLO, which were reached after secret negotiations, without involving Arab states, but a European Christin state, Norway. Arabs also did not oppose the attempts to reach peace between Israel and Arab states such as Syria. The 2002 Arab peace initiative calls for peace with Israel, in return for an Israeli retreat from areas Israel seized in 1967. The UAE agreed to have peace with Israel, without any Israeli withdrawal. However, the positive background of different peace steps to a large extent paved the way for the accord between the UAE and Israel on September 15, 2020.

In 1999 a northwest African–Arab country, Mauritania, became the third Arab state to recognize Israel (after Egypt and Jordan). Yet after a decade, following the confrontation at the Gaza Strip in December 2008–January 2009, Mauritania disconnected its diplomatic ties with Israel. This is a remainder and a precedent. An Arab state started and after a decade ended its official relations with Israel. It might happen with Israel and the UAE or any other Arab state that recognizes Israel, considering the ongoing tension between Israel and Arabs, mostly the Palestinians. However, since the UAE is so far away from Israel, even if the UAE becomes hostile toward Israel, it would not have a huge effect, compared if it happens with one of Israel's neighbors, i.e., Egypt and/or Jordan.

The Response in the Middle East to the Peace Between Israel and the UAE

Iran opposes the relations between the UAE and Israel.[11] The Iranian President Hassan Rouhani condemned and warned the UAE for making a "huge mistake." He rejected giving Israel a "foothold in the region."[12] His response was obvious, demonstrating how Iran was concerned about this matter. Iran has been working on establishing a presence near Israel, by using its proxies. In 2020, by signing accords with the UAE and Bahrain, Israel seemed to return a favor, i.e., arriving in the Gulf, Iran's front yard. Israel did not have proxies there, but the new stage of the relations between Israel and the UAE and Bahrain could contribute to creating an anti-Iranian alliance. However, the UAE has diplomatic ties with Iran and there is quite a lot of trade between them. The UAE is also worried that Iran might hit her hard with missiles, cyber and terror attacks. Therefore the UAE might want to stay kind of neutral, and not to be seen as an Israeli base in the Gulf.

Another regional non-Arab power, Turkey, opposed the agreement between Israel and the UAE. Turkey has relations with Israel, but they have been at a low point for more than a decade, mostly due to the Israeli–Palestinian conflict. At the same time there were quite fertile economic relations between Israel and Turkey. The latter threatened to suspend its ties with the UAE, but not with Israel. In 2021 Turkey made signs it seeks to reconcile with Israel.[13] Turkey therefore has an ambivalent approach toward Israel. Turkey has its concerns about the relations between the UAE and Israel. Turkey certainly would not join them against Iran. On the one hand, Turkey sees Iran as a rival, which competes with Turkey on gaining influence in the region such as in Syria. On the other hand, Turkey cooperates with Iran in several levels.

The peace accords shocked the PA, considering it as a betrayal.[14] The PA tried to stop this process, but failed. In that sense the PA and Iran had the same interest. In early December 2020, the Emirati Foreign Minister Sheikh Abdullah Bin Zayed claimed the agreement with Israel, "will enable us to continue to stand by the Palestinian people, and realize their hopes for an independent state within a stable and prosperous region."[15] It was an attempt to calm the PA without criticizing Israel.

Following the announcement by the UAE and Israel on normalizing their relations, the Saudi Foreign Minister Faisal bin Farhan mentioned that his country will not make its ties with Israel official, until there is peace between Israel and the Palestinians. He added that "Saudi Arabia affirms its commitment to peace as a strategic option based on the Arab Peace Initiatives," which call for a full Israeli withdrawal from the West Bank.[16] Saudi Arabia did not like the UAE taking its own initiate, boosting its international status, in a way at the expense of its powerful neighbor, Saudi Arabia. The latter, by sticking to its positions, supported the Palestinians in order not to aggravate the Palestinians and their supporters in Saudi Arabia and around the Arab world. However, Saudi Arabia, which had developed its secret relations with Israel, did not reject the Emirati–Israeli peace accord. Saudi Arabia understood overall this is the right step in establishing a coalition against Iran.

Should Israel be Concerned if the UAE Gets the F-35?

In early June 2015, US Chairman of the Joint Chiefs of Staff Gen. Martin Dempsey visited Israel. He said Israelis were concerned that the military buildup of Gulf Arab states could erode Israel's military edge (QME).[17] On May 17, 2017, the Trump administration and Saudi Arabia announced a huge arms deal, worth 110 Billion Dollars, which included various weapon systems for the Saudi air, land, and naval forces.[18] Israel has reasons to be worried about the Saudi air force. Other aspects of the arms deal such as border security and particularly missile defense and naval warfare were less of a concern for Israel. It might also work for Israel's benefit, in encouraging Saudi Arabia to assist Israel in attacking Iran's nuclear sites. If Saudi Arabia is better protected, it would help her to deter and defend itself against an Iranian retribution. As to selling vehicles for land combat to Saudi Arabia, the latter doesn't share a border with Israel, so neither of them poses any threat to the other in this sense.

In late 2020 the UAE renewed its request to buy the F-35.[19] Israel, the only state in the Middle East that has the F-35, was concerned about delivering such a highly advanced aircraft to an Arab state. IAF Chief, Major General Amikam Norkin argued in late September 2020 that selling the F-35 to the UAE might be bad for Israel in the long term, since the balance of power would change.[20]

On November 3, 2021 Yousef al-Otaiba, the UAE ambassador to the United States, argued that if the UAE can't get US arsenal, the UAE would buy weapons from other countries. It followed the opposition to an arms deal between the United States and the UAE, one that would include the F-35.[21] The United States had to make sure the hardware it sells would be protected including cybersecurity and security-clearance to those who have access to US technology in that country.[22] Israel on its part had to examine carefully how much its American patron wants to sell the F-35 to the UAE. There are US interests in the strategic, political, and economic levels. One of them is that if the UAE does not receive the F-35 it might turn to Russia for aircraft, which would frustrate the United States, due to its competition with Russia, including in arms sales. The United States might blame Israel for helping Russia, at the expense of the United States. In addition the reports about the possibility of selling the F-35 to the UAE appeared during the summer of 2020. Israel could have waited for the US elections in November that year, to see if there is a change in the administration and in congress, which would affect US policy in the Middle East. After that it could have been easier for Israel to evaluate if and how much political capital to invest in preventing and at least to slowing down and limit the sale of F-35 to the UAE.

In early December 2020 the Israeli Ambassador to the United States, Ron Dermer, said the UAE is an ally against Iran and the arms deal would not violate US commitment to Israel's QME.[23] At the same time AIPAC (The American Israel Public Affairs Committee) announced it does not oppose the sale of the F-35 to the UAE, because of the peace agreement between Israel and the UAE and since the Trump administration would ensure Israel's QME.[24] The Biden administration suspended this deal in late January 2021, but on April 13 President Biden approved it.[25]

In late August 2020, the Emirati Minister of State for Foreign Affairs Anwar Gargash said its country has the right to receive F-35, since the probability of "war with Israel no longer exists."[26] From the Emirati's perspective since the UAE did not see Israel as a foe, then Israel was expected to allow the UAE to protect itself, i.e., to acquire the F-35. Israel had to decide if it is worth opposing the sale, according to the risks of allowing the UAE to obtain the F-35, the probability of success in stopping the UAE from getting this aircraft and if such Israeli policy undermines the relations with the UAE.

There were several reasons why Israel did not have to be worried that much about delivering the F-35 to the UAE. First of all, the sharp decline in the military might of Israel's traditional enemies, Syria and Iraq, together with the peace with Egypt and Jordan, drastically reduce the probability of an Arab coalition against Israel, to which the UAE can theoretically join. As to pro-Iranian proxies such as Hezbollah and Hamas the IDF enjoys a clear advantage over them.

The United States could sell the UAE F-35 inferior to the ones Israel assimilated. It was done before when US F-16 were given to Egypt and Jordan. Furthermore, the UAE might purchase the F-35 or any top US arsenal and then other Arab states such as Saudi Arabia, might ask to acquire this weapon hardware too. Later on the policy or the regime in those Arab states might turn against the United States and Israel. However, then they will lose US military aid (training, ammunition, spare parts, etc.) Without it the armed forces of those Arab states would struggle to maintain and operate their sophisticated American weapons, such as the F-35.

In August 2020 it was estimated that delivery of the F-35 "to the UAE could take up to a decade due to production backlogs and prioritized deals with nations that are partners in the production of the F-35."[27] Meanwhile the IAF has been assimilating the F-35 since 2016, so it would have much more experience, including in combat, of using the F-35, compared to its counterpart at the UAE.

The F-35 is a very sophisticated aircraft, but maximizing its capabilities require high quality pilots and ground crews, and many other military personnel who are involved in getting the best out of the F-35. Here the IAF has an impressive reputation, better than its counterpart at the UAE. In addition, the F-35 could do much by itself, but it still might require assistance from other aircraft such as command and control aircraft and drones. The Emirati F-35 has to be able to coordinate with all those aircraft.

The F-35 would significantly upgrade the Emirates Air Force. It may increase the UAE's deterrence against Iran.[28] If Iran tries to produce nuclear weapons Israel might strike Iran. Israe lmight need the UAE, including for political support. The UAE has to feel secure enough in countering possible Iranian retribution against the UAE. The F-35 would help the UAE in this matter. Furthermore, with or without a clash with Iran, the latter would have to pay more attention to the UAE, due to its growing military strength, and it might be at the expense of investing in Iran's proxies that confront Israel.

The F-35 has combat range of about one thousand km. The distance between the UAE and Israel is more than 2000 km, so the F-35 can't reach Israel from the UAE and return back to the UAE. Drop tanks would increase its range. Yet, it might not be enough if the Emirati F-35 has to spend fuel for example on air to air maneuvers against Israeli fighters. The Emirati F-35 would require to use aerial refueling or to land to refuel in an Arab state nearby Israel, one that would be willing to risk the Israeli retribution.

The UAE's economy depends on oil and natural gas industry. The UAE also had developed its tourism and business centers. All that would be in peril, because if the UAE bombs Israel, the latter will retaliate. The UAE would suffer from both the actual damage it would absorb and from tarnishing its reputation as a safe and reliable place for tourism and making business.

The Israeli reservations about the F-35 don't mean Israel opposes other arms deals. Furthermore, Israel can sell weapons to the UAE; taking into consideration those weapons might end up in the wrong hands. Israel might also sell Saudi Arabia the Iran Dome, to defend the kingdom from Iranian attacks.[29] The UAE might need them too, against the same enemy.

MILITARY COOPERATION BETWEEN ISRAEL AND ARAB ARABS AGAINST IRAN

Itamar Rabinovich claimed in 2014 that "given the ongoing conflict with the Palestinians, the limited scope of its peaceful relationship with Egypt and Jordan, and the absence of a relationship with Saudi Arabia' Israel "could not in fact become part of an effective anti-Iranian bloc."[30] In recent years there were talks about building an alliance against Iran, a kind of an "Arab NATO."[31] In 2020 Israel aimed "to align with the Gulf

Arab states and under US supervision in a wider strategic alliance against Iran."[32] Israel and some Arab states, mostly Gulf Arab states, can reach an understanding about Iran and even to create ah-hoc coalition for a limited campaign against Iran.

In 1990–1 Gulf Arab states allowed hundreds of thousands of western troops, most of them Christians, to deploy on Arab land. Those non-Muslim and non-Arab men and women fought together with Arab Muslims against other Arab Muslims, the Iraqis. In the campaign in Libya in 2011 western forces attacked a Muslim Arab country, while collaborating with local Arab opposition and Arab states, including the UAE. Arabs clashed with Arabs by collaborating with the IDF as well. In 1982, Lebanon's Arab Christians joined Israel against the PLO.[33] In the last decade Palestinian security forces in the West Bank have been collaborating quite well with Israeli security forces, against other Palestinians, mostly Hamas. Although in those cases Israel did not actually fight together, side by side, with its Arab allies, there was a certain precedent in this matter. It follows therefore that since Arabs collaborated with western powers or Israel against other Arabs, they could do it against a non-Arab state, Iran. The latter is Muslim like Arabs, but under Shiite rule, while Gulf Arab states and Israel are not.

In 1981, when Israel destroyed Iraq's nuclear reactor, it could be said this strike also served vital interests of Gulf Arab states like Saudi Arabia, Qatar, UAE, Bahrain, and Kuwait. Although they supported Iraq in its war against Iran, they did not wish to see it becoming too strong, by having nuclear weapons. Two years after the Iran–Iraq war ended, Iraq conquered Kuwait. Saddam Hussein saw that small Gulf Arab state as a district belonging to Iraq, and if he possessed nuclear weapons in 1990 he could have kept Kuwait, and become a threat to other Gulf Arab states. Iran with nuclear weapons could demand the return of Bahrain as some in Iran consider it their lost district, or at least be handed over to the Shiite majority in Bahrain. It might be part of an Iranian future strategy to use its nuclear weapon as a leverage to increase its grip in the Gulf.

The proximity of Gulf Arab states to Iran gives them a comfortable jumping point to attack it. In recent years the relations between Israel and Gulf Arab states were significantly improved. The peak was signing the peace agreements between Israel and both the UAE and Bahrain in 2020. Israeli officers could be invited to Iron Union, joint US–Emirati military exercises, which can improve Israeli–Emirati relations.[34] In April 2021 Israeli and Emirati air crews participated in a "major international aerial exercise hosted by Greece, simulating in-air dogfights, large airstrikes and rescue operations."[35] In October that year a large-scale international exercise took place in Israel. "The UAE did not take part in the drill, but sent its air force commander, Ibrahim Nasser Muhammed al-Alawi, to observe a portion of the exercise."[36] Those are encouraging signs. However, military coordination between Israel and Gulf Arab states, such as joint planning and exercises, let alone in a significant scale, would be almost impossible to carry out, due to political constraints.

Gulf Arabs states can provide Israel with intelligence about Iran and its nuclear program. Israel could also expect not to fight its way to Iran and back against fighters and antiaircraft batteries from Gulf Arab states. The latter could turn a blind eye and bear Israelis crossing over their countries for a couple of hours, to bomb Iranian nuclear sites. Israeli aircraft might even be allowed to land temporally on Arab soil, in some remote and isolated roads, to refuel or in emergency.

Iran, following the Israeli attack, can strike back at Israel with drones, cruise missiles, and long-range surface to surface missiles. The IAF would retaliate and at least would try to destroy Iranian drones, missiles, and their launchers, before more missiles and drones would be fired at Israel. Gulf Arab states might tolerate a one-time Israeli aircraft flying over them to Iran, and back, but not repeatedly. The first sortie would be to wipe out Iranian nuclear sites, a common interest of Gulf Arab states and Israel, but the next would be against drones and missiles directed at Israel, not that much of concern for Gulf Arab states. Furthermore, Iran might avoid striking those Arab states after the first Israeli attack. Iran might change this policy following more Israeli sorties against it, flying again over Arab territory. Gulf Arab states therefore might not take the risk of allowing Israeli aircraft to fly back and forth over their territory, for more than one time.

Iran improved its cyber capabilities.[37] Iran might retaliate with cyber attacks against both Israel and Gulf Arab states. Iran could also launch terror assaults with "sleeper cells" that were created inside Gulf Arab states. Iranian Missiles, cyber and terror attacks on Gulf Arab states might cause havoc there, and in the oil market as well. However, Arab governments might agree to take this chance and bear the cost, if they calculate that the ramifications of a nuclear Iran would be much worse.

Dennis Ross mentioned in late May 2018 that if Israelis attacked from Lebanon and Syria by Iranian missiles, then Israe lmight strike Iran. "In a way designed to inflict a high cost—perhaps hitting Iranian oil facilities.

At that point, the Iranians may choose to hit back at Saudi Arabia or elsewhere in the Gulf."[38] Therefore, not necessarily because of an Israeli raid on Iran's nuclear sites, a war between Israel and Hezbollah could entangle Iran and Gulf Arab states in it.

In October 2021 John Hannah mentioned the accords between Israel and the UAE and Bahrain "have further advanced the security partnership" between them. Yet, "the prospect that either Gulf state would actively participate in an IDF strike on Iran—or even allow Israeli planes to refuel in their territories—remains highly unlikely. It is certainly nothing Israel could count on."[39] Much would depend on Saudi Arabia, which is enormously bigger than the UAE and Bahrain. To begin with in order to reach the UAE and Bahrain, Israeli aircraft have to fly over Saudi territory. Even if the UAE and Bahrain refuse to permit the IAF to cross their air space, but Saudi Arabia accepts that it might be enough for the IAF.

In the bottom line Israel and Gulf Arab states should have an alliance and at least some kind of understating of how they can deal with Iran, including if Israel clashes with Iran.

ISRAEL, IRAQ, AND IRAN

Iraq participated in the Arab–Israeli wars. The peak was in the 1973 war, when Iraq sent a large part of its military to confront the IDF.[40] Until the 1990s Iraq was considered by Israel as a major threat. In the 1980s Iran became Israel's enemy. The Iran–Iraq war (1980–1988) served Israel, because its foes wore down each other.[41] During the war Iranian nuclear sites were bombed a few times, between 1984 and 1987, by the Iraqi air force. At first Iran thought that the IAF bombed it.[42] In that sense Iraq served an Israeli interest, but its attacks on Iran's nuclear sites were not significant and anyway Iran's nuclear project was then in its first stages. Still, it was neither the first nor the last time when Israel had a common interest with a sworn enemy. Following the successes of ISIS in Iraq in 2014, Iran took part in the vast coalition against ISIS. Israel did not participate in the battles, but Israel provided intelligence about ISIS to members of that alliance. In that sense Israel and Iran were on the same side.

In the 1960s and 1970s Israel assisted Iraqi Kurds against their common foe, the Iraqi regime.[43] During the last decades there were contacts between Israel and Kurds. In August 2017 senior Iraqi Kurd officials visited Israel, urging Israel to support an independent Kurdish state. Israel expressed sympathy for the Kurdish cause.[44] If Iraq falls apart, due to its fragile condition, the Kurds there might try to declare independence. Israe lmight recognize this state, which would need help. Iran would oppose a Kurdish state in Iraq, fearing Iranian Kurds might want to join it. The new Kurdish state can therefore cooperate with Israel against Iran. Either way there are up to 30 million Kurds living in Turkey, Iran, Iraq, and Syria. Israel and Kurds can help each other, including against Iran.

In 2019 Israel bombed a site on northern Iraq, which served Iran to transfer missiles to Syria.[45] It was part of the ongoing Israeli strategy, aiming at disrupting the Iranian effort to both create a fire base in Syria and to supply Hezbollah in Lebanon. Iran has quite a lot of influence in Iraq. In recent years there were vast protests in Iraq, due to social and economic hardships. There were many Iraqis who oppose the Iranian grip on their country.[46] There are also some in Iraq, not only Kurds, who consider reconciling with Israel, but so far this approach did not gain much support in Iraq. Israel should help Iraqis who seek to have relations with her and/or to reduce the Iranian influence in Iraq. The Israeli assistance has to be done in secret, so those who have contact with her would not be accused in Iraq as traitors.

If Israel strikes Iran, the IAF might have to cross Iraq on its way to the targets. Flying to Iran over the pro-Iranian Iraq would have been quite easy for Israel, since there was no Iraqi air defense or a strong air force to stop the IAF.

JORDAN, ISRAEL, AND IRAN

The Hashemite kingdom, which is relatively weak, must always be careful about potential or actual rivals. Jordan tries to maneuver between Iran and Gulf Arab states. Iran already has a grip on two of Jordan's neighbors, Syria and Iraq, and could try to increase its influence in the Hashemite kingdom. If Iran has nuclear weapons, it may be prompted to initiate subversion inside Jordan. Nevertheless, Jordan may avoid assisting, let alone participating, in an Israeli attack on Iran, fearing fierce Iranian retribution.

In 1991 the Hashemite kingdom supported Iraq, but without fighting with it against the Anti Iraqi coalition. When Iraq fired long-range missiles at Israel, the latter planned to dispatch aircraft to Iraq both to retaliate and to hit missile launchers. The shortest way from Israel to Iraq is over Jordan, but penetrating its skies could have created a major crisis, possibly even a war, between Israel and the Hashemite kingdom.[47] Eventually Israel avoided any attack on Iraq.

An ongoing exchange of punches between Israel and Iran, in which Israeli planes penetrate Jordanian air space, would cause high tension between Israel and the kingdom, possibly even clashes in the air between their fighters. Jordan would not want to fight for Iran, but it could also not be seen as supporting Israel against Iran. Jordan has to be careful not to get between Israel and Iran. In 2021 Jordan was attacked by Iranian-made drones and missiles. It demonstrated to the kingdom what could be the Iranian retribution, if Iran blames Jordan for assisting Israel in attacking Iran.[48]

Israel and Jordan do have a long history of security cooperation between them, even before they signed a peace treaty in 1994. Therefore perhaps they could manage to form some kind of a creative and secret agreement, in case Israel strikes Iran. Israel can offer Jordan major benefits in areas that are crucial to Jordan such as in water, energy, etc. Israel can also consider concessions in regard to the Palestinians, ones that would serve Jordan. Such a policy would be worth it for Israel, because stopping Iran from producing nuclear weapons is a top priority. If Jordan still reuses to allow Israeli aircraft to pass over its territory, Israel could use other ways. One of them is to jam Jordanian radars without destroying them, preventing thus the Hashemite air force from intercepting Israeli aircraft. Yet, such a method might not work that well, and it would require resources, which would be needed to support the attack on Iran itself.

Jordan and Iraq strive to cooperate with each other and with other Arab states as well. Jordan and Iraq suffer from serious economic and political problems, which might undermine their stability. Chaos in Iraq and mostly in Jordan concern Israel, because it could allow radical Islamic groups such as ISIS to take over territory in Jordan, using it against Israel. However, Israel might also benefit from anarchy in Jordan and Iraq. Jordan and certainly Iraq would not participate in a raid in Iran, and they might even interfere. If those two Arab states are in shambles, their military would collapse or would be too crippled to bother the IAF on its way to Iran.

ISRAEL, EGYPT, AND IRAN

In the late 1950s, Israel strove to collaborate with non-Arab states like Iran in order to block the spreading of influence of both the Soviet Union and Egypt.[49] The 1979 Iranian revolution ended the alliance between Israel and Iran, but in the same year Israel signed a peace treaty with Egypt. Therefore, instead of cooperating with Iran against Egypt, Israel, and Egypt can work together against Iran.

Following the 1991 war against Iraq, Egypt claimed that since Iraq is restrained, Israel does not need its nuclear weapons.[50] It was part of the Egyptian effort, which continued in the upcoming decades, to force Israel to give up its nuclear weapons and at least to allow others to monitor them. Despite the peace Egypt suspects Israel and seeks to reduce Israel's military might as much as possible, let alone in the nuclear field. Egypt is also concerned about Iran, and its nuclear ambitions. Iran replaced Iraq as a threat not only to Israel, but to Arab states, including Egypt.

On September 13, 2021, Egyptian President Abd al-Fatah al-Sisi met in Sinai the Israeli Prime Minister Naftali Bennett. They talked among others on preventing Iran from having nuclear weapons and how to stop Iran's regional aggression.[51] Israel might have to bomb Iran's nuclear sites. Egypt might not support the Israeli raid, certainly not publically. Officially, Egypt might even criticize Israel, but Egypt actually might not oppose the Israeli attack. Egypt can tolerate it, as it did when Israel destroyed Arab nuclear sites in 1981 and 2007. Egypt did not want those Arab states to obtain nuclear weapons, because it would have changed the balance of power in their favor, boosting their status in the Arab world. Egypt, which sees itself as a leading Arab power, wants to prevent any Arab state from undermining Egypt and interfering with her regional ambitions. The same is also true about Iran. Egypt does not want any country in the Middle East, Arab or not, to compete with Egypt. Egypt would not want to be seemed as allowing Israel to bomb other countries. Nevertheless, Egypt accepted such operations over the years, such as during the Israel air campaign in Syria. Egypt can therefore ignore an Israeli attack in Iran, which as the Israeli bombardments in Syria; can reduce Iran's influence and power in the region.

Egypt's nuclear program was frozen in the 1970s.[52] In January 2007, President Hosni Mubarak claimed his country might have to obtain nuclear weapons, due to Iran's effort in this matter.[53] If eventually Iran produces nuclear weapons, Egypt too might try to get nuclear weapons.

Egypt might try to build it by itself, although the complexity and the cost of such a huge project, in several levels, could be quite high. Egypt might not be able to afford it, and its economy is already struggling. As an alternative, Egypt might join forces with other Arab states, building the Arab Bomb, yet the various constraints of such a project and Egypt's national pride and concerns might bring it to make an effort to gain nuclear weapons that would be under its control solely.

In late October 2021, Saudi Arabia "had deposited $3 billion with Egypt's central bank and extended the term of another $2.3 bln in previous deposits."[54] It was part of the Saudi aid to Egypt's economy. Also, their two militaries trained together and Egypt participated in the war in Yemen, against pro-Iranian proxies. If Iran produces nuclear weapons, Saudi Arabia might obtain nuclear weapons too. Egypt, despite its ties with Saudi Arabia, would not want to rely on the Saudi nuclear umbrella in such a crucial matter.

The peace between Israel and Egypt has been cold, due to almost lack of any relations in the economic, social, and cultural levels. Only at the security level there has been a fertile cooperation between the two states. Egypt and Israel should invest in those fields that were neglected. Making the peace stronger would help them also in facing Iran together.

Israel conquered the Sinai Peninsula in 1967 and fought to keep it in her hands in the attrition war in the late 1960s and in the 1973 war, while paying a heavy price. Sinai is a vast area, (60,000 sq. km.) that was highly valuable for Israel because it gave Israel strategic depth, bases, oil, etc. Egypt gradually got the Sinai back, during negotiations with Israel, which reached their peak in the 1979 peace accords. One of the stipulations of that treaty was Egypt's obligation to demilitarize most of Sinai. Following the insurgency in Sinai in the last decade, Israel allowed Egypt to reinforce its troops there. It might undermine the demilitarization of Sinai, a serious concern for Israel. The peace treaty survived many crises, but Israel still seeks to prevent Egypt from deploying large amount of troops and weapon systems near their border. This alone might create friction that would undermine their relations.

ISIS has a presence in Sinai. The Egyptian military has been unable to defeat ISIS. The latter sees both Iran and the Egyptian regime as its sworn enemies. ISIS does not seem powerful enough to undermine Egypt, but ISIS might keep Egypt busy, bothering it from contributing to the effort to contain Iran. ISIS might also strike Israel. The latter assists Egypt in confronting ISIS. Egypt authorized Israel to bomb ISIS in Sinai, since it serves both Israel and Egypt. They kept it a secret, in order not to embarrass the Egyptian government. Despite this joint effort if ISIS manages to inflict painful blows to Israel, it might cause tension and even a rift between Israel and Egypt. Israel might blame Egypt for failing to prevent ISIS attacks and might demand to operate in Sinai, openly, with few restrictions. Egypt would strongly oppose that, because of national pride. A friction between Israel and Egypt would damage the cooperation between them against both ISIS and Iran.

Sisi and Israel have a common enemy, Hamas in the Gaza Strip. Hamas is pro-Iranian. Hamas also assisted ISIS in Sinai. The Israeli blockade of the Gaza Strip means Hamas depends on Egypt, the only Arab state that has a border with the Gaza Strip. Egypt used it as leverage and acted aggressively to block smuggling of weapons from Sinai to the Gaza Strip. Egyptian pressure convinced Hamas to reduce its cooperation with ISIS. In addition, Hamas is associated with the MB, (Muslim Brotherhood) although Hamas claimed in 2017 it cut its ties with the MB. Sisi toppled the MB regime in 2013 and has been suppressing them.[55] Hamas might help the MB to undermine the Sisi regime. ISIS and the MB are also Israel's enemies. Therefore Israel and Egypt have several reasons why to see Hamas as a threat, not only because of its ties to Iran.

Egypt has been trying to handle Hamas with diplomacy, including serving as a broker between Israel and Hamas. Israel too rather relies on diplomacy in dealing with Hamas, even if it is done indirectly. Israel and Egypt could not convince Hamas to end its relations with Iran, but a combination of carrot and stick could urge Hamas to reduce the Iranian influence in the Gaza Strip.

In Libya there has been an ongoing civil war between the Tripoli-based Government of National Accord (GNA) that is supported mainly by Qatar and Turkey their foe is General Khalifa Haftar, who controls eastern Libya and commands the Libyan National Army (LNA). He enjoys the support of several states including Israel, Egypt, Saudi Arabia, and the UAE, which cooperate between them in this matter.[56] It is another aspect of the secret cooperation between Israel and Arab states. Even if it is not connected to Iran, developing the ties between Israel and Arabs can also help in building their cooperation against Iran.

Egypt and Israel take into consideration that there might be a war between them "regardless of its unlikelihood."[57] In spite of the 1979 peace treaty, Egypt has poured funds into its military, instead of investing more in solving its enormous economic and social problems. Such hardships destabilized Egypt in the past and it might happen again, with all its negative implications, including on the peace with Israel.

Israel is concerned since Egypt's military buildup is focused on preparing to run a high intensity war. Egypt does not face such a threat from its weaker neighbors, Sudan and Libya. Israel also shares a border with Egypt, and Israel has a powerful military, but Israel has no intentions of fighting Egypt. Furthermore, the IDF made a major shift in the last decade, from getting ready to run a high intensity war to training to confront pro-Iranian NSAs such as Hezbollah and Hamas. Israel therefore is concentrated on fighting Egypt's enemies. Egypt should do the same, since its main security threat is not the IDF, but NSA and the Egyptian military has difficulties in defeating ISIS.

If there is a reason for Egypt to keep a strong military is to assist Saudi Arabia against Iran. Iran does not share a border with Saudi Arabia, so Iran can't invade the kingdom, unless Iran launches an amphibious assault. Iran would probably rely on hitting Saudi Arabia with a barrage of missiles and drones. If Egypt deploys its forces, including aircraft, in Saudi Arabia, it can help its ally. In 1991 Egypt dispatched two of its best divisions to Saudi Arabia, to protect the kingdom from Iraq.

By 2021, since 1978, Egypt received from the United States "over $50 billion in military and $30 billion in economic assistance."[58] The aid started after the United States lost Iran as one of its most powerful partners in the Middle East. The United States hoped Egypt can replace Iran. Egypt, like Iran, has a status of a regional power. In both cases it is based on huge territory, vast population, rich history including as an empire and strategic location. Egypt also controls the Suez Canal while Iran can try to block the Hormuz straits. The United States therefore needs Egypt, among others to contain Iran.

After Sisi brought down the MB regime in July 2013, the Obama administration reduced the military aid to Egypt. Egypt saw that as a humiliation. Israel was worried since Egypt considers the US military aid to be part of the peace with Israel, although it is not, at least not officially. Later on the aid was restored, but the Biden administration, following human rights violations in Egypt, could cut the aid to Egypt. Such disputes brought Egypt to buy weapons from Russia and China, which don't bother Egypt about its internal affairs.[59] Tension between Egypt and the United States can disrupt cooperation against Iran. Sisi toppled the MB regime in Egypt, while Iran undermines regimes in other countries. There are serious Human rights concerns in Egypt. Iran has those issues too, and Iran also creates those problems in other countries. The United States and Egypt can reach a compromise regarding their differences, in order to focus on Iran.

CONCLUSION

Gulf Arab states such as Saudi Arabia and the UAE are much worried about Iran, which can lead to cooperation between them and Israel, against Iran. Israel has been seeking to contain and undermine the bridge Iran has been building, aimed at reaching from Iran all the way to the Mediterranean Sea. Israel also tries to build its own arc, from Israel to the Gulf, based on Arab Gulf states, as part of the conflict with Iran.

Arab states avoided getting their own nuclear weapons, although they know their foe, Israel, has this arsenal. Arabs in that sense believed Israel keeps its nuclear weapon only as a last resort, not in order to force Arabs to accept Israel's terms. In contrast if Iran produces a nuclear weapon, many Arabs would not trust Iran as they do with Israel in this matter. Fearing Iran might use its nuclear weapon not only as a last resort, might convince Arab states such as Saudi Arabia to gain a nuclear weapon too. Arabs might also hope Israel and Iran will mutually destroy each other, leaving Arabs unharmed. Meanwhile Arab states prefer Israel to save them again from having a Middle Eastern Muslim power with a nuclear weapon, i.e., to bomb Iran, as Israel did in 1981, in Iraq, and in 2007, in Syria. Arab Gulf States might assist Israel, but doing it indirectly, in order to prevent Iran from retaliating against them.

Israel is concerned about the Arms deals between its American patron and Gulf Arab states. Despite the ties between Gulf Arab states and Israel there is mutual suspicion. Israel was worried about selling the F-35 to the UAE, but it is not actually a huge concern for Israel. Overall an increase in Arab power in the conventional framework, not the nuclear one, would be less of a problem for Israel. Furthermore, it might shift Iran's focus away from Israel to the Gulf Arab states, who in their turn might feel more confident in their effort to deter Iran.

Iraq struggles with internal problems. Many Iraqis oppose the Iranian influence in their country. Some might also consider having relations with Israel. The latter can help those Iraqis, without putting them at risk. Jordan strives to stay out of an Israeli–Iranian conflict. Yet, maybe Israel can reach a deal with Jordan, allowing Israeli aircraft to cross Jordan on their way to Iran. Egypt, Israel, and the United States can overcome their differences, so they can work together against Iran.

NOTES

1. David Rundell, *Vision or Mirage: Saudi Arabia at the Crossroads* (I.B. Tauris: London, 2020).
2. On the Israeli nuclear project see: Avner Cohen, *The Last Taboo* (Or Yehuda: Kinneret, Zmora—Bitan, Dvir, 2005). Shlaomo Aronson, *Nuclear Weapons in the Middle East* (Jerusalem: Akademon, 1995).
3. *CBS News*, March 15, 2018. https://www.cbsnews.com/news/saudi-crown-prince-mohammed-bin-salman-iran-nuclear-bomb-saudi-arabia/.
4. Times of Israel staff, "Saudi Minister Says Nuclear Weapons 'An Option' for Kingdom if Iran Gets Them", *The Times of Israel*, November 18, 2020. https://www.timesofisrael.com/saudi-minister-says-nuclear-weapons-an-option-for-kingdom-if-iran-gets-them/.
5. *Reuters*, April 13, 2021. https://www.reuters.com/article/us-iran-nuclear-saudi/saudi-arabia-says-it-is-concerned-about-iran-uranium-enrichment-idUSKBN2C11MZ.
6. George Perkovich, Brian Radzinsky and Jaclyn Tandler, "The Iranian Nuclear Challenge and the GCC", *Carnegie*, May 31, 2012. http://carnegieendowment.org/2012/05/31/iranian-nuclear-challenge-and-gcc/b67p.
7. Yehuda U. Blanga, "Saudi Arabia's Motives in the Syrian Civil War", *Middle East Policy*, Winter 2017, Number 4, pp. 45–62.
8. Ebtesam Al Ketbi, "Contemporary Shifts in UAE Foreign Policy: From the Liberation of Kuwait to the Abraham Accords", *Israel Journal of Foreign Affairs* (Vol. 14, No. 3, 2020), p. 398.
9. On the Emirati armed forces see: Kenneth M. Pollack, "Sizing up Little Sparta: Understanding UAE Military Effectiveness," *American Enterprise Institute*, October 27, 2020. https://www.aei.org/research-products/report/sizing-up-little-sparta-understanding-uae-military-effectiveness/. See also: Eleonora Ardemagni, "The UAE's Military Training-Focused Foreign Policy", *Carnegie Endowment for International Peace*, October 22, 2020. https://carnegieendowment.org/sada/83033.

10. *Reuters*, August 13, 2021. https://www.reuters.com/world/mid dle-east/dubai-expo-focus-uae-racks-up-700-mln-trade-with-isr ael-since-normalisation-2021-08-13/.

11. Maysam Bizaer, "How the UAE—Israel Deal can Change the Regional power Balance", *Middle East Institute*, November 2, 2020. https://www.mei.edu/publications/how-uae-israel-deal-could-change-regional-power-balance.

12. *Reuters*, August 15, 2020. https://www.reuters.com/article/us-israel-emirates-iran/irans-president-says-emirates-made-huge-mis take-in-israel-deal-idUSKCN25B0BE.

13. Karel Valansi, "Turkey is Seeking a Fresh Start with Israel", *Atlantic Council*, March 10, 2021.
    https://www.atlanticcouncil.org/blogs/turkeysource/turkey-is-seeking-a-fresh-start-with-israel/.

14. *Reuters*, September 15, 2020. https://www.reuters.com/article/us-israel-emirates-palestinians-factions/rival-palestinian-factions-hold-rare-joint-meeting-over-israel-uae-deal-idUSKBN25U31R.

15. *CNN*, December 3, 2020. https://www.cnn.com/2020/12/03/middleeast/israel-uae-wedeman-intl/index.html.

16. Lahav Harkov, "Saudi FM Says No Ties with ISRAEL until Peace with PALESTINIANS", *The Jerusalem Post*, August 19, 2020. https://www.jpost.com/arab-israeli-conflict/saudi-fm-says-no-ties-with-israel-until-peace-with-palestinians-639205.

17. Tamar Pileggi, "Israel's Regional Military Edge is Safe, Top US General Assures", *The Times of Israel*, June 9, 2015. http://www.timesofisrael.com/dempsey-says-israel-will-not-lose-regional-mil itary-edge/.

18. US Department of State, May 20, 2017. https://www.state.gov/r/pa/prs/ps/2017/05/270999.htm.

19. Kylie Atwood and Zachary Cohan, "Kushner's Secret Push to Sell F-35 Jets to UAE Causes Frustration Among US Agencies and Lawmakers", *CNN*, August 20, 2020. https://www.cnn.com/2020/08/20/politics/kushner-uae-israel-f-35-fighter-jet/index.html.

20. The Times of Israel staff, "Air Force Chief: UAE F-35 Sale Could Be 'Less Optimal' for ISRAEL in Long Term", *The Times of Israel*, September 24, 2020. https://www.timesofisrael.com/air-force-chief-uae-f-35-sale-could-be-less-optimal-for-israel-in-long-term/.

21. Jacob Magid, "UAE Envoy: If US Unwilling to Supply Weapons, We'll Have to Turn Elsewhere", *The Times of Israel*, December 4, 2020. https://www.timesofisrael.com/uae-envoy-if-us-unwilling-to-supply-weapons-well-have-to-turn-elsewhere/.
22. James Stavridis, "Selling Fighter Jets to the UAE Is All About Israel", *Bloomberg*, September 24, 2020. https://www.bloomb erg.com/opinion/articles/2020-09-23/selling-f-35-fighter-jets-to-the-uae-is-all-about-israel.
23. Jacob Magid, "Envoy: Israel 'Comfortable' with US Arms Deal to UAE, Keeps Military Edge", *The Times of Israel*, December 7, 2020. https://www.timesofisrael.com/israel-very-comfortable-with-us-sale-of-f-35s-to-uae-ambassador-dermer-says/.
24. *Jewish Telegraphic Agency*, December 8, 2020. https://www.jta. org/quick-reads/aipac-no-longer-opposes-f-35-sales-to-the-uni ted-arab-emirates.
25. *US News*, April 13, 2021. https://www.usnews.com/news/ world/articles/2021-04-13/exclusive-biden-administration-pro ceeding-with-23-billion-weapon-sales-to-uae.
26. On selling Iron Dome to Saudi Arabia see: (no Author), "UAE: Israel Deal Should Remove Any Hurdle to F-35 Sales", *Aljazeera*, August 22, 2020. https://www.aljazeera.com/news/2020/08/ uae-israel-deal-remove-hurdle-35-sales-200821120108765.html.
27. Neri Zilber, "Peace for Warplanes? How Domestic and Foreign Disputes over the Potential Sale of F-35 Jets to the UAE Could Complicate the Country's Normalization Deal With Israel," *The Washington Institute for Near East Policy*, August 21, 2020. https://www.washingtoninstitute.org/policy-analysis/ view/peace-for-warplanes.
28. Christine McVann, "How to Balance Competing Priorities with an F-35 Sale to the UAE", *The Washington Institute for Near East Policy*, September 23, 2020. https://www.washingtoninstitute. org/policy-analysis/view/how-to-balance-competing-priorities-with-an-f-35-sale-to-the-uae.
29. On the Iron Dome see: Seth Frantzman, "Israel Should Provide Saudi Arabia with Iron Dome Batteries", *The Jerusalem Post*, March 22, 2021. https://www.jpost.com/middle-east/israel-sho uld-provide-saudi-arabia-with-iron-dome-batteries-662715.

30. Itamar Rabinovich, "A Jewish State in an Arab World", *Hoover Institute*, May 13, 2014. http://www.hoover.org/research/jewish-state-arab-world Hoover Institute.

31. Dima Abumaria, "An Arab NATO Hoover Institute in the Making", April 11, 2019. https://www.jpost.com/middle-east/an-arab-nato-in-the-making-586524.

32. Nora Maher, "Balancing Deterrence: Iran-Israel Relations in a Turbulent Middle East", *Review of Economics and Political Science*, March 2020, p. 14.

33. On 1982 see: Zeev Schiff and Ehud Ya'ari, *A War of Deception* (Tel Aviv: Schocken 1984).

34. On this issue see: Bradley Bowman and Jacob Nagel, "Why Not Add Israel to this Year's US-UAE Iron Union Exercise?" *Defense News*, September 10, 2020. https://www.defensenews.com/opinion/commentary/2020/09/10/why-not-add-israel-to-this-years-us-uae-iron-union-exercise/.

35. Judah Ari Gross, "Israeli, UAE Fighter Jets Fly Together in Large International Exercise in Greece", *The Times of Israel*, April 21, 2021. https://www.timesofisrael.com/israeli-uae-fighter-jets-fly-together-in-large-international-exercise-in-greece/.

36. Judah Ari Gross, "In landmark Visit, UAE Air Chief in Israel to Observe 'Blue Flag' Exercise", *The Times of Israel*, October 25, 2021. https://www.timesofisrael.com/in-landmark-visit-uae-air-chief-in-israel-to-observe-blue-flag-exercise/.

37. Mariam Baksh, "CISA Warns About Iran's Offensive Cyber Capabilities", *Defense One*, December 7, 2020. https://www.defenseone.com/threats/2020/12/cisa-warns-about-irans-offensive-cyber-capabilities/170548/. James Andrew Lewis, " Iran and Cyber Power", *CSIS*, June 25, 2019. https://www.csis.org/analysis/iran-and-cyber-power.

38. Dennis Ross, "The Next Mideast Explosion", *The Washington Institute for Near East Policy*, May 20, 2018. http://www.washingtoninstitute.org/policy-analysis/view/the-next-mideast-explosion.

39. John Hannah, "Israel Needs Weapons to Stop Iran's Bomb", *Foreign Policy*, October 15, 2021.

40. Avi Kober and Zvi Ofer (ed.), *The Iraqi Army in the Yom Kippur War* (Tel Aviv: Ministry of Defense, 1986).

41. On sending weapons to Iran: Avi Shlaim, *The Iron Wall* (Tel Aviv: Ydiot Ahronot, 2005), p. 418.
42. Yossi Melman and Meir Javedanfar, *The Sphinx: Ahmadinejad and the Key for the Iranian Bomb* (Tel Aviv: Ma'ariv book Guild, 2007), p. 108.
43. Shlomo Nakdimon, *Broken Hope* (Tel Aviv: Yediot Aharonot, 1996). Eliezer Tzafrir, *Ana Kurdi* (Tel Aviv: Ma'ariv Book Guild, 1998).
44. Herb Keinon, "Kurds Hope Israel Can Nudge US to Support Independence", *The Jerusalem Post*, August 16, 2017. http://www.jpost.com/Israel-News/Kurds-hope-Israel-can-nudge-US-to-support-independence-502425.
45. Allisa Rubin and Ronan Bergman, "Israeli Airstrike Hits Weapons Depot in Iraq", *The New York Times*, August 22, 2019. https://www.nytimes.com/2019/08/22/world/middleeast/israel-iraq-iran-airstrike.html.
46. Report no. 223, "Iraq's Tishreen Uprising: From Barricades to Ballot Box", *The Crisis Group*, July 26, 2021. https://www.crisisgroup.org/middle-east-north-africa/gulf-and-arabian-peninsula/iraq/223-iraqs-tishreen-uprising-barricades-ballot-box.
47. On the possibility of war see: Moshe Arens, *Broken Covenant* (Israel: Yedioth Ahronoth, 1993), pp. 205–6.
48. On the attack on Jordan see: Tzvi Joffre and Tovah Lazaroff, "Jordan Has Been Attacked by Iranian-Made Drones—King Abdullah", *The Jerusalem Post*, July 21, 2021. https://www.jpost.com/middle-east/jordan-has-been-attacked-by-iranian-made-drones-king-abdullah-674911.
49. Shlaim, *The Iron Wall*, p. 196.
50. Hossam Eldeen M. Aly, "Prospects for Arms Control in the Middle East", Theodore A. Couloumbis and Thanos P. Dokos, (eds.), *Arms Control and Security in the Middle East and The CIS Republics* (Hellenic Foundation for Europe and Foreign Policy, 1995), p. 169.
51. Tovah Lazaroff, "Bennett and Sisi Talk Hamas, Iranian Threats in Rare Meeting", *The Jerusalem Post*, September 13, 2021. https://www.jpost.com/breaking-news/israeli-prime-minister-visits-egypt-in-first-official-trip-for-a-decade-679334.
52. Anthony H. Cordesman, *The Military Balance in the Middle East* (London: Praeger, 2004), p. 137.

53. Steven A. Cook, "The Unspoken Power: Civil-Military Relations and the Prospects for Reform" (The Brookings Project on U.S. Policy towards the Islamic World, September 2004), p. 13.
54. On the 3 Billon $ see: *Reuters*, October 31, 2021. https://www.reuters.com/world/middle-east/saudi-deposits-3-bln-egypts-central-bank-extends-previous-facilities-2021-10-31/.
55. On the MA in Egypt see: Eric Trager, *Arab Fall—How the Muslim Brotherhood Won and Lost Egypt* (Georgetown University Press, 2016).
56. Yosi Melman, "Israel's Little-Known Support for Haftar's War in Libya", *Middle East Eye*, April, 15, 2020. https://www.middleeasteye.net/news/israel-little-known-support-haftar-war-libya.
57. David M. Witty, "Egypt's Armed Forces Today: A Comparison with Israel", *MECRA*, September 26, 2020. https://www.mideastcenter.org/post/egypt-s-armed-forces-today-a-comparison-with-israel.
58. "US Relations with Israel", Us Department of State, January 5, 2021. https://www.state.gov/u-s-relations-with-egypt/.
59. On buying from Russia and China see: David Schenker, "Getting Tough with Egypt Won't Work", The Institute for Near East Policy, March 25, 2021. https://www.washingtoninstitute.org/policy-analysis/getting-tough-egypt-wont-work?fbclid=IwAR0fFfjQ-ZinOO8SWZrkmfsSvqe06rfz70hJ92llUHyXtkdx08uLLAt5doI.

CHAPTER 4

Iran, Hezbollah, and the Palestinians

Iran has different kinds of allies, states like Russia and Syria and NSAs such as Hamas and Hezbollah. There was friction between Hamas and Iran, following the Syrian civil war. Hezbollah, which kept its loyalty to Iran, continued to receive massive Iranian aid, but Hezbollah still has major hardships, including economic ones. In the West Bank the PA has its concerns about Iran, since the latter supports the PA's rival, Hamas. Israel cooperates with the PA against Hamas in the West Bank, while in the Gaza Strip Israel deals with Hamas by itself. Israel tolerates Hamas rule in the Gaza Strip, for lack of a better option.

HAMAS AND HEZBOLLAH AS IRANIAN ALLIES

For Iran the United States is "the big Satan" while Israel is "the small Satan."[1] It could be argued that for Israel Iran is "the big Satan" and the Hezbollah and pro-Iranian Palestinian organizations such as the Islamic Jihad and Hamas are a "small Satan" each. Israel perceives them as the military and political vanguard of Iran in the Levant. Their location gives Iran a springboard to attack Israel, mostly by firing rockets and missiles. Iran also needs them to gather support in the Arab world, since Iran is mostly Persian and mostly Shiite, while the Hezbollah is Arab and the pro-Iranian Palestinian groups are not only Arabs but Sunnis too, as are most of the Arabs. Iran supports those organizations as part of its cold

© The Author(s), under exclusive license to Springer Nature Switzerland AG 2022
E. Eilam, *Israeli Strategies in the Middle East*,
https://doi.org/10.1007/978-3-030-95602-8_4

war with Israel. If Israel had attacked Iran, those groups would have been called to fire at Israel. Iran needs Hezbollah for other tasks as well such as to train Shi'a militias and to assist Iran across the region. It gives Iran a tool the latter can use without risking its own men while also avoiding taking responsibility for Hezbollah's actions.[2]

Hezbollah confronted Israel in Lebanon in the 1980s and in the 1990s, and again in 2006, for 34 days. The ongoing conflict between Hamas and Israel started in the late 1980s. The peak was in the 2008–2009 and 2014 wars. Both Hamas and Hezbollah see themselves as part of "Resistance" (muqawama), and believe that in spite of Israel's military might, it is weak both mentally and socially, while they (Hamas and Hezbollah) are stronger due to their "deep religious faith." They further insist that the struggle against Israel must continue, aiming to drain it "mentally and physically" until it is annihilated. This goal will be achieved through resilience, patience (sabr), and endurance, arising from the Resistance fighter's mental strength and the use of low intensity warfare.[3] "Hezbollah, Hamas, and the Houthi insurgency have been able to circumvent their fundamental inferiority vis-à-vis stronger states, such as Israel or Saudi Arabia. The nonstate actors have used their arsenals to constrain the ability of the states to intervene in their strongholds."[4]

Israel was willing to negotiate officially with pro-Iranian Arab states like Syria, but not talk openly with pro-Iranian Arab non-state actors like Hamas and Hezbollah. Those groups don't want to talk directly to Israel either. Yet Israel, Hamas, and Hezbollah, have had all kinds of understandings between them over the years. Israel, due to its military might, could have destroyed the base of those groups. But Israel has accepted the rule of the Hamas in the Gaza Strip since 2007, as well as the fact that the Hezbollah has been the dominant force in Lebanon.

On June 25, 2006, an Israeli soldier was taken captive by Hamas on the border of the Gaza Strip. In response, but not only because of that assault, the IDF launched a series of attacks in the upcoming months. Their scale was limited compared with a much bigger confrontation that started on July 12, 2006, after the Hezbollah captured two Israeli troops, when their patrol ran into an ambush on the border with Lebanon. Since then there was 2014 war between Israel and Hamas that started after three Israeli teenagers had been kidnapped and murdered. Another provocation by the Hamas/Hezbollah, such as grabbing Israeli troops, might lead to another round, which might be longer and more destructive to both sides. Hamas and Hezbollah are well aware that Israel is very sensitive about its soldiers.

Israel proved it was willing to pay a huge price for releasing its troops from captivity. Hamas also use psychological warfare in order to put pressure on Israel in this matter.[5]

"The potential loss of its logistics hub and supply line in Syria would place Hezbollah at a significant disadvantage in the event of another conflict with Israel." This reason and Iran's demand to assist Assad brought Hezbollah to fight in Syria.[6] Hamas refused to do the same, which caused a rift between Hamas and Iran. The former lost much of the Iranian aid. It was not the first time Hamas was required to help a major Iranian ally. In the 2006 war in Lebanon, when Israel confronted Hezbollah the latter tried to open a second front in the West Bank and the Gaza Strip. However, Israeli security forces managed to prevent assaults. Many of the attempts were carried out by Fatah and not by Hamas. The latter did launch rockets from the Gaza Strip, but only a few dozens. Even this fire was gradually reduced and eventually stopped, following Israeli retribution, and Hamas assuming that world attention was focused on the war in Lebanon. Hamas could have continued and even intensified its assaults against Israel, but they did not deem it worthwhile. Hamas therefore avoided taking a decisive military initiative that might have affected Israel's fight in Lebanon, and would have showed solidarity with another Iranian partner.

The relations between Iran and Hamas were not rattled by the 2006 war in Lebanon, but they ran into a crisis because of the civil war in Syria. For Iran the absence of Hamas from the war against Israel in 2006 was not as severe as the Hamas's refusal to stand by Assad against other Muslims. In 2006 the Hezbollah might not have been at risk as Assad has been since 2011, but in Lebanon in 2006 there was after all a confrontation, where the Hamas could have demonstrated its full commitment to the "resistance," the alliance against Israel to which the Hamas belongs. Furthermore, Hamas did not have too much to lose in 2006. In spite of its victory in the municipal elections inside the PA in 2005, and the fact that one of its leaders, Ismail Haniyeh, was the prime minister of the PA, Hamas did not actually hold any territory Israel might have taken from it as retribution. After 2007, when Hamas captured the Gaza Strip, this factor influenced its calculations.

"Hezbollah's raison d'etre has always been to fight Israel, not other Arabs (even if they are Sunnis)." Hezbollah's involvement in the war in Syria "distracted Hezbollah from what is allegedly its top priority."[8] In contrast, Hamas kept its focus on Israel. Hamas could have also sought to abandon the Iranian camp, in favor of another bloc, an anti-Iranian one. However, as a relatively weak player in the Middle East, Hamas needs all the help it can get, without losing current aid. Hamas might have hoped that its position regarding Syria would not antagonize Iran too much, since to begin with Hamas did not carry much weight inside Syria, and its ability to assist Assad was limited. Hamas leaders might have calculated that Iran would not punish them severely, and risk losing its investment in it. Hamas might have believed it is possible to continue keeping a partnership with Iran while strengthening its ties with Arab states that oppose Iran. Either way, Hamas assumed that supporting Assad would have caused a rift between it and Arab Sunni states that wanted to topple Assad. Those states might have turned against Hamas and this would have made it more vulnerable to an Israeli action. Hamas wished to avoid a danger to its rule in the Gaza Strip, and was willing to do so at the expense of Assad. But Hamas decision to rely on Sunni states proved to be a mistake at least with regard to Egypt. The toppling of President Mohammed Morsi from the MB, an ally of the Hamas, and the rise of Abdel Fattah al-Sisi, in early July 2013 was a major blow to the Hamas.

It could perhaps be possible for Hamas to upgrade its ties with Iran, without automatically jeopardizing its control of the Gaza Strip, in case of a confrontation between Iran and Israel. Being aware, however, of its location, on the border with Israel not far away as Iran is, and bearing in mind its weakness compared to Iran, Hamas would realize its exposure to an Israeli retribution. The 2014 war proved that "Hamas once again went toe-to-toe with the Middle East's strongest military and survived." However Hamas is also aware of the cost of that war, which might convince Hamas not to start another confrontation.[9]

In early January 2020 the head of Hamas political bureau, Ismail Haniyeh, visited Tehran, for the first time since 2012, "thus giving the current visit exceptional importance." He was the only non-Iranian figure who spoke during the service of the top Iranian official Qasem Soleimani. Haniyeh called him a "martyr of Jerusalem," "which caused intense controversy and debate, even within Hamas itself."[10] Iran also continued to send money to Hamas. In December 2020 Israel moved to seize $4 million that were transferred from Iran to Hamas.[11] However, Hezbollah receives much more because of its loyalty to Iran.

In January 2020 the United Kingdom, after already declaring that Hezbollah movement is a terrorist organization, "expanded the scope of its asset-freezing measures...to cover the entire organization as well as its military wing."[12] The Director of the US national intelligence claimed in mid-April 2021 that Hezbollah "maintains the capability to target, both directly and indirectly, US interests inside Lebanon, in the region, overseas, and—to a lesser extent—in the United States."[13] Therefore Israel and its American patron have to contain Hezbollah as much as possible, including in Lebanon (Map 4.1).

Hezbollah and Lebanon

The end of the Lebanese civil war in 1989 gave the state an opportunity to recover by reducing the power of armed groups.[14] However, Hezbollah established itself as a major player in Lebanon by taking care of the basic needs of Shiites there such as by providing education, food, and medical services, as long as the Shiites were willing to obey the group without question.[15] South Lebanon is a Hezbollah stronghold due to its large Shiite population, where Hezbollah would stand its ground.

The Syrian–Iranian axis strengthened Hezbollah by allowing it to receive aid from Iran through Syria.[16] In addition in 2019 Iran continued to pay part of Assad's debts to Russia. In return, millions of dollars in cash that were taken out of Syria's central bank were passed to Hezbollah. Still the sanctions on Iran forced it to cut its aid to Hezbollah, which used to be almost one billion a year. Hezbollah experienced financial hardships also due to the need to take care of thousands of its wounded from the Syrian war, families of those who were killed there and those who retired. Hezbollah tried to deal with it by taking austerity measures, calling it an "economic jihad." Yet "as patron of the Shiite people in Lebanon and as a 'Dawah' group that sponsors educational, cultural, and welfare activities as a way of bringing people closer to its goals." Hezbollah had to be careful not to undermine its support among its public in Lebanon.[17]

In 2020 Hezbollah was in decline because of the group's "economically strangled sponsor," i.e., Iran and Lebanon's bankruptcy. Furthermore rifts and unrest inside Lebanon meant that there was "no discernible consensus to back Hezbollah in going to war"[18] against Israel. "Hezbollah's financial difficulties have also weakened its support. Reduced, or suspended, salaries, smaller pensions to families of 'martyrs,' and public appeals for donations to the 'resistance' have undermined Hezbollah's reputation by creating an atmosphere of vulnerability and fiscal unreliability. It also breeds resentment among the populace who look to Hezbollah for a living. The Lebanese Shia business community, once

64   E. EILAM

Map 4.1 Lebanon, Map No. 4282, January 2010, UNITED NATIONS
https://www.un.org/geospatial/content/lebanon

a significant donor, is distancing itself from Hezbollah to avoid being tarnished as a 'terrorist financier' and potentially targeted by US sanctions."[19]

In November 2019 the United States rejected Israel's request that US financial aid to Lebanon will be given only if Lebanon prevents Hezbollah from assimilating precision-guided missiles.[20] Hezbollah's buildup makes Iran more powerful. Israel and the United States wish to avoid that and also to help Lebanon to function, particularly following the deep economic crisis in that country, so it will not crumble. Some claim Lebanon is already a failed state. If it continues "the Lebanese army could collapse as well, with Hezbollah being the only entity that could assume control. The country could end up with a partition among its main confessional groups or, worse, descend again into civil war." Such an outcome would be bad for Israel too.[21]

In 2020 US aid to the Lebanese military was supposed to professionalize it and "to mitigate internal and external threats from non-state actors, including Hizballah... preventing the use of Lebanon as a safe haven for terrorist groups."[22] On June 7, 2021, General Kenneth McKenzie, Commander of the U.S. Central Command, said the United States remains "committed to supporting the Lebanese armed forces. They're one of the elements of the Government of Lebanon that actually functions very well, and we believe they should continue to be the sole expression of military power of the state in Lebanon."[23] There is also a need to assist the Lebanese military in preventing cross-border smuggling, a severe problem since it harms the economy and benefits Hezbollah. The Lebanese armed forces avoid carrying out this mission, fearing of provoking Hezbollah.[24] Israel and the United States strive to strengthen the Lebanese military, so it can suppress Hezbollah. However the latter is part of the Lebanese government, which controls the armed forces, and there are also ties between the Lebanese military and Hezbollah. The weapons the Lebanese military assimilated, mostly its anti-tank missiles, could be aimed at Israel, particularly if they fell into the hands of Hezbollah. Nevertheless, it might be for Israel a calculated risk, if the Lebanese military eventually help to contain and hopefully to disarm Hezbollah, as part of stabilizing Lebanon. When Hezbollah is at a low point, its rivals in Lebanon might be able to reduce its influence and to break Iran's grip on Lebanon. Under such circumstances a more robust Lebanese military will serve as an important national tool in restraining the Hezbollah.

The economic meltdown in Lebanon has affected its military as well, bringing deep cuts, including in providing food supply for the soldiers. Furthermore the monthly salary of the troops is worth much less. This grim reality causes resentment among soldiers, some seek to be discharged.[25] Such a crisis can cripple the Lebanese military, making it more difficult to use it to stabilize the country, including in confronting Hezbollah.

In late October 2021, there was a crisis between Lebanon and Saudi Arabia. From the Saudi point of view the origin of the rift is the "Lebanese political setup that reinforces the dominance of the Iran-backed Hezbollah armed group and continues to allow endemic instability."[26] The Saudi position reflects the Israeli approach too, which sees Hezbollah as a threat to Lebanon. The economic catastrophe in Lebanon might bring a change that could weaken Hezbollah and by that reducing the Iranian grip on that country.

THE PA AND IRAN

Iran's supreme leader, Ali Khamenei argued that in the Palestinian matter the goal should be to return the territory, where there is now Israel, to Islamic hands. Khamenei's so-called solution is to allow Palestinian refugees to return and then "Muslims, Christians and Jews could choose a government for themselves, excluding immigrant Jews."[27] Therefore almost all the Israelis can't vote in those "elections." Khamenei's plan is of course meant to ensure the Arabs will win. It is a biased and ridiculous idea, which was ignored not only by Israel but by Arabs too.

There were signs of tension between the Fatah-led PA and Iran.[28] PA Officials were "openly fearful of increasing Iranian influence over Palestinian politics, mainly with respect to Hamas." Some in the PA claimed that the stalemate in the talks with Israel and the Israeli settlement activity "would amplify calls for Iranian involvement in the region."[29] On July 11, 2021 "Azzam al-Ahmad, a member of Fatah's Central Committee and the PLO's Executive Committee, participated in the annual general conference of the Iranian Mujahedeen-e-Khalq (MEK) resistance group." He expressed there "his support for the Iranian opposition and reiterating the strength of relations between the two sides." The PLO ruled out that Ahmad's position reflects its own official position. Ahmed Majdalani, a member of the PLO's Executive Committee, said "the relationship with the Iranian opposition is not a substitute for the relationship with the regime and is not directed against it." However, in recent years the PA and the Iranian opposition have tightened their toes.[30] It is a message to the Iranian regime, which assists Hamas, the PA's opposition.

The PA and Hamas are sworn enemies. The PA and Hamas tried several times to reconcile, by using brokers, but it did not work. The PA and Hamas have disagreements about many issues, including about Israel. Both the PA and Hamas wish to replace Israel with a Palestinian state. Yet, the PA and Hamas have different approaches. The PA is more moderate than Hamas. Unlike Hamas and its Iranian patron the PA is willing to compromise on a two-state solution. The PA also opposes confronting Israel militarily. Hamas did not abandon the armed conflict. Hamas has been well aware of its military inferiority, in fighting the IDF, but this did not deter it from provoking Israel over and again. However, due to its constraints such as the severe economic crisis in the Gaza Strip, Hamas demonstrated certain flexibility by reaching all kinds of understandings with Israel.

Iran urges the Palestinians to oppose US steps in regard to the Israeli–Palestinian conflict.[31] It is part of the Iranian strategy to both weaken US influence in the region and to increase the Iranian sway. Iran also encourages Palestinians to confront Israel, not only in the Gaza Strip, but in the West Bank as well. In the Gaza Strip it is easier since there Iran's protégés, Hamas and the Palestinian Islamic Jihad (PIJ), have a much stronger position than the one they have in the West Bank. Iran is obviously against the cooperation between the PA and Israel against Hamas. Iran rather replaces the PA with Hamas.

The PA is quite fragile. Israel is concerned that if the PA crumbles then Hamas might try to take over parts of the West Bank. Israel tolerates Hamas rule in the Gaza Strip, but Israel would certainly not allow Hamas to seize any territory in the West Bank, close to the heart of Israel, the Tel Aviv area. Although Hamas already fired at the Tel Aviv area from the Gaza Strip, if Hamas can use the West Bank it would become much more dangerous to Israel. Blocking Hamas, and therefore also Iran, from establishing a fire base in the West Bank is a red line for Israel.

The PA lost the Gaza Strip to Hamas, in 2007. Israel could seize the Gaza Strip and bring down Hamas, paving the way for the PA to regain its hold over the Gaza Strip. The PA, however, might refuse to be seen as returning to power in the Gaza Strip by depending on the IDF, although the PA's survival in the West Bank is to a large extent due to the deployment of the IDF there. Even if the PA takes over the Gaza Strip, it might not manage to hold its ground there. Israel would probably not want to join, let alone replace, the PA in running the Gaza Strip because of political, military, and economic constraints. As much as Israel wants to get rid of Hamas, among others because of the ties between Hamas and Iran, Hamas stays in power in the Gaza Strip.

THE TENSION BETWEEN ISRAEL AND HAMAS

Hamas is contained in the Gaza Strip,[32] but it still manages to hold on against Israel. The results of the 2006 war between Israel and Hezbollah did not convince Hamas of the need to avoid provoking Israel. It therefore led to the clash in 2008–2009. Consequently, other fronts where Israel faced an Arab NSA were affected, when Israel looked relatively successful, or vice versa when it looked as though it failed.

Iran arms Hamas, in order to deter Israel from attacking Iran. The 2014 war between Israel and Hamas did not occur because Iran urged Hamas to strike Israel. In a way from Iranian perspective it was a waste of resources and an unnecessary risk, since Israel did not attack Iran. Although Israel did not try to topple Hamas it was a major confrontation, which could have undermined Hamas rule and by that jeopardizing Iran's grip in the Gaza Strip.

One of Israel's biggest concerns in the 2014 war was the tunnels that led from the Gaza Strip into Israel. Hamas used them to infiltrate into Israel several times, which cost Israel some casualties. The IDF, during that war, improvised,[33] but the tunnels stayed. They were remembered by Israel as a serious problem. Hamas, acting by itself or because of Iran, presented a threat. Hamas could have launched hundreds of fighters into the south of Israel. Therefore since 2014 Israel had invested heavily, up to a Billion $ in discovering and blocking tunnels. In the upcoming years tunnels were discovered and destroyed one after another. Without the 2014 war the tunnels might not have received much attention from Israel, which would have allowed Hamas and Iran to keep them for retribution, if Israel had attacked Iran. It was another reason why the 2014 confrontation did not serve Iran's interests.

On March 30, 2018, thousands of Palestinians confronted the IDF on the border of the Gaza Strip. Fifteen Palestinians were killed and hundreds were wounded, the deadliest day since the 2014 war. The IDF claimed its troops were attacked by stones and in one case also with live fire. This clash was organized by Hamas. The IDF got ready in advance by reinforcing its forces across the border, including with snipers and Special Forces. Those clashes continued in the upcoming years, with heavy casualties to the Palestinians. Hundreds of them were killed and thousands were wounded, during what was a mixed of demonstrations, provocations, and attempts to reach the border, to which Israel did not allow them to approach. Israel was worried they might breach the fence, cross it and then they will attack its troops there or infiltrate to one of the nearby villages.

From Iranian perspective those clashes made Israel look bad. However, as long as there were not major skirmishes with high casualties among Palestinians, the international community, including Arab states, got used to them. Hamas might serve Iran by keeping such a policy after an Israeli raid on Iran. Iran could then use its proxies to confront Israel as much as possible on several fronts. Hamas, by using wild and violent demonstrations, can pin down Israeli troops, bother Israel and help Iran to show that Arabs, including Sunnis, are on her side.

The Clash in November 2019: Israel Against the PIJ

Israel, for lack of a better choice, prefers to keep Hamas in charge of the Gaza Strip. Hamas, in order to keep its control, monitors and when needed suppresses other radical groups, which are smaller than Hamas. The PIJ is one of them, the second most powerful group in the Gaza Strip. There is cooperation but also mutual suspicion and competition between the PIJ and Hamas.

The PIJ and Hamas are Iranian proxies. The PIJ might not want to seize the Gaza Strip or part of it. Nevertheless, if Hamas becomes weaker than the PIJ, with or without encouragement from their Iranian patron, might change their position.

Israel rather Hamas stays the ruler of the Gaza Strip. The PIJ is more radical than Hamas and also does not have any experience in running a territory, unlike Hamas, which could bring chaos, and this does not serve Israel. Hamas does a bad job in running the Gaza Strip, but the PIJ might be worse. Hamas also had gained knowledge in communicating with Israel, indirectly, since 2007 while absorbing major blows from the IDF. Therefore Hamas could be more careful and responsible than the PIJ. Hamas refuses to openly negotiate with Israel, but Hamas might be convinced not to obey Iran, which could help in eventually reaching both a solution to the Israeli–Palestinian conflict and in Israel's struggle against Iran.

In November 2019 Hamas watched how two of its foes, the PIJ and Israel, encountered each other, yet they did not absorb many casualties and damages. No one was killed in Israel and the cost to its economy was mild, certainly compared with a war. The PIJ lost a few dozen men and some facilities and arsenal. The fight was basically between the PIJ rockets; more than 400 of them were launched at Israel, and the Israeli Iron Dome system, which performed quite well in shooting them down. The PIJ was focused on the south of Israel, although it has the capability to strike farther north, i.e., in the Tel Aviv area. The IAF bombed targets in the Gaza Strip, but did not carry a large-scale campaign. There was also no ground offensive in the Gaza Strip or infiltrations from there into Israel. Both sides, mostly Israel, therefore did not use their full military potential, since they strove to avoid an escalation.

The PIJ and Hamas compete with each other. The PIJ does not challenge Hamas's rule, yet each group wishes to prove that it is the one that better fights for the Palestinian cause. Hamas took a risk by standing from the side in the 2019 November collision. Hamas could have been seen in the Arab world and particularly in the Gaza Strip as fearing Israel and even worse: as collaborating with it against the PIJ. Hamas does not want to have the image of the PA that maintains security cooperation with Israel. This is why it might have been just of matter of time until Hamas would have been forced to join the skirmish. Then it would have been a different fight.

The clash in mid-November 2019 started after a senior figure from the PIJ, a brigade commander, was killed by Israel, since he caused many problems to Israel and actually to Hamas as well. Israel had assumed the assassination might bring an escalation, but Israel did not get ready for a major showdown. For example the IDF did not call in its reserves and avoided a massive reinforcement of its units around the Gaza Strip, such as by sending there its elite infantry and armor brigades, a necessary step that was done during previous crises there.

THE CONFRONTATION OF MAY 2021

IDF Chief of Staff Aviv Kohavi said in late December 2019 that he knows a war in the Gaza Strip "would mean fighting in highly complicated urban areas, where Hamas has established many military facilities, believing that Israel would be more cautious and hesitant in such a densely populated location, full of civilians." He added "the enemy decided to base itself in an urban environment, but we will respond forcefully…We will warn the civilians who live there and give them time to evacuate."[34] Hamas would again use its population as human shield. Israel must do its best to avoid harming civilians, but some of them might still be hurt. Iran, which assisted Assad in a war that cost the lives of hundreds of thousands of people, many of them Syrian Sunnis, would not care that much if Palestinian Sunnis are killed during a fight with Israel. Yet, Iran would use it to present Israel as an enemy of Arabs.

Maj. Gen. Tal Kalman argued in March 2021 that Israel wants Hamas to be contained and weak militarily.[35] Israel wants to disarm Hamas, as part of reducing Iran's strength. Yet, Israel could compromise on allowing Hamas to keep light arms, just to handle and contain its enemies in the Gaza Strip, which are Israel's foes too. Israel has the same concept regarding the PA in the West Bank, where the PA suppresses Hamas and other groups, more radical than the PA. In the West Bank the Palestinian security forces openly cooperate with their Israeli counterparts. Hamas in the Gaza Strip does not do that. Nevertheless, the Israeli concept is that rational Arab groups should be in charge, since by following their own interest they would fight other Arabs, who are more dangerous to Israel, also since sometimes they are pro-Iranian. This is why Israel can tolerate the PA and Hamas to be strong enough to deal with their Arab enemies, without possessing an arsenal, such as rockets, that would jeopardize Israel.

In mid-May 2021, Israel and Hamas had a confrontation that lasted 11 days. It was basically exchange of fire, as the confrontation in November 2012. Hamas fired rockets while Israel as usual relied on the IAF. The latter's biggest achievement was destroying major part of Hamas's underground network, an attack that was supposed to kill many Hamas gunmen. Yet Hamas did not absorb many losses. This confrontation, like the former ones, ended in a tie, although it seems to have boosted Hamas's position among Palestinians, at the expense of the PA.[36] In that sense it benefited Iran as well.

Hamas and PIJ have significantly upgraded their arsenal, including improving their ability in launching a barrage of rockets to the Tel Aviv area, which is 70 km north of the Gaza Strip.[37] Khaled al-Qaddumi, Hamas representative in Iran, said then that Iran gave significant help by providing both knowledge and rockets to Hamas. He emphasized that Iran and Hamas are partners, but Hamas is not an Iranian proxy.[38] Hamas showed again its desire to be considered as an independent player and at the same time it gave Iran compliments, in order to continue to receive Iranian aid.

Brig. Gen. Dror Shalom served as the head of the Research and Analysis Division for Israeli Defense Intelligence. He argued in August 2021 that Hamas rule might crumble following internal hardships, without Israel's intervention.[39] In late October 2021 the IDF conducted a two-day exercise "simulating war in the Gaza Strip."[40] If Hamas assumes its economic situation in the Gaza Strip is desperate, the group might initiate an escalation, even a war, if it seems to its leadership as their only way to survive. Iran will assist Hamas, in order not to lose its investment in this group.

CONCLUSION

Israel fought Iran's protégés, Hezbollah and Hamas, although it was not always because of Iran. Hamas has its own agenda. Furthermore there was a rift between Hamas and its Iranian patron since Hamas refused to assist Iran during the Syrian civil war. As to Hezbollah, the United States and Israel wish to reduce Hezbollah's influence as much as possible. One option is to strengthen the Lebanese military so it can contain Hezbollah, although it will not be easy due to the ties between the Lebanese armed forces and Hezbollah.

There is an ongoing coordination between the Palestinian security forces and their Israeli counterparts. They managed to contain Hamas in the West Bank. However, the PA is vulnerable. If it crumples Israel will prevent Hamas, and its Iranian patron, from getting a foothold in the West Bank. In the Gaza Strip Israel would continue to tolerate Hamas rule, since it is better than chaos. Hamas is also less radical and more responsible than other groups there, such as the PIJ.

Notes

1. Ali Hashem, "Iranians Look for Change in US Policies", *Al Monitor*, October 18, 2013. http://www.al-monitor.com/pulse/originals/2013/10/iran-observe-us-change-policy.html.
2. Matthew Levit, "Hezbollah Regional Activities in Support of Iran's Proxy Networks", Middle East Institute, July 26, 2021. https://www.mei.edu/publications/hezbollahs-regional-activities-support-irans-proxy-networks. Kaunert Christian and Ori Wertman, "The Securitisation of Hybrid Warfare Through Practices Within the Iran-Israeli Conflict: Israel's Practices for Securitizing Hezbollah's Proxy War", *Security & Defence Quarterly* (Vol. 31, 2020), pp. 99–114.
3. Uzi Rabi and Harel Chorev, "To Deter Hamas: Expect the Unexpected", *The World Post*, August 12, 2014.
4. Jean-Loup Samaan, "Nonstate Actors and Anti-Access/Area Denial Strategies: The Coming Challenge" (US Army War College Press, June 2020), p. 12.
5. (No Author), "Hamas Releases Audio Allegedly of Israeli Soldier it Holds", *Aljazeera*, June 7, 2021. https://www.aljazeera.com/news/2021/6/7/exclusive-audio-recording-of-israeli-soldier-held-by-hamas.
6. Bilal Saab and Daniel Byman, "Hezbollah in a Time of Transition", The Atlantic Council, November 17, 2014. http://www.atlanticcouncil.org/publications/hezbollah-in-a-time-of-transition.
7. Hanin Ghaddar, "A Strategy to Contain Hezbollah: Ideas and Recommendations", The Washington Institute for Near East Policy, August 24, 2021, p. 4. https://www.washingtoninstitute.org/policy-analysis/strategy-contain-hezbollah-ideas-and-recommendations.
8. Coli Clarke, "A Glass Half Empty? Taking Stock of Hezbollah's Losses in Syria", *The Rand Blog*, October 17, 2017. https://www.rand.org/blog/2017/10/a-glass-half-empty-taking-stock-of-hezbollahs-losses.html.
9. Grant Rumley and Neri Zilber, "A Military Assessment of the Israel-Hamas Conflict", The Washington Institute for Near East Policy, May 25, 2021. https://www.washingtoninstitute.org/policy-analysis/military-assessment-israel-hamas-conflict.

10. Adnan Abu Amer, "Hamas and Iran: More Than an Understanding, Not Quite a Complete Alliance", *Middle East Monitor*, January 17, 2020. https://www.middleeastmonitor.com/202 00117-hamas-and-iran-more-than-an-understanding-not-quite-a-complete-alliance/.
11. The Times of Israel staff, "Defense Minister Orders Seizure of $4 Million Sent by Iran to Hamas", *The Times of Israel*, December 22, 2020. https://www.timesofisrael.com/defense-minister-orders-sei zure-of-4-million-sent-by-iran-to-hamas/.
12. Reuters, January 17, 2020. https://www.reuters.com/article/us-britain-treasury-hezbollah/uk-expands-hezbollah-asset-freeze-tar gets-entire-movement-idUSKBN1ZG1DT.
13. Director of national intelligence, "2021 Annual Threat Assessment of the U.S. Intelligence Community", April 13, 2021. https://www.dni.gov/index.php/newsroom/reports-publicati ons/reports-publications-2021/item/2204-2021-annual-threat-assessment-of-the-u-s-intelligence-community.
14. Michael Hudson, *Trying Again: Power-Sharing in Post-Civil War Lebanon* (Brill, 1997). Imad Salamey, "Failing Consociationalism in Lebanon and Integrative Options", *International Journal of Peace Studies* (Vol. 14, No. 2, 2009), pp. 83–105.
15. Joseph Daher, *Hezbollah: The Political Economy of Lebanon's Party of God* (London: Pluto Press, 2016).
16. Ahmad Nizar Hamzeh, *In the Path of Hezbollah* (Syracuse University Press, 2004), p. 26.
17. Yoav Limor, "The Battle to Dry Up Hezbollah's Cash Flow", *Israel Hayom*, August 23, 2019. https://www.israelhayom.com/ 2019/08/23/the-battle-to-dry-up-hezbollahs-cash-flow/.
18. On its decline see: Michael Rubin, "Hezbollah Has Become the Middle East's Weak Horse", AEI, December 2, 2020. https:// www.aei.org/op-eds/hezbollah-has-become-the-middle-easts-weak-horse/.
19. Nicholas Blanford and Assaf Orion, *Counting the Cost—Avoiding Another War Between Israel and Hezbollah* (The Atlantic Council, May 2020), p. 18.
20. Raphael Ahren, "US Rejects Israeli Request to Condition Lebanon Aid on Disarming Hezbollah", *Times of Israel*,

November 13, 2019. https://www.timesofisrael.com/us-rejects-israeli-request-to-condition-lebanon-aid-on-disarming-hezbollah/.
21. Marco Carnelos, "Lebanon Is a Failed State: When Will the World Step in?" *Middle East Eye*, July 16, 2021. https://www.middleeas teye.net/opinion/lebanon-failed-state-when-will-world-step-in.
22. Bradley Bowman, "Lebanese Armed Forces Must Act Against Hezbollah to Retain America's Military Aid", *Defense One*, April 1, 2020. https://www.defensenews.com/opinion/commentary/2020/04/01/lebanon-must-act-against-hezbollah-to-retain-ame ricas-military-aid/.
23. US Department of State, June 7, 2021. https://www.state.gov/special-briefing-with-general-kenneth-mckenzie-commander-of-the-u-s-central-command/.
24. Hanin Ghaddar, "To Push Past Hezbollah Stonewalling, Leverage the LAF", The Washington Institute for Near East Policy, March 18, 2021. https://www.washingtoninstitute.org/policy-analysis/push-past-hezbollah-stonewalling-leverage-laf.
25. Reuters, March 9, 2021. https://www.reuters.com/article/us-leb anon-crisis-security-crime/lebanons-collapse-piles-strain-on-army-security-forces-idUSKBN2B11F2.
26. Reuters, October 30, 2021. https://www.reuters.com/world/middle-east/crisis-with-lebanon-rooted-hezbollah-dominance-saudi-minister-2021-10-30/.
27. CNN, December 15, 2000. https://web.archive.org/web/20070405205037/ http://archives.cnn.com/2000/WORLD/meast/12/15/mideast.iran.reut/.
28. Ahmad Melhem, "Fatah Slams Iran for Funding Gaza Strip While Skirting PA", *Al—Monitor*, December 11, 2018. https://www.al-monitor.com/originals/2018/12/palestinian-authority-iran-fatah-palestinian-division-.html#ixzz7AXfkGqmh.
29. Jack Khoury, "Iranian Supreme Leader Khamenei: Support for Palestine Resistance Forces Is Vital", *Haaretz*, February 21, 2017. https://www.haaretz.com/middle-east-news/iranian-supreme-lea der-khamenei-support-for-palestine-resistance-forces-is-vital-1.543 9504.

30. Ahmad Melhem, "Palestinian Authority, Hamas Divided on Iran", *Al—Monitor*, August 9, 2021. https://www.al-monitor.com/ori ginals/2021/08/palestinian-authority-hamas-divided-iran#ixzz78 X9gRF5s.
31. Reuters, March 29, 2019. https://www.reuters.com/article/ us-usa-golanheights-iran/iran-urges-palestinians-to-resist-trumps-pro-israel-moves-idUSKCN1RA1TK.
32. Tareq Baconi, *Hamas Contained: The Rise and Pacification of Palestinian Resistance* (Stanford University Press, 2018).
33. Raphael D. Marcus, "'Learning Under Fire': Israel's Impro-vised Military Adaptation to Hamas Tunnel Warfare", *Journal of Strategic Studies* (Vol. 42, Nos. 3–4, 2017), pp. 344–370.
34. Judah Ari Gross, "IDF Chief Warns Israelis: The Next War Will Hit Our Home Front Extremely Hard", *The Times of Israel*, December 25, 2019. https://www.timesofisrael.com/idf-chief-isr ael-alone-in-the-fight-against-iran-in-syria-iraq/.
35. Yoav Limor, "Israel Has the Ability to Completely Destroy Iran's Nuclear Program", *IsraelHayom*, March 30, 2021. https://www. israelhayom.com/2021/03/29/israel-has-the-ability-to-comple tely-destroy-irans-nuclear-program/.
36. On boosting Hamas see: Patrick Kingsley and Ronen Bergman, "Israel's Military Inflicted a Heavy Toll: But Did it Achieve Its Aim?" *The New York Times*, May 21, 2021. https://www.nytimes. com/2021/05/21/world/middleeast/israel-gaza-war-ceasefire. html?fbclid=IwAR3B3ZS3gs7lJgPZTW-EzgiJjADIOhxUvWpGP 8mpRfeD7kueA3QlQ0ABdQo.
37. Fabian Hinz, "Iran Transfers Rockets to Palestinian Groups", Wilson Center, May 19, 2021. https://www.wilsoncenter.org/art icle/irans-rockets-palestinian-groups.
38. Ali Hashem, "Hamas Representative in Iran: Latest Round of Fighting Is Strategic Shift for Group", *Al Monitor*, May 17, 2021. https://www.al-monitor.com/originals/2021/05/hamas-repres entative-iran-latest-round-fighting-strategic-shift-group?amp=&__ twitter_impression=true&s=03&fbclid=IwAR1bmr7dpw5kYAH0 ygVfyZ8Jz0_BhRDiTTPLu5lUEelcslbkeM8EUtyT3GU.

39. Dror Shalom, "Last Call for Gaza? Proposing an Alternative to Israeli-Palestinian 'Conflict Management'", The Washington Institute for Near East Policy, August 30, 2021. https://www. washingtoninstitute.org/policy-analysis/last-call-gaza-proposing-alternative-israeli-palestinian-conflict-management.

40. Judah Ari Gross, "IDF Launches 'Southern Storm' Training Exercise on Gaza Border", *The Times of Israel*, October 26, 2021. https://www.timesofisrael.com/idf-launches-southern-storm-training-exercise-on-gaza-border/.

CHAPTER 5

How the IDF Prepares to Confront Hezbollah

Hezbollah confronted Israel in Lebanon in the 1980s and in the 1990s, until the IDF left that country in 2000. In 2006 the two sides have clashed again, for 34 days,[1] in a war that ended in a tie. Since then, they have been preparing for another round between them that might occur any time. It will be a war between one of the strongest militaries in the Middle East and an NSA that has developed impressive hybrid capabilities, following massive Iranian aid.

ACHIEVING VICTORY

Some in Israel assume it could not achieve decisive victory against NSAs.[2] Yet on August 13, 2015, the IDF released to the public its first official doctrine: "IDF Strategy" that was updated in 2018. According to it the IDF seeks to win by making Israel's enemy unable or unwilling to continue the fight.[3] The IDF is eager to break the series of draws it had since the 2006 war, including the wars against Hamas in 2008–2009 and in 2014, by finally gaining a decisive victory. However, Israel might end up with another tie, more or less because of the nature of the fight against an NSA. Even if the IDF manages to inflict Hezbollah heavy losses the latter can continue to fight, relying on guerrilla and terror tactics. Destroying that group will be hard since Hezbollah is rooted inside the Lebanese Shiite community. Hezbollah is known for taking care of the

E. Eilam, *Israeli Strategies in the Middle East*, https://doi.org/10.1007/978-3-030-95602-8_5

79

needs of its people by providing them with food, medical service etc. At least Israel is aware the IDF's overwhelming superiority guarantee the IDF will not be defeated in any case, which allows the IDF to take some risks in both preparing and conducting the war. The IDF took significant risks in the past, in many cases, including as part of the conflict with Iran and Hezbollah. One of them was blocking Hezbollah tunnels in December 2018, those that led from Lebanon into Israel. Hezbollah might have responded, but it did not.[4]

The IDF always sought to shorten the war, before the international community gets involved, which often did not serve Israel's interest.[5] Israel has been very sensitive to casualties. One of the reasons for striving for a quick victory is the assumption that it will reduce the human cost. Indeed, prolonging the war would have increased the price Israel would have paid. However sometimes the pressure to win as soon as possible brought the IDF to make mistakes, attack hastily, etc., which cost it drearily.

Hezbollah holds up to 150,000 rockets and missiles, which have various ranges.[6] A few of them cover almost all of Israel, where there is only 420 km from its north to its south. Hezbollah might fire more than a 1000 rockets and missiles a day. The IDF's main mission will be therefore to destroy those rockets as fast as possible.

Israel, with US support, has developed highly advanced weapon systems such as the Arrow, David Sling and the Iron Dome, aimed at intercepting rockets and/or missiles. Yet Israel's air defense does not have enough missiles to shot down many of Hezbollah's rockets and missiles. The IDF also recognizes that its air defense can't protect every civilian and military site in the country. Therefore, the air defense will shield key infrastructure, which means that many Israelis will have to absorb Hezbollah's fire. In addition, the air defense itself might become a target. Israel therefore can't rely on defense, and it must carry out a full-scale air and ground offensive into Lebanon.

THE ISRAELI OFFENSIVE

One typical war scenario is that an incident between Hezbollah and Israel escalates rapidly. Hezbollah will try to seize a village inside Israel. In response the IDF carries out a counterattack that recaptures any land it lost and then the IDF transfers the battle into Lebanon. Yet meanwhile it gives Hezbollah time to get ready for the Israeli offensive.

The solution could be an Israeli preventive war or a preemptive strike i.e., to attack Hezbollah before its men can take their positions. Yet the IDF ruled it out, at least in mid-2020.[7] Surprise is crucial in capturing Hezbollah off guard. In such a situation the IDF can inflict a major blow to Hezbollah. However, political constraints i.e., Israel's concern it will be seen as aggressive by the international community, might prevent such an Israeli attack.

The IAF "continues to build up its capability to accurately strike thousands of enemy targets per 24 hours during a full-scale conflict."[8] "It is estimated that the currently active fast jet F-15/16/35 squadrons of the IAF can almost immediately sustain the generation of about 620 short-range combat sorties per day. When fully mobilized, these same squadrons can sustain the generation of about 1600–1800 short-range sorties per day."[9]

Yet the IAF might not be able to stop the pounding of Israel. Furthermore Hezbollah's missiles and rockets might hit Israeli airfields. The IAF has been preparing for this but Hezbollah's fire might still slow down air operations. The IDF "knows that it will not be able to rely solely on the air force, but will need to use its ground troops to neutralize Hezbollah." It means launching a massive ground offensive.[10]

The ground offensive would be required to annihilate objectives that could not be destroyed by firepower.[11] The offensive could be launched on a wide front, in order to reach as many objectives as possible, before Hezbollah could react effectively. The IDF will try to create momentum while bypassing pockets of resistance, if conquering them is not essential at that stage. In the 1982 war, in less than a week, the IDF reached all the way to the Lebanese capital, Beirut, about 90 km north of the border with Israel.

The IDF prefers destruction of targets to seizing territory.[12] Israel is well aware that it is very difficult to annihilate completely an elusive foe such as Hezbollah. The IDF therefore will only seize an area in order to destroy military targets there. Then the IDF, gradually or quite fast, will withdraw from there. In 1985, after three years of fighting deep inside Lebanon, the IDF retreated to the south of Lebanon, staying there for the next 15 years. The northeast point the IDF held at that time was a few dozen miles north of the border with Israel. The IDF struggled to stop Hezbollah incursions in the rugged terrain. Hezbollah also bombed Israeli posts, by using mortars. The clashes there, which cost Israel a few hundred casualties has been a bitter memory for Israel. There was also severe criticism, in and outside Israel, about the Israeli presence in Lebanon. Therefore when the IDF retook part of south Lebanon in the 2006 war its troops withdrew from there at the end of the war. The same might happen in the next war. Despite the political and military advantages of this approach it deprives Israel of assets that can be used as bargaining chip in negotiations during and after the war ends.

Maj. General (Ret.) Giora Eiland, former head of Israel's National Security Council, argues that the Lebanese military "is fully subordinate to the word of Hezbollah. ... That is why it is much more just and moral to hold the government and the people of Lebanon as accountable for Hezbollah." He claimed that Israel should clarify that "if there is fire from Lebanon ... Lebanon will be destroyed in a few days." According to Eiland threat should both urge Lebanese public opinion to turn against Hezbollah and to convince the international community to compose "a cease-fire favoring Israel."[13] Yet Lebanon is almost a failed state, suffering from a deep economic crisis. If Israel destroys key Lebanese infrastructure that country might collapse completely. This outcome will be terrible for its people and bad for other states as well, including Israel. Lebanon will serve as a base not only for Hezbollah but for other radical Islamic groups that will attack others, including Israel.

Furthermore it is doubtful how much Hezbollah will care about Lebanese public opinion let alone the international community, if they demand Hezbollah to stop fighting Israel, for the sake of the Lebanese population. Hezbollah has been ignoring the needs of its own people for many years now, by continuing to upgrade its arsenal. Hezbollah claims it is only meant to protect Lebanon but it is well known this pro-Iranian group arms itself as part of Iran's regional ambitions. Hezbollah is a powerful group and it is quite independent but it is still an Iranian protégé, following its orders, in Lebanon and in other countries as well. If there is an attempt by the Lebanese public to put pressure on Hezbollah it might "resort to force to maintain its hold on power in Lebanon." Therefore Hezbollah could not be convinced by others in Lebanon to end the war with Israel.[14]

In former wars with Israel, when Hezbollah did not enjoy the powerful position it has now, the group still acted according to its own interests, at the expense of Lebanon. Hezbollah will exploit its vast influence in Lebanon, to continue with this policy. The group does hear what is said in Lebanon and it can be pragmatic but in the bottom line Hezbollah will do what is good for Iran and Hezbollah, even if it causes a catastrophe for Lebanon. Therefore putting pressure on Lebanon and even bombing it heavily is not the best way to bring a cease-fire on Israel's terms.

The Infantry and the Armor

When the IDF was established in 1948 the infantry was its main corps, and this stayed like that until the late 1950s. Since then the armor corps took center stage, after playing a key role in the 1956 and 1967 wars, when the IDF confronted Arab armored divisions and brigades, mostly in open areas. The Israeli armor demonstrated its capabilities to overcome its rivals in all kinds of situations, despite the difficulties it faced in the battlefield such as confronting high quality tanks.[15] In the last decade the Israeli infantry has been regaining the status of the leading corps since Israel's enemies such as Hezbollah are NSAs that fight on foot, in tiny details, inside urban areas, where the Israeli infantry is more valuable than the armor.

The IDF improved the cooperation between its corps like the infantry, armor, and combat engineers, following past lessons in this matter. The IDF, after struggling with this issue for several decades,[16] managed to achieve some improvement during its fight against Hamas, in the Gaza Strip, in the 2008–2009 and 2014 wars. The experience that was gained there will serve the IDF against Hezbollah.

The IDF's crack armor and infantry units and its Special Forces will be sent to Lebanon. However, as a lesson from the 1982 war, the IDF should not gather too many armored forces at the narrow and often winding routes of Lebanon. If the roads are overcrowded then vehicles will be trapped in long columns, vulnerable to Hezbollah fire. Only the troops at the head of the columns might be able to somehow maneuver and fight back.

The IDF created in 2015 the 89th commando brigade which together with other airborne units can land from CH-53 and UH-60 helicopters. The goals of those air assaults will be to destroy rockets and Hezbollah headquarters, secure vital crossroads and bridges etc. Israeli naval commando can strike from the sea yet the IDF does not have the capability to carry out a major amphibious operation due to lack of landing crafts.

The IDF has ammunition that is especially useful against NSAs like Hezbollah. Israeli infantry possesses Spike antitank missiles, to wipe out fortified positions in urban areas. Israeli tanks have the 120 mm APAM-MP-T cartridges that are effective against enemy infantry. Israel's best tank, the Merkava Mark 4, has the new armored shield protective-active that destroy antitank projectiles before they reach their target. The IDF should also rely on APCs (armored personnel carriers) with heavy armor. Israel produces those kinds of APCs: the Achzarit and the Namer, since Israel's M-113 is too vulnerable to enemy fire. In 2020 Israel started to produce its new APC, the "Eitan," which is fast and supposed to be well-protected.

BUILD UP

The IDF's new multi-year plan, "Momentum" (for the years 2020–2024) replaces the "Gideon" multi-year plan, which began in 2015. "Momentum" is a result of "recognition that Iran, Hezbollah, Hamas, and others have been collectively reducing the qualitative gap with Israel."[17] The IDF is supposed to be able to deliver "a series of multidimensional strikes" that will "destroy a maximum number of targets in as short a time as possible." Intelligence gathering and communications systems will be upgraded so "every part of the IDF can communicate with every other part."[18] "Momentum" is supposed to create "a sharper, more lethal IDF in which field units receive the wealth of capabilities that are currently enjoyed by IDF Central Headquarters in Tel Aviv."[19]

Increasing the "lethality" of the IDF[20] is actually a body count approach. It is part of the process of destroying maximum amount of military targets, aiming at weakening the foe to such a degree that it will accept Israel's terms for a cease-fire. This strategy might work but striving to kill as many enemy combatants as possible might increase collateral damage. Israeli officers might also focus too much on inflicting casualties, at the expense of other tasks, more important ones. It might also cause credibility issues if there are exaggerating in the number of Hezbollah's fatalities. The IDF has to adopt a more flexible approach in which other missions such as breaking Hezbollah's formations might be sometimes more useful than going after its fighters.

"Momentum" can't be implemented without increasing the IDF's budget. The ongoing political uncertainty in Israel, which had four elections in less than three years, delayed the approval of the state budget.

Furthermore the fallout of the Covid-19 pandemic that caused the Israeli economy significant losses, might require budget cuts, including in the IDF, which obviously could cripple "Momentum."

Another possible concern is a major security problem that might happen in any time such as a Palestinian outburst in the West Bank. From time to time there are signs of what is called the "third Intifada" (a Palestinian uprising. The first two occurred in 1987–1993 and in 2000–2005). It might start because of one incident that would escalate rapidly. It might be limited in scale and time, but if not it would require the IDF to invest many resources in suppressing it. This means deploying troops, maybe thousands of them, for weeks, months if not longer. It will disrupt training and require budgets, at the expense of executing "Momentum".

The IDF had assimilated sophisticated C4I (Command, Control, Communications, Computers and Intelligence) network, which allows ground, air and sea units to share information and to watch the same picture of the battle. The IDF is aware that its troops must not rely too much on cutting edge technology. Therefore in exercises the troops sometimes train without certain systems, in case they fail because of cyber warfare, technical problem, enemy fire, etc.

In the confrontation of May 2021 between Israel and Hamas the IDF used a "combination of a wide variety of intelligence sources with artificial intelligence" to upgrade the intelligence provided to its officers. This effort was also effective in both targeting dozen top operatives and in reducing collateral damage.[21]

In September 2020 the 7th armored Brigade and the 1st infantry brigade ran an exercise at the Golan Heights,[22] an area that is similar to parts of nearby Lebanon. Hezbollah, since it is based in Lebanon, is obviously much more familiar with the topography of Lebanon than the IDF. Only Israeli troops, who are now in their 40s and 50s, have experienced how it is to fight in Lebanon, during their regular service in the 1990s. Therefore the IDF has been training in the north of Israel such as in the Golan Heights, where there is similar terrain to the one in Lebanon.

In IDF's exercises that took place in recent years, armor, infantry, combat engineers, artillery, the logistical corps, the IAF and sometimes the navy too trained with each other in order to improve the cooperation between them that will be needed in combat. In addition the IDF has established new ground units, such as the Multi-Dimensional Attack Brigade and the so called Ghost Unit, the multi-faceted unit, which include troops from various corps, mostly from ground forces but also from the IAF.

The IDF had conducted in late October 2020 a vast exercise "dubbed "Deadly Arrow" focused "on how various headquarters and command centers work together and communicate in wartime." Air, ground, and naval forces maneuvered, simulating a "multi-front scenario" since Israel might fight Hezbollah not only in Lebanon but in Syria as well. It was the largest exercise in 2020 yet it was "scaled back due to restrictions," following the Covid-19 pandemic.[23] The IDF carried out in mid February 2021 a surprise exercise called "Galilee Rose," simulating a war against Hezbollah.[24]

In late October 2021 the IDF ran an exercise imaging how Hezbollah launches large-scale barrages, including CW, as a result of "direct hits on toxic chemical storage facilities within Israel." The exercise examined also "overwhelmed hospitals, and nationwide power outages." Emergency units, including police, fire and medical services participated in the exercise.[25] In other exercises at that time troops were drilled up to division level, training in cooperating between ground forces and the IAF.

The IDF's new Brigade and Battlegroup Mission Training Center simulates Lebanese villages together with Hezbollah bunkers. "The system documents failures in the field and virtual casualties inflicted to help units learn from mistakes...this digital battlefield aids in improving coordination. It is supposed to close gaps between battalion and company levels." The simulator allows more than 100 officers to use "logistics, drones, helicopters, artillery, aircraft and all the other combined arms and elements that may be present on the battlefield."[26] Such kind of exercise saves money and its safer compared with a drill in the field let alone one that involves live fire.

The IAF has been based on fighter-bombers such as F-15/16. The IAF started to assimilate the F-35 in 2016. The IAF needs the F-35 to overcome advanced air defense systems, which Hezbollah doesn't have. Therefore the F-35 is not that important in a war against Hezbollah. In such a fight the IAF requires aircraft that specialize in close air support like the AH-64, which has been in service in the IAF since the 1990s. The IAF can also use other aircraft, ones it does not possess like the A-10. In the past the IAF had the A-4 and maybe it should consider having again a pure attack plane.

Israel's Ramat David airbase in the north of country "will act as a focused F-16 jet center, while Hatzor airbase in central Israel will become the center of the IAF's intelligence-gathering drone activities. The IAF's drone array today conducts 75% of the air force's flight hours, indicating how central it has become to daily operations."[27] Those changes will assist the IAF against Hezbollah.

The Israeli navy is based on the 3rd Flotilla (missile ships), 7th Flotilla (Submarines) and the 13th Flotilla (naval commandos). The navy had "developed new systems and combat doctrines" and "operational plans that combine our new perception with the new technologies and weapons, and they are being exercised."[28] It will serve the IDF in a war against Hezbollah.

THE RESERVES: MOBILIZATION UNDER FIRE

Any large-scale Israeli offensive requires the mobilization of tens of thousands of Israeli reserves. They might be called in under fire. Some of them would have to leave their families behind while Hezbollah missiles and rockets target where they live. This would cause some of Israel's civilian—soldiers to hesitate. If their home is directly hit let alone if their families or close friends are hurt then taking care of them will come first. Israeli soldiers will also be in harm's way when they drive to their bases, where they receive their weapons, vehicles, and equipment. Those camps might not have enough shelters and bunkers to protect all the troops there. The danger will remain on the roads from the base to the frontline, where there will be no cover. The troops might be delayed if roads and crossroads are jammed because of traffic and not only military one. Civilians will escape their homes in northern Israel, mostly those who reside near Lebanon, fearing incursions and bombardments. Roads like road 6, the Trans-Israeli highway, might be divided, for routes serving only military vehicles and those serving civilian cars solely.

Staging areas will not be safe. Israeli troops might be sitting ducks there, without bunkers to shield them. They will have to dig fox holes, which they are not used to do. Without it, during a bombardment, they will have to fall to the ground or stay in their armored vehicles. Their helmets and body armor will help too.

Hezbollah, in order to direct its fire, might follow IDF movements inside Israel by using collaborators, drones, and by listening to communications. Hezbollah's goal will be to fire at Israeli troops all the way from their homes to the frontline, aiming at inflicting casualties and damage, undermining motivation and disrupting Israeli operations. The IDF had done some drills in this matter, preparing its troops to function under fire. It would be a challenge since Hezbollah might fire "1,000 to 3,000 rockets and missiles every day for at least the first week of fighting, far more than the few hundred" that were fired each day during the confrontation in May 2021 between Israel and Hamas.[29]

THE FIGHT IN URBAN AREAS

Hezbollah hides its rockets in about 200 villages and towns in Lebanon. Senior Israeli officials, from the military and the government, warned several times that turning populated areas in Lebanon into a fire base will have severe ramifications for Lebanon. Israeli firepower might cause huge collateral damage in those places, unless the civilians there evacuate their homes. When the war starts Israel will warn them to leave as soon as possible, this makes it much more difficult for Israel to carry out a preemptive strike. Israel might wait but while Lebanese noncombatants are getting ready to flee their homes Hezbollah could open fire from there, targeting Israeli cities.

The IDF, mostly with air power, can hit Hezbollah's positions in villages and towns across south Lebanon but in some cases Israeli ground units will have to reach those places. The IDF gained vast experience in urban warfare since 2000, mostly during clashes with Palestinians in the West Bank and the Gaza Strip. The IDF also has been training in close combat, including in underground warfare, by building specific facilities for that purpose. The IDF can learn in this field from the experience gained in former wars in Vietnam and Iraq and from its own lessons from the 2014 war in the Gaza Strip. In fighting underground IDF's advantages in firepower are not relevant, when the troops enter the tunnel. Since inside the tunnel only one soldier can take the lead he will be alone while his friends behind him can't use their weapons. Therefore it is better to seal the tunnel / or to destroy it from the outside. In the confrontation of May 2021 the IAF managed to bomb and destroy a large part of Hamas' underground network. The IAF might not be able to repeat it against Hezbollah since the terrain in Lebanon is different than the one in the Gaza Strip.

Hezbollah's Capabilities

In the 2006 war Hezbollah had up to 5000 fighters. In 2020 Hezbollah had about 30,000 fighters, 7000 of them belong to its Special Forces division. Hezbollah's best units might try to infiltrate into Israel, by tunnels.[30] In early 2019 "the IDF carried out a six-week operation to destroy several Hezbollah tunnels stretching from southern Lebanon into northern Israel, but it conceded that more secret passages likely remained undetected."[31] Hezbollah might also try to penetrate into Israel, exploiting the rough terrain to approach the border. Some Israeli villages and towns are at the border itself.[32] Hezbollah's elite "Radwan Brigade units could carry out acts of sabotage against infrastructure, mount roadside bomb ambushes, and cut communication lines. They may pursue a propaganda advantage by including a cameraman among them to film the fighters entering Israeli communities and then beam the images around the world. Hezbollah may attempt to infiltrate Israel from the Golan Heights as well as south Lebanon."[33] In fighting Hezbollah the IDF would have to deal with IED (Improvised explosive device) and antitank missiles, some of them are quite advanced such as the 9M133 Kornet.

Hezbollah has been deeply involved in the Syrian civil war, which cost the group up to 2000 dead,[34] a significant price for a group that does not have more than 50,000 men, including reserves. Hezbollah will need time to recover from those losses. Furthermore Hezbollah recruits its men from the Lebanese Shiite community that amounts to around a million people and its birth rate is in decline. Those constraints affect Hezbollah's manpower. The group might be careful not to be entangled in another war, this time against Israel.

Lebanon was overall kept out of the Syrian civil war, despite some battles that occurred on the border between the two states. In contrast a war with Israel will be destructive to large parts of Lebanon and particularly to villages and towns of the Shiite community, where Hezbollah stores its arsenal. By turning its own community into a giant fire base Hezbollah shows its willingness to put its people at risk, although for now Hezbollah seems to wish to avoid a war. In addition following the 2006 war Iran helped Hezbollah and its supporters to recover by providing funds. After the next war Iran might find it hard to allocate the huge sums of money needed to rebuild Lebanon, because of Iran's economic problems and since the damage to Lebanon will be much bigger compared with the 2006 war.

Hezbollah, by implementing guerrilla and terror tactics, managed many times in the past to be elusive and to avoid Israeli attacks. However Hezbollah grew and became more like a military during the Syrian civil war, which will make it easier for the IDF to target Hezbollah. The latter also got accustomed to have air superiority and to receive air support from the Russian and the Syrian air forces while fighting Syrian rebels who had no aircraft. In a war against Israel Hezbollah will be like Syrian rebels i.e., Hezbollah will fight without aircraft against a rival that possesses a powerful air force. Those differences could cost Hezbollah dearly in a war against Israel.

Hezbollah has invested in its naval unit, with Iranian help. Hezbollah has been "developing capabilities to carry out seaborne commando raids and sea mine attacks on Israeli ports using Iranian midget submarines and diver transportation vehicles. These can be launched from Hezbollah's permanent bases along the Lebanese coast or even through merchant ships." Hezbollah has also anti ship missiles. In the 2006 war Hezbollah hit an Israeli missile corvette, which was caught off guard.[35] The Israeli navy will be very careful in the next war. Hezbollah's missiles also threat Israel's gas rigs in the Mediterranean Sea, a highly valuable asset. The Israeli navy has the Barak 8 missile, aimed at intercepting anti ship missiles. Hezbollah might also fire rockets at Israel's sea rigs. The IDF's new C-dome, a maritime version of its Iron Dome, is meant to shoot down those rockets.

In the 2021 war Hamas failed to surprise the IDF in certain fields. Its drones that were supposed to drop bombs or to serve as suicide drones were shot down. Tiny "unmanned submarines were laden with up to 30 kilograms of ordnance in order to target ships and gas platforms," but they were destroyed in time. Hamas elite units ("Nukhba") were not able to infiltrate Israel. Hezbollah will learn those lessons.[36]

CONCLUSION

In the next war between Israel and Hezbollah the latter will launch barrages of rockets and missiles that will hit all over Israel. The IDF's air defense would contribute their share by intercepting some of those projectiles. However, especially in a war against Hezbollah, Israel's air defense could not shoot down most of the rockets because there are too many of them. Therefore Israel will have no choice but to conduct a massive offensive against Hezbollah.

The IDF has an overwhelming superiority over Hezbollah. The IDF will strive to use its advantage to achieve a quick and decisive victory yet the IDF might end up with another draw. The IDF might penetrate several dozen miles into Lebanon, staying there for a limited amount of time, enough to both annihilate Hezbollah's infrastructure and cause the group substantial casualties. The IDF will then retreat back to the border. The IDF will avoid seizing areas, which will prevent the various problems of holding a hostile territory. However by that Israel gives up in advance a valuable bargaining chip for post war negotiations.

The IDF might be focusing too much on both destroying targets and body count. The IDF should also be aware that depending too much on air power might not bring the best outcome for Israel. A massive ground offensive could be needed, aiming at Hezbollah's centers of gravity and by that taking the group out of balance.

Each side will be harmed in the next war but Lebanon will absorb much more casualties and damages than Israel. The latter must compose a plan how to defeat Hezbollah and at least to shorten the war as much as possible in order to reduce the cost to Israel and to Lebanese population as well.

Notes

1. Raphael D. Marcus, Israel's *Long War with Hezbollah: Military Innovation and Adaptation Under Fire* (Georgetown University Press, 2018). Kaunert Christian and Ori Wertman, "The Securitisation of Hybrid Warfare through Practices within the Iran-Israeli Conflict: Israel's Practices for Securitising Hezbollah's Proxy War", *Security & Defence Quarterly* (vol. 31, 2020), pp. 99–114.
2. Avi Kober, *Practical Soldiers—Israel's Military Thought and Its Formative Factors* (Boston: Brill, 2015), p. 144.
3. "Israel Defense Forces Strategy Document", Belfer Center, https://www.belfercenter.org/israel-defense-forces-strategy-doc ument#:~:text=The%20IDF%20Strategy%20is%20the,of%20mili tary%20thinking%20and%20action.

4. BBC, December 4, 2018, https://www.bbc.com/news/world-middle-east-46437629.

5. IDFA (Israel Defense Force Archives) 52/854/96. Ghani Abdel Mohamed El Gamasy, *The October War* (The American University in Cairo, 1993), p. 136.

6. About the 150,000 rockets see the testimony submitted to House Foreign Affairs Committee hearing "Israel Imperiled: Threats to the Jewish State," a joint meeting held by the Subcommittee on Terrorism, Nonproliferation, and Trade and the Subcommittee on the Middle East and North Africa. David Makovsky, Ziegler Distinguished Fellow and Director, Project on the Middle East Peace Process, The Washington Institute for Near East Policy. April 19, 2016.

7. Jack Khoury and Yaniv Kubovich, "Israel Not Planning Preemptive Strike Against Hezbollah, Army Source Tells Al Jazeera", *Haaretz*, August 2, 2020. https://www.haaretz.com/israel-news/israel-doesn-t-intend-to-carry-out-preemptive-attack-against-hezbollah-report-says-1.9039738.

8. Yaakov Lappin, "The IDF in the Shadow of the Pandemic", The Begin-Sadat Center for Strategic Studies, October, 22, 2020. https://besacenter.org/perspectives-papers/israel-pandemic-idf/.

9. Kenneth S. Brower, "Israel versus Anyone: A Military Net Assessment of the Middle East", The Begin-Sadat Center for Strategic Studies, Mideast Security and Policy Studies No. 178, August 2, 2020, p. 8.

10. Anna Ahronheim, "Hezbollah to Pay a 'heavy price' if War Breaks Out—Northern Command Head", *The Jerusalem Post*, July 15, 2021. https://www.jpost.com/arab-israeli-conflict/northern-command-head-hezbollah-to-pay-a-heavy-price-if-war-breaks-out-673812.

11. Michael Herzog, "New IDF Strategy goes Public", The Washington Institute for Near East Policy, August 28, 2015. http://www.washingtoninstitute.org/policy-analysis/view/new-idf-strategy-goes-public.

12. Yaakov Lappin, "The IDF's Momentum Plan Aims to Create a New Type of War Machine", The Begin-Sadat Center for Strategic Studies, March 22, 2020. https://besacenter.org/perspectives-papers/idf-momentum-plan/.

13. NBC News, September 16, 2017. https://www.nbcnews.com/news/world/hezbollah-s-new-strength-leaves-israeli-border-tense-n801596.
14. (No author) "Facing Domestic Criticism, Lebanon's Hezbollah May Opt for Violence", Stratfor, August 13, 2021. https://worldview.stratfor.com/article/facing-domestic-criticism-lebanon-s-hezbollah-may-opt-violence.
15. Amiad Brezner, *Wild Broncos—The Development and the Changes of the IDF Armo—1949–1956* (Tel Aviv: Ministry of Defence, 1999). Avi Kober, *Military Decision in the Arab–Israeli Wars 1948–1982* (Tel Aviv: Ministry of Defense, 1995). Chaim Herzog, *The War of Atonement* (Jerusalem: Edanim, 1975).
16. On this subject see: David Rodham, *Combined Arms Warfare in Israeli Military History: From the War of Independence to Operation Protective Edge* (Sussex Academic Press, 2019).
17. Yaakov Lappin, "The IDF in the Shadow of the Pandemic", The Begin-Sadat Center for Strategic Studies, October 22, 2020. https://besacenter.org/perspectives-papers/israel-pandemic-idf/.
18. (No author) "Chief of Staff Launches Plan for "more lethal" IDF", Globes, Israel Business News, February 13, 2020. https://en.globes.co.il/en/article-chief-of-staff-launches-plan-for-more-lethal-idf-1001318466.
19. Yaakov Lappin, "The IDF's Momentum Plan", https://besacenter.org/perspectives-papers/idf-momentum-plan/.
20. (No author) "Chief of Staff...". https://en.globes.co.il/en/article-chief-of-staff-launches-plan-for-more-lethal-idf-1001318466.
21. Jodah Ari Gross, "IDF Intelligence Hails Tactical Win in Gaza, Can't Say How Long Calm Will Last", *The Times of Israel*, May 27, 2021. https://www.timesofisrael.com/idf-intel-hails-tactical-win-over-hamas-but-cant-say-how-long-calm-will-last/.
22. Seth Frantzman, "An Inside Look at How Israel Trains for the Next War With Its Best Units", *The National Interest*, October 7, 2020. https://nationalinterest.org/blog/buzz/inside-look-how-israel-trains-next-war-its-best-units-170281.
23. Jodah Ari Gross, "IDF Launches Its Largest Drill of the Year, Simulating War against Hezbollah", *The Times of Israel*, October 25, 2020. https://www.timesofisrael.com/idf-launches-its-largest-drill-of-the-year-simulating-war-against-hezbollah/.

24. Jodah Ari Gross, "IDF Launches Surprise Air Exercise, as It Reportedly Strikes Sites in Syria", *The Times of Israel*, February 25, 2021. https://www.timesofisrael.com/idf-launches-surprise-air-exercise-as-it-reportedly-strikes-sites-in-syria/.
25. Judah Ari Gross, "Learning from May War, IDF Simulates Hezbollah Battle Alongside Domestic Strife", *The Times of Israel*, October 31, 2021. https://www.timesofisrael.com/learning-from-may-war-idf-simulates-battle-with-hezbollah-amid-domestic-strife/.
26. Seth Frantzman, "Israel Increases Training via Virtual Battlefield Center Amid Hezbollah tensions", Defense News, July 27, 2020. https://www.defensenews.com/global/europe/2020/07/27/isr ael-increases-training-via-virtual-battlefield-center-amid-hezbollah-tensions/.
27. Yaakov Lappin, "The IDF in the Shadow of the Pandemic", The Begin-Sadat Center for Strategic Studies, October, 22, 2020. https://besacenter.org/perspectives-papers/israel-pandemic-idf/.
28. Udi Shaham, "Israel's Navy Ready to Attack Hezbollah from the Sea Like Never Before", *The Jerusalem Post*, April 22, 2021. https://www.jpost.com/arab-israeli-conflict/israels-navy-ready-to-attack-hezbollah-from-the-sea-like-never-before-666083.
29. Jodah Ari Gross, "IDF: In Future War, Hezbollah Could Fire up to 3,000 Rockets a Day for a Week", *The Times of Israel*, July 14, 2021. https://www.timesofisrael.com/liveblog_entry/idf-in-future-war-hezbollah-could-fire-up-to-3000-rockets-a-day-for-a-week/.
30. Nicholas Blanford and Assaf Orion, "Counting the Cost—Avoiding Another War between Israel and Hezbollah", *The Atlantic Council*, May 2020, p. 22.
31. Brian Katz, "Will Hezbollah's Rise Be Its Downfall?", *Foreign Affairs*, March 8, 2019.
32. Eado Hecht, "War on the Northern Front", *Infinity Magazine*, Summer 2018, volume 6, Issue 2, pp. 23–29. https://www.milita rystrategymagazine.com/article/war-on-the-northern-front/.
33. Blanford and Orion, *Counting the Cost*, p. 22.
34. Coli Clarke, "A Glass Half Empty? Taking Stock of Hezbollah's Losses in Syria", The Rand Blog, October 17, 2017. https://www.rand.org/blog/2017/10/a-glass-half-empty-taking-stock-of-hezbollahs-losses.html.

35. Eyal Pinko, "The Unique Intelligence Challenges of Countering Naval Asymmetric Warfare", April 1, 2021, CIMSEC. https://cimsec.org/the-unique-intelligence-challenges-of-countering-naval-asymmetric-warfare/.
36. Grant Rumley and Neri Zilber, "A Military Assessment of the Israel-Hamas Conflict", The Washington Institute for Near East Policy, May 25, 2021. https://www.washingtoninstitute.org/policy-analysis/military-assessment-israel-hamas-conflict.

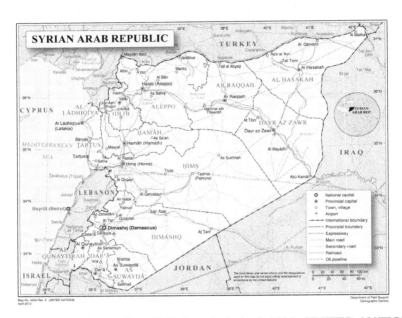

Map 6.1 Syria, Map No. 4204 Rev. 3, 1 April 2012, UNITED NATIONS
https://www.un.org/geospatial/content/syrian-arab-republic

CHAPTER 6

Iran and Israel Fight Over Syria

Bashar al Assad managed to win the Syrian civil war,[1] but Syria is almost a failed state. Israel did not support any of the sides. Israel was involved in Syria, as part of its conflict with Iran. Israel has been striking targets inside Syria since 2012. It was first aimed at slowing down the delivery of weapons to Iran's protégé in Lebanon, Hezbollah. Later on Israel tried to stop and at least to delay the establishment of an Iranian base inside Syria. Israel is aware it probably could not prevent Iran from having a grip on Syria. If Iran insists on holding on to Syria then Israel has to tolerate that. Yet, Israel makes sure Iran will pay a significant price while trying to reduce the Iranian presence in Syria, without getting dragged into a war. It is a major part of Israel's "campaign between the wars" (Map 6.1).

Iran supports the Assad regime since the latter is part of Iran's coalition against Israel. However, Assad might stay out of a war between Israel and Iran, fearing Israeli retribution that could bring down Assad's regime. Iran paid heavily in blood and treasure for its involvement in Syria. If Iran continues to pour money into Syria, at the expense of the Iranian people, it would increase the frustration and criticism in Iran against their regime. It might contribute to undermining the Iranian regime. In that sense, Israel can benefit from the Iranian involvement in Syria.

E. Eilam, *Israeli Strategies in the Middle East*, https://doi.org/10.1007/978-3-030-95602-8_6

THE SYRIAN CIVIL WAR

Hafez al Assad, who ruled Syria in the years 1970–2000, was a "savvy politician." He came from Alawites, a sect in Shia Islam. They are a small minority in Syria. He depended on them, yet he also promoted Christians and Druze and some Sunnis. His security services kept a tight grip on the country, cracking down on the opposition.[2] In 1982 the Assad regime killed more than 20,000 civilians, as part of suppressing a mutiny of the MB in the city of Hama. Despite that, most of the Sunnis in Syria, who are the majority there, tolerated Assad since he brought stability.[3]

Hafez al Assad died in 2000. His son, Bashar al Assad, inherited him. He succeeded in keeping stability, despite his lack of experience in running a state. In 2005 Syria was forced to withdraw from Lebanon, a country memorized in Syria's old dream as a torn-off piece of "Great Syria." Practically, Lebanon was vital to Syria not only economically, but militarily as well. Lebanon could have served as a springboard to invade Galilee, the northern part of Israel, thus cutting off Israeli troops in the Golan Heights. Yet, such an offensive was unlikely. It seems Lebanon was more important to the Assad regime as Syria's west flank defense area, in case of an Israeli offensive inside Lebanon. This might have happened during another round between Israel and the Hezbollah. It could be said that from the Syrian point of view, before or during a future campaign against the Hezbollah, Israel would decide that besides confronting an NSA, Hezbollah, the IDF should seize the opportunity to attack Syria as well. The Assad regime remembers that in the 1982 war in Lebanon Israel struck both Syria and an NSA, the PLO. However, at that time Syria was deployed in Lebanon. In the 2006 war in Lebanon, a year after Syria left that country, Israel focused on Hezbollah solely. If there's another round in Lebanon between Israel and Hezbollah, Israel will probably seek to avoid any confrontation with Syria, although such a collision could still happen, as a result of miscalculations by one or both sides. On the other hand, there might be reconciliation between Israel and Syria. The last time they had peace talks was in 2008. They might not negotiate on peace, but they can try to improve their relations and mostly to avoid misunderstandings.

The Syrian civil war, which started in early 2011, almost toppled Assad. Nevertheless, he did not give up or compromise, in spite of the huge cost to the population and to cities like Homs and Aleppo. Bashar al Assad did not want to lose his father's heritage, certainly not without a fight to the finish. Gradually, with strong support from Iran, Hezbollah and Russia he was able to defeat his rivals. He and his allies implemented very brutal methods such as using chemical weapons, conducting heavy bombardments, imposing starvation, etc. Eventually, Assad stayed in power and regained control of most of Syria, after losing most of it, in the early years of the war.

The Syrian rebels did not succeed in uniting and coordinating their efforts, and they often fought with each other. Militarily speaking the rebels had troops, mostly those who deserted Assad's military, but they lacked professional skills needed to build well organized and trained units. Their groups were basically light infantry. They had no aircraft or air defense. They had at most several armored vehicles. Their mobility was based on civilian vehicles. Their arsenal was mostly small arms with some antitank missiles and rockets, mortars, etc. Therefore, they were not a conventional military. They had better chances in conducting guerrilla warfare, but gradually they were pinned down in cities, where they were pounded into submission. Although rebels held on for years their many mistakes, in the strategic and tactical levels made it easier for Assad to win.

How Important Is Syria to Iran?

The 1979 revolution might have brought Iran to join Arabs against Israel, in the name of Muslim solidarity. However, during most of the 1980s Iran was the one facing Arab Sunni collaboration against it, due to many Arab states supporting Iraq in its war with Iran. The latter had Syria on its side, which was vital for Iran,[4] maybe more than having Syria as a partner against Israel, at least in the 1980s.

The magnitude of Iran's population, territory, and natural resources, compared with those of Syria, make the latter the smaller, but not necessarily the weaker partner. Sometimes Iran needed Syria quite badly, because of its location and status as a key Arab state. They both had a common enemy like Iraq until recent years, and obviously Israel. Yet, Syria did not open a second front against Iraq during the Iran–Iraq war in the 1980s.

During the mutiny in Hama in 1982, Hafez al Assad did not require Iranian support. In contrast, during the Syrian civil war, Bashar al Assad needed Iran to assist and actually to save him from defeat. Iran not only provided political support and economic aid but also dispatched

Hezbollah and even Iranian troops to fight in Syria. Iran did it due to Syria's strategic importance, but there are question marks in this matter.

Syria is part of Iran's strategic depth. Syria has a vital location, due to its borders with several states. Syria serves as a major component in the arc Iran created, stretching from Iran to the Mediterranean Sea, through Iraq, Syria, and Lebanon. However, in both Lebanon and Iraq, there is a strong anti-Iranian resentment, following Iran's deep involvement in their internal affairs. In 2005, vocal protests in Lebanon were strong enough to force Assad to withdraw his troops from there. If Lebanon and/or Iraq eventually succeed in significantly reducing the Iranian presence in their territory, that will undermine the Iranian arc, affecting Syria's importance as well.

Iran lost more than 2000 soldiers in Syria.[5] Nakissa Jahanbani argued that "Iran's soft-power investments and indirect military engagement in Syria have grown since 2015. Before that, Tehran relied on direct military engagement, but heavy losses forced the IRGC to shift to more indirect methods to achieve its aims."[6] The sensitivity of the Iranian public to Iranian casualties in Syria brought the Iranian regime to intensify its propaganda efforts, explaining how the war serves Iran's national security interests and also the need to protect holy Shiite sites located in Syria. Iran's losses in Syria are immeasurably smaller compared with the Iran-Iraq War (1980–1988). It shows Iran's high sensitivity in this matter that indicates Iran's willingness to pay a heavy price fighting Israel, including over Syria.

Iran had invested in Syria 30 and maybe up to 105 billion Dollars.[7] Iran declared over and again it will help Assad. However, Iran has its constraints, due to Iran's own economic weakness, following ongoing sanctions, corruption, and poor management, the cost of handling the Covid-19 virus crisis, etc.

Iran, after investing so much in Syria, wants to get at least some of its money back, such as from the reconstruction of Syria. However, Syria is in very bad shape. Even if Assad controls all of Syria's natural resources such as oil, they are not enough to finance the huge reconstruction projects Syria needs. Furthermore, the US "Caesar Law" from June 2020 imposes heavy sanctions on the Syrian regime and those who have contact with it. This will deter states, companies, etc., from investing in Syria, which disrupts Iran's plans to benefit from the rehabilitation.

The EU keeps a firm stance against the Assad regime while maintaining "lower-level diplomatic contacts with Syria." Some EU members strive to develop their ties with Syria.[8] European States busy dealing with refugees, can hope that rebuilding both Syria and the relations with Assad will help in the return of Syrian refugees to their homeland. If refugees eventually go back to Syria, in mass, it could assist in making Syria stronger. This would serve Iran since it would increase the chances Iran can get back at least some of the enormous investment it made in Syria. However, if Assad is more powerful, he would not rely so much on Iran. Also, Iran and Assad might hesitate in allowing millions of refugees, many of them Sunnis, to return to Syria.

Overall, many states are still hostile toward Assad, some of them tried to topple him. Therefore, they will not wish to help him to recover, even if it is at the expense of the Syrian people. Part of the aid that can be delivered to Syria might reach and help its population, but much of the aid will find its way to the hands of corrupted and/or those who support Assad. Such outcomes make it harder to assist those in Syria who desperately need help. In addition, some countries that are not necessarily hostile to Assad, such as China, may be reluctant to pour money into projects, as long as there is uncertainty and fighting in Syria.

In mid-2021 some in the Arab world, such as in Egypt, thought Assad could be allowed to return to the Arab league. This "would gradually accentuate its 'Arabism,' while moving Syria away from Persian Iran."[9] However, Assad, who had an alliance with Iran before he was kicked out of the Arab league, would not cut his ties with Iran, even if Syria is again a member of the Arab league. Assad still needs Iran. He also fears Iran's retribution, if the latter assumes he turned against her, after all the aid Iran provided him.

Since 2019 and until early 2021 Israel attacked in the eastern Mediterranean and in the Red Seas 10 ships carrying fuel/military equipment from Iran to Assad. Israel also strove to harm Iran economically, by reducing Iran's oil revenues.[10] However, having another front with Iran, at sea, could have been another factor that might have brought escalation, and maybe even a war. Israel also hit Iran in sea sectors that are relatively close to Israel, since Israel's sea capabilities are limited. Those Israeli operations, which started because of Iranian aid to Syria, give Iran a kind of justification to strike Israel at sea, on terms that are convenient to Iran. For example, the Red Sea is Israel's shortest sea route to East Asia and east Africa. The Bab al—Mendab Strait is the southern gate to the Red Sea, near Yemen, where pro-Iranian Houthis can strike Israeli ships. The Bab al-Mendab Strait is about 2000 km from Israel. The IAF and the Israeli navy can reach there, but it would not be easy to run there an ongoing fight. It is therefore an Israeli weak spot. Iran can exploit it.

FRICTION BETWEEN IRAN AND ASSAD

Mehdi Khalaji argued in March 2021 that Iranian "leaders consistently define Syria as a "province" that they have the right and capability to control as they see fit."[11] Some Syrian military and security unites "are financed and under complete Iranian control."[12] Top Syrian officers were forced to accept orders from their Iranian counterparts, during the Syrian civil war. A power struggles between the Syrian elite and Iranian officials caused friction. Some Syrians fear Iran trying to take over their country. It seems Iran considers Syria, due to its low point, less as a partner and more like a proxy.

Iran has other allies such as Hezbollah, Hamas etc. that are NSAs, while Syria is a state. Despite its fragile situation the Syrian regime clearly sees itself as the head of a state. Assad did praise the contributions of Hezbollah and Iran to the fight in Syria, but textbooks in Syrian schools, controlled by the Assad regime, emphasize Syrian national pride and manifest certain hostility toward Iran. In mid-July 2020, Syria and Iran signed an agreement designed to upgrade the military cooperation between them, and also to refute rumors of the weakening in their ties. It was an indication that both Iran and Assad were aware of their need to display an image of allies.

Assad might be persuaded to substantially reduce Iran's military presence in Syria, the one target Israel. The decline of the Syrian civil war means that Assad does not need that much Iranian military support, to fight rebels, especially if the Iranian deployment is directed against Israel and not against rebels. Moreover, Assad wants to strengthen his independence, and not be a puppet of Iran.

CAN IRAN USE ASSAD'S MILITARY AGAINST ISRAEL?

Despite the cost of its Syrian project, its possible negative implications and attempts by Assad to call the shots in Syria, Iran sticks to its guns. Iran is determined to expand its influence in Syria. Syria does not only increase Iran's grip in the Arab world but also gives Iran another base near Israel (besides the one in Lebanon. In the Gaza Strip Hamas does not always obey Iran). Syria is needed for Iran to contain and deter Israel from attacking Iran's nuclear sites.

From Syria Iran can attack Israel by launching drones, rockets, and missiles and also to mount ground incursions in the Golan Heights. Iran also seeks to get a hold in Syrian seaports, where Iran can deploy midget submarines, capable of launching torpedoes, mines, and short-range missiles. Egypt, by controlling the Suez Canal, can make it difficult for Iran to send vessels from Iran to Syria and vice versa.

Iran could use its leverage over Assad, to urge Assad to attack Israel, if Israel clashes with Hezbollah, let alone if Israel strikes Iran. Assad could refuse, fearing severe Israeli retribution would cripple his military, leaving him vulnerable to his foes inside Syria. It is important to remember that Assad avoided fighting Israel when his country and military were in much better shape, prior to the civil war.

Assad used CW against its people. Following US pressure Assad was forced to sign an agreement, in late 2013, that got rid of most of Assad's CW.[13] During the war, Assad lost also a large part of its weapon systems. In recent years there has been an effort to rebuild the Syrian military. The goal is to reconstruct it for internal purposes, to defeat rebels, not to confront Israel.[14] This alone rules out using the Syrian military in conducting a massive attack in the Golan Heights. Even if Assad's military would return to focus on Israel, it might need many years, maybe even a decade or more, to fully recover from the civil war, before it can be ready to confront Israel.

Assad has limited military options against Israel. One should also bear in mind that Assad did not retaliate after Israel destroyed the Syrian nuclear reactor in 2007. Therefore he would not want to jeopardize his regime, reacting after Iran's nuclear sites are attacked. Although Iran would be eager to hit Israel, following an Israeli raid in Iran, the latter might not risk losing Assad, and all its investment in him. Iran could be satisfied with a symbolic Syrian strike against Israel, limited enough to prevent Israel from hitting Assad too hard, but sufficiently effective to present Assad as standing together with Iran against Israel.

During the Syrian civil war, Israel was not sure what to do with Assad. By avoiding inflicting a significant blow to Assad's military, Israel served a vital Iranian interest i.e., keeping Assad in power. Yet, if Assad allows Iran to use Syria as a base to strike Israel then the latter might hit Assad hard, in order to punish him and to urge him to convince Iran to stop confronting Israel from Syria. Even if Assad is not much involved in

Iran's effort to harm Israel, the latter can still exploit his weakness and his importance to Iran, by going after Assad. Overall, the extent of the Israeli pressure on Assad would be according to the effect on Iran and Assad and to how much Israel is willing to risk replacing Assad with the unknown.

THE SYRIAN: ISRAELI WARS, 1948–1982

Israel and Syria have been enemies since 1948, which led to several wars and numerous violent incidents between them.[15] In the 1967 war Israel seized the Golan Heights.[16] In the 1973 war Syria launched a surprise attack. Israel managed to recover and eventually it kept the Golan Heights in its hands. The IDF also advanced toward Damascus, but it was a tough fight.[17]

In 1982 a large part of Lebanon was under Syrian influence. Lebanon protected Syria's western flank.[18] In 1982 IDF's Intelligence branch did not assume that Syria plans to attack Israel.[19] Yet, Israel strove to weaken Syria.[20] In the 1982 war, Israel had plans to confront Syria in Lebanon,[21] and a clash indeed happened. There were fierce battles between Israeli and Syrian forces inside Lebanon. The war did not spread to Syria, because Israel did not seek that. Both Syria and Israel had considered Lebanon as a separate theater of operations, where they can fight outside their own states. At the time Syria was Israel's main enemy. Israel decided to confront Syria in a third country, Lebanon. During the Syrian civil war, Israel has been fighting its current arch-enemy, Iran, in another country, in Syria.

In the late 70's and early 80's Syria invested heavily in the military buildup, by relying on massive Soviet aid. The collapse of Syria's patron, the Soviet Union, in 1991 led to a decline of Syria's military might.[22] Furthermore, the peace treaties between Israel and Egypt (1979) and Jordan (1994) together with the blows Iraq took in 1991 and 2003 left Syria basically without its traditional Arab allies. Nevertheless, Israel was very careful not to confront Syria that still possessed a powerful military.

The 1982 war was the last time the Israeli and the Syrian militaries confronted each other in a major clash. Since then both sides prepared for another war between them. For the IDF, in spite of all its confrontations and skirmishes with Palestinians and Hezbollah, Syria was its main challenge, due to its military might. Israel and Syria maintained a status quo that sometimes seemed fragile, but it held on. There were periods of high tension in the Golan Heights, yet both sides managed to avoid a war. Syria did harm Israel by supporting NSAs such as Hamas and Hezbollah, but in a limited way. Syria never joined those groups when they fought Israel.

ISRAEL'S DILEMMA AND BENEFITS FROM THE SYRIAN CIVIL WAR

Since 1982 there was not a war between Israel and Syria. Israel did bomb inside Syria in a few cases, in the two decades prior to the Syrian civil war. The most famous and important Israeli raid was the destruction of Assad's nuclear reactor in 2007, after Israel suspected that Assad plans to produce nuclear weapons.[23] Israel decided it could not allow it, even at the risk of war. Israel took steps in order to avoid an escalation to war, such as keeping the raid a secret. Assad, who also did not seek war, did not retaliate. Nevertheless, it was a huge gamble by Israel, a justified one, which paid off.

During the Syrian civil war Israel was not sure what would better serve its national interest: if the pro-Iranian Assad stays in power, or if he is toppled by the rebels, many of them were Muslim extremists who hate Israel. Israel did not want to see Syria becoming a country that most of it is under the rule of radical Islamic groups. In that sense, Israel preferred that Assad stays in office, even if it means he keeps his alliance with a radical Shiite state, Iran, instead of dealing with radical Sunni groups. At least Assad is well known to Israel. Ideologically, Iran opposes Israel's right to exist, and the Assad regime has the same opinion. Yet, unlike Iran Assad negotiated with Israel on achieving peace i.e., was willing to recognize and have some kind of normal relations with Israel. Furthermore, even without peace Assad could be deterred and Israel can reach an understating with him. It might be more difficult to achieve that with radical Sunni groups that are associated with Al-Qaida, ISIS, etc. Militarily speaking, Syrian radical Sunni groups are weaker than Assad and Iran. Compared to those Sunni groups, Iran could allocate much more resources and manpower to Syria, as part of the conflict with Israel. Nevertheless, for Israel defeating those groups would have been a tall order too, from which Israel sought to avoid.

Israel was well aware that if the IDF intervenes in the battles in Syria, Israel will pay with blood and treasure. In spite of the severe criticism in Israel about the atrocities and mass killing in Syria, there was no public support in putting Israeli troops in harm's way, in order to protect Syrians. Furthermore, sadly Arabs, including many Syrians, would not have seen the IDF as one that comes to save Syrians, but as another side in the conflict that seeks to exploit Syria's weakness, to harm Syrians and to exploit their country. Israel could have been dragged into the quagmire there, unable to leave. Israel experienced that before, when it got bogged down in Lebanon in 1982, which led to a deployment of 18 years in that torn country. Israel remembered that grim experience, and its heavy cost. Israel was determent to avoid making the same mistake again, this time in Syria.

The best outcome of the Syrian civil war, from the Israeli perspective, is that Assad stays in power. He should be strong enough to suppress radical groups, but too weak to challenge Israel. The latter has the same approach about another Iranian ally, Hamas in the Gaza Strip. Israel also wishes that Assad would be independent, without relying on Iran, but Israel wants Assad to be vulnerable, so Israel can deter and contain him. Since Israel decided not to intervene in the war it left it to others, including Iran, to set the outcome, hoping it would please Israel.

There were those in Israel who assumed the longer the Syrian civil war is, the better it is for Israel, since Israel's enemies in Syria would not be available to turn against Israel. The same line of thought was in Israel during the war between Iran and Iraq in the 1980s. It made sense in regard to the Syrian civil war too. However, since the Syrian civil war went on for years, it paved the way for Iran, Hezbollah and Russia to increase their presence in Syria, which did not serve the Israeli interest.

Israel strives to prevent "Hezbollah from becoming so heavily armed with game-changing weaponry that it becomes overconfident and reckless."[24] Since 2012 the IAF conducted sorties inside Syria, aiming to destroy deliveries of advanced weapons such as antiaircraft missiles that were on their way to Hezbollah in Lebanon. By that Israel has been striving to delay the outbreak of the next war, although its strikes inside Syria might have ignited a war with Hezbollah.

Israel was frustrated when Hezbollah assimilated more and more rockets and missiles since 2006, arsenal which came from Syria. Israel was aware that bombing those weapons inside Syria might have brought war with the powerful Syrian military. Following the Syrian civil war and the gradual decline of Assad's armed forces, Israel dared to bomb inside Syria. In that sense, the Syrian civil war not only substantially crippled the Syrian armed forces but also gave Israel an opportunity to delay Hezbollah's military buildup.

Israel was not involved in igniting the Syrian civil war. The entire Arab turmoil that started in 2010 was a complete surprise for Israel. On one hand, this gigantic Arab wave of protests and wars had its risks for Israel. One of them was when the Mubarak regime was toppled, which might have undermined the peace between Egypt and Israel. On the other hand, the Syrian civil war significantly weakened the IDF's biggest rival since the 1980s, the Syrian military. The IDF invested a lot in preparing for a war with Syria. The IDF was stronger than the Syrian military, and the latter was in a decline, following the collapse of its Soviet patron. Nevertheless, for Israel the cost of a war with Syria might have been very high. Syria would have suffered more than Israel, yet hundreds and maybe a few thousand Israelis might have been killed in such a war, including in the rear. Therefore the meltdown of Assad's armed forces was for Israel one of the most important and positive developments in the last decades. For Israel it was kind of a strategic miracle, to see its main rival destroys itself. In a certain way, it was frustrating for Israel, especially considering all the huge budgets, energy, special projects, and time Israel invested in getting ready for a possible war with Syria. Yet, it was not in vain, because Israel's capabilities deterred Syria and some of the knowledge and lessons Israel gained from preparing to confront Assad, are useful for other purposes. Above all, of course, it was a tremendous relief for Israel, knowing it avoided a highly costly war. During the Syrian civil war the Syrian military had huge losses, in men, weapons systems, etc., but the IDF did not have to fight at all. Basically, Israel did not have to pay any price let alone in human lives, to achieve this outcome.

The sharp decline of the Syrian military showed the importance of strategic patience. Israel was concerned since 1973 that the Assad regime might try again to retake the Golan Heights by force. In certain situations, Israel suspected Syria might attack. Israel could have conducted a preemptive strike, assuming since war is about to start, Israel must take the initiative, in order to fight on its own terms. Israel avoided that, taking a risk the Syrian military would strike first. Israel took a calculated risk that paid off, since Assad did not attack.

The probability of a large-scale Syrian offensive was quite low since 2000. Reforms in the Syrian military made it rely much more on defense and firepower, and less on launching massive armor attacks. However, the risk of a major war remained, until the Syrian civil war. Israel strove to deter Assad and by that to avoid a war. Israel almost never used force against Assad, and demonstrated restraint. This strategy proved itself. It might work also with Hezbollah and Iran, if eventually there is some crucial change with Iran or Hezbollah that would reduce dramatically the danger to Israel, as it was with Assad. It might be the results of an internal outburst in Lebanon or Iran.

In 1980–1988 Iraq and Iran fought each other. It kept Iraq busy, so it could not have sent a large expeditionary force to confront Israel. The cost of the war to Iraq was significant, including at the economic level, but Iraq was in better shape than Syria is now. In additions, both the Iraqi military in the 1980s and the Syrian military in the last decade gained vast combat experience. However, Assad's forces confronted rebels, while Iraq clashed with a conventional military. Iran's military had then problems following purging, as a result of the 1979 revolution, and the US embargo, which made it difficult to operate its American weapon systems such as the F-14. Nevertheless, the Iranian military managed to hold on and even invade Iraq. In contrast, Assad's troops clashed with a foe that had no aircraft, tanks, artillery, etc., so the knowledge Assad's military acquired was in suppressing rebellion, not confronting a conventional military. Overall the Iraqi military in the late 1980s was better fit to confront the IDF, than Syria's military is, in its current stage. It could be added that by fighting Iraq in the 1980s Iran helped to upgrade the Iraqi military, which could have been used against Israel. In the Syrian civil war Iran assisted the Syrian military, improving its ability in handling insurgents, not in confronting the IDF.

THE ISRAELI AIR CAMPAIGN IN SYRIA

On December 7, 2014, following an Israeli airstrike inside Syria, Israel's Defense Minister, Moshe Ya'alon, warned that "those who try to arm our enemies should know that we will reach every place, anytime, by any means, to thwart their plans."[25] On April 11, 2016, Israeli Prime Minister Benjamin Netanyahu admitted that Israel had bombed deliveries of weapons that were on their way from Syria to Hezbollah in Lebanon.[26] Until then Israel did not officially take responsibility for those strikes, in order to make it easier for Assad to avoid retribution against Israel. Even when Israel referred to this issue it was in kind of a vague way. Assad continued to restrain himself due to his weakness. Still, it was a wise decision not to provoke and humiliate Assad in public. He could have tried to conduct a terror attack against Israel, with the help of Hezbollah and Iran, somewhere around the world.

Israel bombed Syria 12 times in 2013; 8 times in 2014, 21 times in 2015, 10 times in 2016, 22 times in 2017, and more than 28 times in 2018.[27] Israel did try to avoid killing Hezbollah operatives "seeing little benefit from the deaths of a small number of low-level operatives at a cost of having to divert resources to ready for a Hezbollah retaliation." The IDF care less about harming Iran-backed Shiite militias in Syria who come from countries such as Afghanistan, "and are less likely to retaliate or to be able to do so significantly."[28] In some cases the IAF fired warning shots, giving its foe an opportunity to disperse, before the target was destroyed.[29] The idea was therefore to focus on the weapons, not on personal, and by that to try to reduce the probability of an escalation.

By 2018 Indirect contacts between Israel and Iran failed in reaching an understanding in regard to Syria. Iran refused to restrict its operations inside Syria or to tone down its announcements against Israel.[30] On February 10, 2018 a major incident occurred, after an Iranian drone that was sent from Syria, penetrated Israel. The drone was shot down almost immediately after it passed the border into Israel. Israel responded by destroying the drone's command and control center, which was stationed in T4, a base deep inside Syria. Iran ignored that attack. Assad did not retaliate against Israel directly, fearing to start a war, one he did not want since his military was too weak. Yet his air defense launched a barrage of about 26 missiles, which brought down an Israeli F-16I, over the skies of Israel. Following that Israel conducted a major attack on Syria's air defense.

On May 9, 2018, the IRGC fired more than 32 rockets into Israel, to the Golan Heights. The rockets were intercepted or they hit empty areas, without causing any casualties or damage. Nevertheless, Israel responded by conducting quite a massive air attack. Dozens of Israeli fighters bombed around 75 Iranian targets across Syria. Syrian air defense fired back. The IAF did not lose any aircraft and it also destroyed several antiaircraft batteries. It was a serious skirmish, yet without escalating, since both sides sought to avoid that.

"From 2010 to 2013, two Syrian surface-to-air missiles were fired at Israeli aircraft, compared to the 844 that were launched at IAF jets from 2017 to 2020." The IAF estimated it "destroyed a third of Syria's advanced air defense systems...However, much of those anti-aircraft weapons have already been replaced or even upgraded by more advanced models from either Russia or Iran."[31] The IAF was successful due to its new combat doctrine, vast experience and its F-35.[32] Israel's tactical achievements could also assist the IAF in a major war with Iran. In that sense, the sorties in Syria help to prepare the IAF to bomb Iran. Israel does not conduct strikes in Syria in order to examine how her aircrews function under fire, as it would be in Iran. Israel puts its aircrews in harm's way in Syria because of the need to disrupt the Iranian presence in Syria. However, preparing air crews for a raid in Iran is a kind of a by-product of the air campaign in Syria.

The IAF did not confront a formidable air defense since 1982, until the Syrian civil war. The IAF ran since 1982 many sorties across the Middle East that had to deal with strong air defense. However, the Israeli aircraft had to avoid this air defense, not to confront it, let alone not in an ongoing campaign, as the one that takes place in Syria in the last decade. This factor emphasizes the importance of the clashes in Syria, including in regard to a possible strike in Iran. The main similarity between a raid in Iran to the strikes in Syria is the challenge of overcoming a strong air defense. The main differences are the distance to the targets and the scale of the Israeli attack. Bombing in Syria, especially when the Israeli aircraft launch their missiles from nearby Lebanon, requires much less fuel, compared with reaching Iran, which would require air refueling. In Syria, the campaign also has been running since 2012, while in Iran it would be one raid, although some more strikes might follow later on. In addition in Syria the IAF carried out a few massive attacks, as the one that would be in Iran, but the attack in Iran would probably be on a bigger scale.

By March 2021 the IAF launched up to 1500 airstrikes against Iranian targets in Syria.[33] In 2021 Israeli air operations run into difficulties. The Syrian air defense was improved, "in part due to upgraded Iranian-made components, allowing it to respond more quickly." Also "air defense batteries — the radars, missile launchers and command centers — can be spread out across large geographic areas, making it nearly impossible to destroy them entirely in one counterattack." The IAF responded by "using larger formations with more aircraft to conduct strikes on more targets at one time, instead of carrying out more strikes using smaller formations."[34]

The IDF could theoretically replace air strikes in Syria with firing surface to surface missiles or by conducting an airborne assault. Yet, those options are more problematic than an air attack. Israel's surface to surface missiles are kept for strategic missions such as carrying nuclear warheads. Airborne attacks are risky. During all the air strikes Israel did not lose any of its air crews. If the IDF lands troops from helicopters some of them might be harmed or captured, an outcome Israel strongly wishes to avoid. A ground raid was also not an option, since the targets were deep inside Syria.

If Israel strikes Iran's nuclear sites, the IAF might have to cross Syria. The IAF is familiar with the Syrian air defense, which would help the IAF in handling it. However, the IAF might prefer to save its resources to Iran. Assad can also use its fighters, but he would hesitate to risk his planes in an almost hopeless fight against the IAF.

WAS THERE A PROBABILITY OF A WAR?

On February 20, 2019, Iran's Foreign Minister Mohammed Javad Zarif warned the Israeli strikes in Syria might ignite a war between Israel and Iran.[35] IDF Chief of Staff Aviv Kohavi said in late December 2019 Israel "won't allow Iran to establish a military presence in [Syria], or even in Iraq."[36] In late April 2020 Israeli Defense Minister Naftali Bennett argued that Israel strives to push Iran out of Syria.[37] Israel needs a clear exit strategy from its campaign in Syria, but meanwhile it continues to bomb there. Israel is aware of the risks. Israel's desire to annihilate and at least to limit Iran's base in Syria might bring a severe retaliation and in the worst case it might start a war. Iran, Hezbollah and Assad avoided massive retribution against Israel, such as striking it with a barrage of missiles. Yet, there is no guarantee this pattern would repeat itself each time Israel conducts a raid in Syria. Iran, Syria or Hezbollah might seek to turn the attention from them toward Israel. An Israeli attack gives them a pretext for that.

A war let alone a full-scale one was against the interest of all parties. This was the logic behind the Israeli strikes. Even when the Syrian civil war came to an end and Iran, Assad and Hezbollah had the upper hand, the winner side needed time to recover. Assad and his allies did not strive for another war, this time with Israel. Such a confrontation might be quite demanding for Syria, Iran, and Hezbollah. Assad, Iran, and Hezbollah had other priorities, internal and external ones. Despite their hate toward Israel, they knew it was not the right time to confront it. Iran had to focus on getting rid of the sanctions, in order to allow its economy to recover. A war with Israel was not the way to do it. Furthermore, Iran was concerned that during a war, Israel would bomb its nuclear sites. Iran was also busy with other countries such as Iraq and Yemen.

Iran's forces in Syria are no match to the IDF. Iran has long-range surface to surface missiles that can reach Israel from Iran itself. "Iran's medium-range missiles are designed to impress, threaten and deter its neighbors and rivals." Israel certainly takes that into account.[38] However, the front with Israel in Syria is more than 1000 kilometers from Iran. It is a major logistical challenge to dispatch, maintain and secure such as long line of communication. This "Tehran express" might not run so smoothly. Israel would bomb convoys not only in Syria, but in Iraq as well. In contrast, Israeli bases are much closer to the frontline and the IAF could protect Israel's ground forces from Iranian air strikes. In addition Iran's armed forces, including the IRGC, are not built for conducting a full-scale war against a military like the IDF, let alone so far away from Iran. At most Iran can run an attrition war based on a symmetric warfare. Iran's shortcomings would make it easier for Israel to inflict Iran a humiliating defeat, which might undermine the Iranian regime.

Israel, despite the advantages it enjoys in fighting Iran in Syria, wants to avoid a full-blown war. Israel seeks to destroy the Iranian base in Syria, but Israel still prefers a much more restrained confrontation. The Israeli campaign in Syria requires some effort, but a relatively limited one. Most importantly for Israel, the IAF has been bombing in Syria since 2012, without absorbing any casualties. A major war would be more demanding and more costly for Israel.

Can Israel Benefit from the Iranian Presence in Syria?

The Israeli air strikes were supposed to reduce the Iranian presence in Syria, but there were other factors in this matter. Israel might have benefited from the Iranian intervention in Syria. Israel was not sure if it wants Assad to survive. Either way, Israel sought that Iran's intervention in Syria, in favor of Assad, would fail, because Israel opposed an Iranian deployment in Syria. Iran could have stayed in Syria even if Assad had lost the war, but Iran needs him, despite his low point. In that sense, Israel wanted to topple Assad, although he might be more of a burden than an asset for Iran.

In late March 2021 Oula Alrifai claimed that "Iran currently spends at least $6 billion annually to prop up Assad."[39] In a way, Israel might want Iran to invest more and more in Syria, at the expense of taking care of the Iranian people, who already expressed their disappointment of this poor choice of priorities. Iran's economic hardships could increase the frustration there, which would eventually undermine the stability of the Iranian regime. Syria could therefore serve Israel in achieving a much more important goal than kicking Iran out of Syria i.e., to bring down the Iranian regime.

Israel obviously would be very pleased if the Iranian regime is toppled. Without its Iranian ally Assad too might not survive. Even if he stays in power, Syria would not serve as an Iranian base against Israel. It will end Israel's campaign in Syria, bringing calm between Israel and Syria, A collapse of the Iranian regime might also disrupt the ties between Assad and Hezbollah, which would cripple the latter.

Israel is concerned about Iran's presence in Syria. Yet, it should be remembered that Syria was never friendly toward Israel. The two states have been enemies since Israel was established in 1948, and Syria's military has been Israel's main threat since the 1980s. Iran's deployment in Syria during the civil war there has been much less intimidating, compared with the power Assad had possessed prior to the civil war. Assad had more troops and weapon systems like tanks, aircraft, etc., than Iran ever had in Syria, even before Israel destroyed a significant part of the Iranian arsenal there.

Israel is concerned Iran can build in Syria a fire base similar to the one Hezbollah has in Lebanon, but it would take a long time to do it. Even then the threat from the Syrian military pre civil war was bigger. Israel also has to be careful not to be seen as weak i.e., that a regional power like Israel is worried too much about a limited Iranian deployment near it.

One of Israel's basic strategic approaches over the years was to try to "contain threats or keep them as distant as possible from Israeli borders and society."[40] It has to do with Iran as well. Israel has satellites, aircraft, and intelligence services that collect information and operate all over the Middle East. Nevertheless, there is a clear advantage of having the foe close to Israel, since it is easier to both monitor and strike it. In that sense, the Iranian presence in Syria helps Israel in watching Iranian steps in a country that has been well familiar for Israel. The latter's control of the Golan Heights and its technological edge assists Israel in observing and attacking Iranian targets in Syria. It also allows Israel to humiliate

Iran, which might cause deterioration, but also to diminish Iran's position in the region.

Iran helped Assad to fight a war that since 2011 cost 500,000 lives, "more than five times greater than the approximately 90,000 Palestinians killed in the last 70 years of the Palestinian-Israeli conflict, while more than twice as many Syrians (12 million) as Palestinians have been displaced. Indeed since 2011 far more Palestinians have been killed by Assad (nearly 3,700) than by Israel, including by chemical weapons."[41] Iran's support of Assad not only cost the Palestinian dearly but also showed how far Iran will go in accomplishing its regional ambitions, at the expense of Arabs. Israel hoped Iran would look bad in the Arab world since Iran backs Assad and most of the Arabs are against him. Iran's intervention in Syria did cause some damage to Iran's image, but it did not prevent Iran from increasing its influence in Arab countries such as Yemen and Iraq.

Eventually, Iran might not be able to benefit much from Syria, if the Assad regime does not survive or turns against Iran. Even if Assad stays an Iranian ally, Iran might calculate its Syrian project is too costly and decide to cut its losses and basically to give up on Syria. Without a grip in Syria Iran's bridge to the Mediterranean would be broken. Iran might accept it, especially if Iranian influence in Iraq and Lebanon is diminished. Iran might reconsider all its complicated and expensive involvement in the Arab world. Iran might turn toward other regions, where Iran could expand its influence, such as Central Asia, instead of continuing to focus on the Arab world, including on Israel. Such a shift would obviously be in favor of Israel. Iran would still be hostile toward Israel, but Iran's activity against Israel would be reduced, maybe significantly, following Iran's pivot to other regions. The Iranian intervention in Syria could therefore be the start of a turning point in Iran's foreign policy. The Iranian regime might also be forced to allocate more resources to address its major domestic distress, at the expense of its aspirations in the Middle East. Iran can therefore make a drastic change that would be a difficult strategic decision. However, the Iranian regime faced other crossroads like ending the war with Iraq in 1988 or signing the nuclear deal in 2015. The bottom line indicates that despite Syria's importance in the eyes of Iran, there are several factors that might lead to Iran loosening its grip on Syria.

THE GOLAN HEIGHTS

The 1948–1973 wars between Israel and Syria were near or in the Golan Heights. The dispute over the Golan Heights is one of the main reasons for the Syrian–Israeli conflict. If Israel had returned the Golan Heights to Syria, it could have ended their conflict. In contrast, Iran and Israel don't share a border, which should reduce the tension between the two sides. However, Iran does not want Israel to give Iran or the Arabs a certain territory. The Iranian regime is not willing to accept Israeli Sovereignty in any part of Israel.

In 2013 Joseph Olmert said that Syria would not have agreed to receive the Golan Heights, in return for "giving up its alliance with Iran."[42] In the late 1990s and in 2008 there were peace talks between Israel and Syria, but they led to a dead end.[43] Even if an accord was signed Syria might have also kept its relations with both Hezbollah and Iran. Assad might have cooled down those ties, waiting until he receives back the Golan Heights. Then he could have again tightened its ties with both Iran and Hezbollah. Assad could have claimed he wants to be a broker between them and Israel. He might have done that, as long it would have served him, which often would not have been necessarily served the Israeli interest. Another problem could have been that as with Egypt the peace with Assad could have been cold too. Still, it is better than a cold war, let alone an actual confrontation. There were therefore all kinds of potential risks and problems, as with other peace accords between Israel and Arab states. In the past, Israel might have been willing to accept it, together with giving up the Golan Heights.

Since 1974 there was complete quiet in the Golan Heights, until 2011. Following the Syrian civil war there were several hundred incidents on the border in the Golan Heights. For example, mortar shells, which were fired from Syria, by either side there, hit Israeli territory in the Golan Heights, often by mistake. Until early 2022 only one Israeli was killed on the border there. Nevertheless, when fire from Syria reached Israel, the IDF shot back at Assad's objectives. Israel saw Assad as responsible for any attack from Syria, even if it was not Assad's fault. Assad tolerated the ongoing Israel's strikes since the latter has been much more powerful than him, he did not absorb many casualties in the incidents on the border and he had much more urgent issues on his plate. Stopping rebels from striking Israel, assuming he wanted to, was not much of a priority for him, to put it mildly. Iran wants to use the border against Israel, yet Assad had to focus on other sectors in Syria, which were more important both to Assad and Iran. Therefore Iran could not have relied much on Assad in confronting Israel in the Golan Heights.

In late January 2015, in the Golan Heights, near the border, Israel killed several Hezbollah combatants, including one of their commanders and an IRGC General, Mohammed Allahdadi. The latter might have been assassinated by mistake. A few days later Hezbollah retaliated by killing two Israeli soldiers.[44] Hezbollah and Iran tried in recent years to strike Israel in the Golan Heights, but without much success. Nevertheless, Israel took steps to secure the Golan Heights by building a new high fence, adding surveillance measures, etc. The IDF also ran some minor ground operations on the Syrian side. It might do it again, including in a large scale, if this is required.

During the 1980s and the 1990s often up to six Syrian divisions were deployed near the Golan front.[45] The Syrian military was severely weakened in the civil war. Even after it regained its positions on the border in the Golan Heights, in 2017–2018, the Syrian armed forces lacked the manpower to have the same massive presence it had there in the 1990s. Therefore, the threat to Israel was greatly diminished. Israel's top priority in the Golan Heights is to secure its population there, where 25,000 Israeli Jews reside. Iran, after it helped Assad to get back most of Syria, could devote more effort to the border with Israel.

Israel, during the Syrian civil war, in order to both keep the Golan Heights quiet and to prevent waves of Syrian refugees, provided since 2013 a humanitarian-aid program that lasted until 2018. By then Israel took care of several thousand Syrians. Furthermore, Ehud Yaari mentioned in April 2018 that some Israeli officers supported a plan, in which rebels will seize southern Syria and "create a wide buffer zone between Israel and Iran-sponsored forces." The Israeli Prime Minister Benjamin Netanyahu rejected this idea, because he did not want to get drawn into the Syrian civil war.[46] It is worth mentioning that over the years, before and after Israel seized the Golan Heights, there were all kinds of ideas in Israel, calling to create a Druze state that will include the Golan Heights or part of it. This state was supposed to serve as a buffer between Israel and Syria. It was a risky adventure that should have been avoided. If the Druze in Syria would have made a joint and significant effort to build their own state, then Israel could have considered helping them, if they had asked for that. Overall, cooperation, including a military one, between Israel and Syrians might happen if the Syrian civil war rages again. Israel and Iran would strive to gain local allies, as part of the fight over the Golan Heights. However, Israel has to be very careful in this matter.

In late March 2019, President Trump recognized Israel's sovereignty over the Golan Heights. Trump changed "standing U.S. policy that held—in line with U.N. Security Council Resolution 497 from 1981—the Golan was occupied Syrian territory whose final status was subject to Israel-Syria negotiation."[47] No other state joined this declaration, yet also no one tried to take steps against Israel, following the US decision. Iran would continue to try to build a fire base against Israel, including near the Golan Heights.

CONCLUSION

The Syrian civil war destroyed that country. Iran has had an alliance with the Assad regime since the early 1980s. Usually, each state handled its own internal problems, like in 1982, when Hafez al Assad crashed a mutiny. Since 2011 Bashar al Assad desperately needed Iran, Hezbollah and Russia.

In 1982 Israel strove to establish a friendly regime in Lebanon, but this attempt failed. It was a bitter experience for Israel. As a result, Israel did not try to be involved in regime change during the Syrian civil war. Israel did not support any of the sides, yet by that Israel basically allowed Assad and his allies to win. Israel strove to stay out of the Syrian quagmire, but Israel launched hundreds of sorties inside Syria, aiming at delaying the delivery of advanced weapons to Hezbollah in Lebanon. Israel also has been determent to stop Iran from establishing a base in Syria. Assad did not retaliate, since he had preferred to focus on his other enemies. Assad certainly did not seek to start a war with Israel. He has been well aware of the balance of power between him and Israel. The IDF is much stronger than its Syrian counterpart; especially following the latter's meltdown during the civil war. Israel would have crushed Assad's forces in a matter of days. Nevertheless, the Israeli bombardments in the heart of Syria humiliated Assad. Assad will wait for the right opportunity to settle the score with Israel. Iran might help him in this matter. Meanwhile, Assad's air defense has been trying to shoot down Israeli aircraft. Only in one incident, on February 10, 2018, Syrian antiaircraft fire intercepted an Israeli F-16.

Since 2011 Israel had to adjust to the unrest on the border between Israel and Syria, in the Golan Heights. However, it was relatively a very low cost to pay considering that the Syrian civil war devastated the Syrian military, Israel's biggest challenge since the 1980s, and a close Iranian ally. Israel provided some humanitarian aid to several thousand Syrians who live close to the border, including giving intensive medical care inside Israel. By that Israel might have hoped to build some kind of military cooperation with Syrian armed groups, against Assad and Iran's protégés in Syria. This project ended in 2018, after Assad took back control of the border. If Assad agrees or maybe forced to allow Iran to use that border to provoke Israel it could lead to an ongoing conflict there. The border between Israel and Syria in the Golan Heights might turn into a battlefield between Israel and Iran and its proxies like Hezbollah. Israel might try to reach Syrians who would be willing to cooperate with it.

Iran seeks to turn Syria into a fire base, aimed against Israel. Israel tries to prevent it, which might cause a war. In such a case Iran is at a clear disadvantage, because its supply lines, from Iran to Syria, stretch over more than a thousand kilometers. Israel is still concerned about the Iranian deployment in Syria, but Israel does not have to be terrified about that. It is bad for Israel's image and deterrence in regard to Iran.

Iran invested tens of billions of dollars in Syria. It is highly doubtful that Iran will get back its money in an economically devastated country, which lacks natural resources. Iran hopes to benefit from the reconstruction of Syria, but many countries and companies avoid investing in Syria. Iran also suffers from its own severe economic difficulties, which would make it harder on Iran to continue to pour funds into Syria. If Iran insists on this policy, it might increase the frustration inside Iran, which might undermine the regime there. In that sense Israel wants Iran to allocate big budgets to Syria.

Iran sees Syria as a base to fight against Israel, but Iran has already paid a high price during the war in Syria. A confrontation between Iran and Israel on Syrian soil might well add to that heavy toll, including in human lives. Considering Iran's sensitivity to casualties, this is an important consideration.

Iran needs Syria's strategic location, as part of the Iranian arc that stretches from Iran to the Mediterranean Sea, which includes also Lebanon and Iraq. Yet the anti-Iranian opposition in Iraq and Lebanon, along with severe problems in Syria itself, raises serious questions about the Crescent's stability.

Assad still needs Iran, but he also wants to reduce both his dependence on Iran, and Iran's hold on Syria. It creates friction between them. Iran's rivals can take advantage of this to drive a wedge between Iran and Assad. In light of all these factors, Iran must carefully consider whether and to what extent it should continue its support and deployment in Syria.

Notes

1. Eyal Zisser, *Syria at War—the Rise and Fall of the Revolution in Syria* (Maarachot—the IDF's Publishing House and the Moshe Dayan Center for Middle Eastern and African Studies, Tel Aviv University, 2020). Fouad Ajami, *The Syrian Rebellion* (Stanford University Press, 2012).
2. Christopher Phillips, *The Battle for Syria: International Rivalry in the New Middle East* (Yale University Press, 2016), p. 12.
3. Itamar Rabinovich and Carmit Valensi, *Syrian Requiem: The Civil War and Its Aftermath* (Princeton University Press, 2021), pp. 15–16.
4. On the benefits of the alliance to Iran see: Yair Hirschfeld, "The Odd Couple: Ba'thist Syria and Khomeini's Iran," in Avner Yaniv, Moshe Maoz and Avi Kober, (eds.), *Syria and Israel's National Security* (Tel Aviv: Ministry of Defence, 1991), pp. 188–192. On their relations see also: Jubin M. Goodarzi, "Syria and Iran: Alliance Cooperation in a Changing Regional Environment", *Middle East Studies* (Vol. 4, No. 2, 2013), pp. 31–59.
5. (No Author), "Tehran: 2,100 Iranian Soldiers Killed in Syria and Iraq", *The Middle East Monitor*, March 7, 2018. https://www.middleeastmonitor.com/20180307-tehran-2100-iranian-soldiers-killed-in-syria-and-iraq/.
6. Oula Alrifai, Nakissa Jahanbani, and Mehdi Khalaji, "Iran's Long Game in Syria", The Washington Institute for Near East Policy, March 29, 2021. https://www.washingtoninstitute.org/policy-analysis/irans-long-game-syria.
7. Waleed Abu al-KhairI, "Impoverished Iranians Bristle at $100 Billion Price Tag for Syria 'investments'", Diyaruna, April 19, 2021. https://diyaruna.com/en_GB/articles/cnmi_di/features/2021/04/19/feature-01.
8. Sandrine Amiel, "Which EU States Are Rebuilding Diplomatic Relations with Assad's Syria?" Euronews, June 17, 2021. https://

www.euronews.com/2021/06/17/which-eu-states-are-rebuil
ding-diplomatic-relations-with-assad-s-syria.

9. David Schenker, "Rehabilitating Assad: The Arab League
Embraces a Pariah", The Washington Institute for Near East
Policy, May 4, 2021. https://www.washingtoninstitute.org/pol
icy-analysis/rehabilitating-assad-arab-league-embraces-pariah?fbc
lid=IwAR1OyrviA8lzAd4HvE9RJdRqbL9OFkqwP1v0PMmgVTc
vANKAtk9EAUldHNw.

10. Patrick Kingslev, Ronen Bergman, Farnaz Fassihi, and Erik
Schmitt, "Israel's Shadow War with Iran Moves Out to Sea", The
New York Times, March 26, 2021. https://www.nytimes.com/
2021/03/26/world/middleeast/israel-iran-shadow-war.html?fbc
lid=IwAR3momNXj_eQnVGT-i0-EtY2Xv7SzgOqtSHyJla0rwmR
J5eN_4lKik5yQdo.

11. Oula Alrifai, Nakissa Jahanbani and Mehdi Khalaji, "Iran's Long
Game in Syria", The Washington Institute for Near East Policy,
March 29, 2021. https://www.washingtoninstitute.org/policy-
analysis/irans-long-game-syria.

12. Samir Altaqi, "The Many Paths to Syrian-Israeli Reconciliation",
The Atlantic Council, March 16, 2021. https://www.atlanticc
ouncil.org/blogs/menasource/the-many-paths-to-syrian-israeli-
reconciliation/.

13. Wyn Bowen, Jeffrey W. Knopf, and Matthew Moran, "The
Obama Administration and Syrian Chemical Weapons: Deter-
rence, Compellence, and the Limits of the "Resolve plus Bombs"
Formula", Security Studies (Vol. 29, No. 5, 2020), p. 798.

14. Anat Ben Haim, "Rebuilding the Syrian Military: Significance for
Israel", INSS, Insight No. 1519, September 15, 2021. https://
www.inss.org.il/publication/syrian-army/.

15. Mohse Ma'oz, Syria and Israel: From War to Peace-Making (Tel
Aviv: Ma'ariv Book, 1996).

16. On the 1967 war see: Matitiahu Mayzel, The Golan Heights
Campaign June 1967 (Tel Aviv: Ministry of Defense, 2001).

17. On the 1973 war see: Dani Asher, The Syrians on the Borders (Tel
Aviv: Ministry of Defence 2008). Oren Elchnan, The History of
Yom Kippur War (Tel Aviv: Ministry of Defense, 2013).

18. Naomi Joy Weinberger, Syrian Intervention in Lebanon (Oxford
University Press, 1986), p. 271.

19. Zeev Schiff and Ehud Ya'ari, *A War of Deception* (Tel Aviv: Schocken, 1984), p. 101.
20. Uri Bar-Joseph, "The Paradox of Israeli Power", *Survival* (Vol. 46, No. 4, Winter 2004–2005), p. 150.
21. Trevor N. Dupuy and Paul Martell, *Flawed Victory* (Fairfax, Virginia: Hero Books, 1986), p. 81.
22. Aharon Yariv, *Cautious Assessment* (Tel Aviv: Ministry of Defense, 1998), pp. 175–176.
23. On the 2007 strike see: Yaakov Katz, *Shadow Strike: Inside Israel's Secret Mission to Eliminate Syrian Nuclear Power* (New York: St. Martin's Press, 2019).
24. Yaakov Lappin, "The Low-Profile War Between Israel and Hezbollah, Begin Sadat Center for Strategic Studies", Mideast Security and Policy Studies No. 138, August 2017, p. 35.
25. On Ya'alon see: Marrissa Newman, "West Bank Violence, Fueled by Hamas, in Decline, Defense Chief Says", *The Times of Israel*, December 9, 2014. http://www.timesofisrael.com/west-bank-vio lence-fueled-by-hamas-in-decline-defense-chief-says/.
26. About what he said see: Reuters, April 11, 2016. http://www.reu ters.com/article/us-mideast-crisis-syria-israel-idUSKCN0X81TO.
27. Seth Jones, "The Escalating Conflict with Hezbollah in Syria", Center for Strategic International Studies (CSIS), June 20, 2018. https://www.csis.org/analysis/escalating-conflict-hezbollah-syria.
28. Judah Ari Gross, "Israeli Air Force Scaling Back Its Strikes in Syria as Southern Border Heats Up", *The Times of Israel*, August 13, 2020. https://www.timesofisrael.com/israeli-air-force-scaling- back-its-strikes-in-syria-as-northern-border-heats-up/.
29. Ilan Goldenberg and Kaleigh Thomas, "How the US Can Learn from Israel to Counter Iran", Defense News, April 23, 2020. https://www.defensenews.com/opinion/commentary/ 2020/04/23/how-the-us-can-learn-from-israel-to-counter-iran/.
30. Ehud Yaari. "Bracing for an Israel-Iran Confrontation in Syria", The American Interest, April 30, 2018. https://www.the-ame rican-interest.com/2018/04/30/bracing-israel-iran-confronta tion-syria/.
31. Judah Ari Gross, "Israeli Air Force Scaling Back Its Strikes in Syria as Southern Border Heats Up", *The Times of Israel*, August 13, 2020. https://www.timesofisrael.com/israeli-air-force-scaling- back-its-strikes-in-syria-as-northern-border-heats-up/.

32. Yossi Melmen, "Why Syria Isn't Firing Its S-300 Missiles at Israeli Jets", *Haaretz*, May 12, 2020. https://www.haaretz.com/israel-news/.premium-why-syria-isn-t-firing-its-s-300-missiles-at-israeli-jets-1.8841093.

33. Seth Frantzman, "Israel-US Attacks Against Iran in Syria Pave Way for Increased Cooperation", *The Jerusalem Post*, March 1, 2021. https://www.jpost.com/arab-israeli-conflict/israel-us-target-iran-in-syria-could-pave-way-for-increased-cooperation-660571.

34. Jordan Ari Gross, "IAF to Start Training for Strike on Iran Nuke Program in Coming Months", *The Times of Israel*, October 25, 2021. https://www.timesofisrael.com/iaf-to-start-training-for-strike-on-iran-nuke-program-in-coming-months/.

35. Reuters, February 20, 2019. https://www.reuters.com/article/us-iran-israel/iran-will-not-rule-out-possibility-of-military-conflict-with-israel-idUSKCN1Q92WY.

36. Judah Ari Gross, "IDF Chief Warns Israelis: The Next War Will Hit Our Home Front Extremely Hard", *The Times of Israel*, December 25, 2019. https://www.timesofisrael.com/idf-chief-israel-alone-in-the-fight-against-iran-in-syria-iraq/.

37. Tom O'Connor, "Israel Says It 'Will Not Stop' Attacking Iran in Syria, Escalates Military Campaign", *Newsweek*, April 28, 2020. https://www.newsweek.com/israel-says-it-will-not-stop-attacking-iran-syria-escalates-military-campaign-1500768.

38. Assaf Orion, "Iran's Missiles: Military Strategy", Iran Primer, February 17, 2021. https://iranprimer.usip.org/blog/2021/feb/17/iran%E2%80%99s-missiles-military-strategy.

39. Oula Alrifai, Nakissa Jahanbani and Mehdi Khalaji, "Iran's Long Game in Syria", The Washington Institute for Near East Policy, March 29, 2021. https://www.washingtoninstitute.org/policy-analysis/irans-long-game-syria.

40. Alon Paz, "Transforming Israel's Security Establishment", The Washington Institute for Near East Policy, October 16, 2015. http://www.washingtoninstitute.org/policy-analysis/view/transforming-israels-security-establishment.

41. Karim Sadjadpour, "Iran's Real Enemy in Syria", *The Atlantic*, April 16, 2018. https://www.theatlantic.com/international/archive/2018/04/iran-syria-israel/558080/.

42. Joseph Olmert, "Israel and Alawite Syria: The Odd Couple of the Middle East?", *Israel Journal of Foreign Affairs* (Vol. 7, No. 1, January 2013), pp. 24–25.
43. Itamar Rabinovich, *The Lingering Conflict: Israel, The Arabs, and the Middle East* (Brookings, 2012).
44. Reuters, January 20, 2015. http://www.reuters.com/article/2015/01/20/us-mideast-crisis-israel-syria-idUSKBN0KT1HQ20 150120.
45. Ma'oz, Syria and Israel, p. 232.
46. Yaari. "Bracing for an…" https://www.the-american-interest.com/2018/04/30/bracing-israel-iran-confrontation-syria/.
47. Jim Zanotti, "Israel and Syria in the Golan Heights: U.S. Recognition of Israel's Sovereignty Claim," Congressional Research Service, December 6, 2019. https://fas.org/sgp/crs/mideast/R44245.pdf.

CHAPTER 7

Israel and the Russian Presence in Syria

Many states were involved in the Syrian civil war,[1] one of them is Russia. The latter and Iran assisted Assad since the start of the Syrian civil war. Yet, by later 2015 Assad was in a low point, so Russia decided to be directly involved in the war. Russia helped Assad to win the war.

Russia and Iran are partners, they both support Assad, but they do have major disagreements such as on which of them would be the dominant power in Syria. Russia also has been allowing Israeli strikes inside Syria, against Iranian targets, but it causes tension between Israel and Russia. The Israeli campaign in Syria can disrupt its relations with Russia, but also be used as a leverage to convince Russia to push Iran out of Syria.

SOVIET–ISRAELI RELATIONS

The Soviet Union helped Israel when the latter was established in 1948, by both recognizing it and providing weapons that were desperately needed. However, since the 1950s the Soviet Union was the patron of Arab states like Syria and Egypt, giving them political support and massive military aid, including advanced weapon systems such as Mig-21 fighters, T-62 tanks, etc. The Soviet Union kept its relations with Israel, but following the 1967 war the Soviet Union cut diplomatic ties with Israel.[2]

© The Author(s), under exclusive license to Springer Nature
Switzerland AG 2022
E. Eilam, *Israeli Strategies in the Middle East*,
https://doi.org/10.1007/978-3-030-95602-8_7

Israel and the Soviet Union confronted each other during the attrition war in Egypt in 1969–1970. The Soviet Union also resupplied Egypt and Syria, after their huge losses in the 1967 war, helping them to prepare for the next war. At the start of the 1973 war it seemed Israel was losing, but it recovered. Later on in the war there was a certain risk of a Soviet–Israeli confrontation, due to the Israeli advance inside Egypt and Syria. It did not happen, yet the Soviet aid to Egypt and Syria, such as resupplying them with anti aircraft missiles during the war, helped them to hold on.

In the 1970s and 1980s the Soviet Union continued to give substantial military aid to Syria.[3] The Soviet Union did not intervene in the 1982 war, because the battles took place only in Lebanon. If the IDF had approached Damascus in 1982 or in any other war for that matter, then Soviet troops might have been deployed to protect the Syrian capital city. In this sense the collapse of the Soviet Union left Syria vulnerable, but Israel did not try to exploit it to launch a war against Syria.

Since 1991 Russia kept its ties with the Assad regime, but without providing him with significant aid as during the Cold War. Russia was concerned when the Syrian civil war started, not wanting to lose Assad and with it all the Russian investment in Syria over the years. Eventually, since 2015 Russia officially joined Assad.

THE RUSSIAN MILITARY INVOLVEMENT

"Russia has not only been strengthened militarily – its foreign policy also seems to have undergone a form of militarisation, with the use of defence becoming more important and more visible. The bulk of Russia's foreign policy successes in recent years have thus involved the use of military force." Following the Russian intervention in favor of Assad "Russia is emerging as a key player in the Syrian peace settlement and a major player in the Middle East in general."[4]

By 2018 more than 63,000 Russian servicemen, including 434 generals and 25,738 officers, were involved in the war in Syria.[5] In mid-2020 5000 Russian troops were in Syria. The Russian approach "prioritized the use of stand-off tactics (like aerial strikes) and military contractors."[6] High casualties among its troops might have brought criticism at home. Although Russia has an Authoritarian regime it does require pubic support. Without it Russia might have had to limit its operations in Syria, which would have made it more difficult for Assad and Iran. In that sense Iran is pleased that Russia did not absorb many losses. Iran also accepted that the Russian tactics caused casualties among Syrian civilians, even when it meant a non Muslim power kills Muslims.

Russia was more militarily successful in Syria than most analysts, including some Russians, have predicted, in spite of Russia's military constraints. This stands in contrast to the criticism the Russian military absorbed following the 2008 war in Georgia. Serving in Syria became mandatory for Russian officers who seek to be promoted, a tour which supposed to upgrade their skills.[7] Iran and Hezbollah also used the Syrian civil war to gain combat experience and to improve their capabilities.

RUSSIAN–ISRAELI COORDINATION IN SYRIA

Israel and Russia developed their ties such as in trade, tourism, etc. There are more than one million Russian speaking Israelis, which contribute to the relations between the two states. Russia also accepted the normalization between Israel and the UAE in 2020. Nevertheless, Russia is of course well aware Israel has very close ties with Russia's rivals, mostly the United States. This does not prevent Russia and Israel from building their relations, but those ties certainly have their limitations and there are disagreements between Israel and Russia, including about Iran and Syria.

Israel has to take into consideration the Russian influence and military deployment inside Syria. The Russian presence relies on air power and antiaircraft batteries that could jeopardize the IAF, including during a war in Syria between Israel and Iran's proxies. Both Russia and Israel seek to avoid a clash between them. Therefore since 2015 Russia and Israel have been running a coordination mechanism, which has been quite effective in allowing Israel a certain freedom of action in Syria. As long as Israel did not try to topple Assad or to harm other Russian vital interests, the understanding between them can go on. Russia allowed Israel to bomb Iranian targets. Russia needed Iran to assist Assad to fight rebels, but Israel did not disrupt that effort so Russia tolerated the Israeli strikes. In recent years, when Assad seems to be wining, Russia requires less help from Iran. Furthermore Iran competes with Russia on controlling Syria. The Israeli campaign against Iran in Syria can assist Russia in reducing the Iranian influence in Syria.

There was a crisis between Turkey and Russia, after Turkey shot down a Russian fighter in late November 2015. Turkey and Russia avoided an escalation. Israel and Russia also had to be careful not to have a similar incident. Russia is less powerful than the Soviet Union was and only a small part of the Russian air force is deployed in Syria. The IAF is also quite powerful, armed with crack US weapons, including the F-35 stealth fighter. Yet, it is not only a question of military strength; both states can harm each other, even if the fight is only conventional. It is clear such a clash should be avoided. If there is a crisis the tension has to be contained and reduced as soon as possible, including by using brokers. Iran might try to cause the opposite, hoping Israel and Russia become rivals, which would serve Iran, including in Syria. Iran wants to end the Russian–Israeli cooperation and if possible to turn Russia against Israel. Russia then might prevent Israel from bombing Iranian targets, not because Russia would want to protect Iranians, but as part of its steps against Israel.

In late September 2018 a Russian reconnaissance plane was shot down by Syrian antiaircraft fire, following an Israeli bombardment in north-west Syria. It did not end the cooperation between Russia and Israel, but increased the risk of "unintended confrontation between them."[8]. Russia did respond by sending the S-300, an advanced antiaircraft system, to reinforce the Syrian air defense. However, the S-300 batteries "have been under the total control of Russian advisers and operators."[9] Russia has in Syria not only the S-300, but even a more sophisticated antiaircraft battery, the S-400. Russia deploys them not necessarily against Israel, but Russia does use them to warn Israel what could happen if Israel goes against Russia. The IAF might lose aircraft, but it might also manage to defeat the Russian systems, which would humiliate Russia and have a negative affect on its arms sales. Nevertheless neither Israel nor Russian wants to fight each other.

In early May 2020 the IAF bombed in northern Syria, in the Aleppo area.[10] It was a rare strike, due to both the distance from Israel and the relative proximity to the Russian bases in Syria, so a tighter coordination was needed. Usually the IAF bombed in southern and central Syria. Sometimes Israel decided such deep sorties inside Syria are required, with all their risks.

On January 2021, following a major Israeli strike in Syria, Russian Foreign Minister Sergey Lavrov suggested Israel to avoid it. Instead he argued Israel can provide Russia with intelligence about Iranian threats, so Russia will "neutralize" them.[11] Israel was not about to accept this offer, since it did not trust Russia to deliver their promise.

"Much of Syria's airspace is controlled by Russia and Israel, both of whom would oppose, by action or omission, Syria's transformation into an Iranian forward base."[12] Russia seeks to have stability in Syria while keeping Assad as the official ruler of the country. If Assad allows Iran to strike Israel from Syria let alone if he participates in attacking Israel, then the latter could retaliate against Assad and maybe even try to bring him down. Iran and Russia don't wish to risk that Assad would be toppled, after all their effort to save him. Even if Iran is willing to take that risk, Russia would oppose such a gamble, patricianly if it serves only Iran. Therefore, Russia has to restrain both Iran and Assad from provoking Israel. The latter would prefer Russia would leave Syria, but since Russia intends to stay there maybe Israel can use it to its advantage.

Israel would continue bombing in Syria, as long as Israel does not absorb casualties. Israel might tolerate a few of them. The IAF has to accomplish its missions, without taking too many risks, in order to avoid losses in aircraft let alone in air crews. It could be a challenge since Iran improved the air defense in Syria, aiming at intercepting Israeli aircraft or the missiles the IAF fires. Iran also tried several times to retaliate, following the Israeli air attacks, by hitting Israel itself. Iran did not gain much success in both defending Syria and striking Israel, at least until late 2021. If Israel pays a cost in human lives, because of its air strikes, it might change its policy in Syria. Another reason that might bring Israel to revaluate its Syrian strategy is if Russia absorbs casualties in Syria, as a result of an Israeli strike against Iranian or Syrian objectives. The IAF makes a serious effort to avoid such a mistake, but it might happen, especially when Assad forces, Iranians, or their protégés are stationed too close to Russian troops. Israel has to prepare an exit strategy in advance, so if Israel reduces and particularly if it suddenly stops bombing in Syria, it would not be seen as an Israeli defeat.

RUSSIA AND IRAN

There is a power struggle between Russia and Iran over Syria, such as on influencing the Syrian military. "The commander of the Syrian air force, regarded as close to the Iranians, was dismissed from his post in March 2021 at Russia's request, and the previous commander, who is close to the Russians, was reappointed in his place." There were also other "new appointments in the military and the security agencies in order to promote Alawite officers whom it regards as trained well enough and loyal to Moscow, not to Tehran."[13]

The competition between Iran and Russia in Syria is part of their complicated relations. Russia resisted Trump's strategy of increasing the sanctions against Iran, as part of Russia's defiance against Western states in general and the United States in particular. Russia is against any attack on Iran, but Russia opposes letting Iran to possess nuclear weapons. In case of an American or an Israeli raid on Iran's nuclear sites, Russia would not fight to defend Iran.

Iran assimilated the Russian S-300, which would make it more difficult to bomb Iran's nuclear infrastructure. In the 1960s and 1970s Russia delivered to Egypt and Syria high quality weapon systems like antiaircraft batteries. Russia's ties with Iran are not as tight as the relations between the Soviet Union and Egypt and Syria had been. Yet, by giving the S-300 to Iran, Russia helps Iran to protect Iran's nuclear program that could eventually produce a nuclear weapon. This arsenal would threaten Israel more than any Soviet conventional weapon system the Arabs got during the Cold War.

Russia and Iran strive to restore their past glory, spreading their influence in Islamic states in the Caucasus and central Asia. If Iran produces nuclear weapons it might increase its efforts in that area. Some states there might seek the protection of Russia and others might accept the hegemony of Iran, assuming it is a growing power while Russia is declining. Another option, distasteful to both Iran and Russia, would be the reliance of those Islamic states on the United States, similar to what Arab states, such as Saudi Arabia, might do in case Iran has a nuclear arsenal. The worst scenario for almost everyone is nuclear proliferation in the Caucasus and central Asia. Islamic states, particularly relatively rich ones like Kazakhstan, using their vast energy sources, might wish to possess nuclear weapons by buying them instead of going into production. Currently there is the Central Asia nuclear weapons free zones (CANWFZ) treaty. It forbids Central Asian states "to research, develop, manufacture, stockpile, acquire, possess, or have any control over any nuclear weapon or other nuclear explosive device." This reality might change if Iran has nuclear weapons.[14]

THE US PRESENCE IN SYRIA IN REGARD TO RUSSIA AND ISRAEL

Russia seeks to undermine US position in the Middle East, while reemerging Russia as a key player there, particularly in Syria. The Trump administration was involved in Syria, mostly in confronting ISIS, not Assad. This American policy helped in reducing the friction between the

United States and Russia, Assad's patron. There was still tension between them, particularly when the United States attacked Assad directly, after he used CW, on April 14 2018.

Israel and the United States are not officially allies, but they have close relationship. If there is a clash between Israel and Russia it might involve the United States. Whatever would happen between Israel and Syria, including in regard to Iran, it should not cause a serious friction between Russia and the United States. Their relations are already quite strained. Considering the possible horrible ramifications of a crisis and mostly a clash between the United States and Russia, Israel should do its best to help preventing a Russian–American collision. Stopping such a nightmare must be a top priority, including for Israel. A Russian–American confrontation is far more dangerous than any other problem that exists between Israel and Syria. It does not mean that Israel and its American patron have to allow Iran to have a strong presence in Syria. Yet, every step Israel considers in Syria, particularly in regard to Russia, has to take into account this most highly important factor.

In mid-2021 the US military had roughly 900 US troops in Syria "to continue supporting and advising the Syrian Democratic Forces fighting the Islamic State" as the US military did since 2014. US troops also stop Assad from recapturing "oil fields and agricultural resources of northeastern Syria." Another goal is to prevent Iran from establishing "a geographic corridor connecting Tehran with Lebanon and the Mediterranean."[15] It has to do with reducing the Iranian influence in Syria, an interest of both Israel and the United States. Israel has to be careful not to entangle the United States in a war between Israel and Iran, if this occurs, inside Syria. Iran is far less dangerous than Russia, but Iran has enough capabilities that could harm US forces in the Middle East, an outcome Israel should do its best to avoid.

Iran is eager to build a base in Syria, as part of Iran's regional aspirations, aimed against both Israel and the United States and actually against Russia too. Israel and particularly the United States oppose the Russian military presence in Syria, but it is more essential for Israel and the United States to get rid of the Iranian grip on Syria. The end of the war in Syria sharpens the conflict of interests between Russia and Iran. To begin with they were not natural allies let alone when they don't need the other any more to fight a common enemy. Iran strives to call the shots in Syria, at the expense of Russia, and vice versa. Therefore Israel and the United States can collaborate with Russia, officially or not, against the

Iranian forces in Syria. It will be a way to both contain Iran and prevent a dangerous clash between Israel and Russia.

In early October 2021 the US State Department emphasized the Biden administration opposes "efforts to normalise or rehabilitate" Assad, until political transition occurs there. Nevertheless, the Biden administration "has yet to apply sanctions under the so-called Caesar Act," aimed "of adding to the pressure on Assad." Syria is anyway not a priority for the Biden administration, due to its focus on China.[16] Iran, and mostly its nuclear program, is a more important issue for the United States than Syria. The Biden administration might agree, unofficially, to let Iran have a certain presence in Syria, in return to concessions regarding its nuclear program. Israel can accept that too, because it is much more crucial to restrain Iran's nuclear capabilities, than to make Iran give up Syria. Such a deal would help to keep Assad in power, which would be a compromise the United States might have to accept, yet Syria is not that valuable for the Biden administration. Russia might not try to disrupt such an arrangement, since it would keep Assad in office and restrain Iran's nuclear program.

The US military can learn from the war in Syria, as part of preparation for possible war against Russia/China. The battlefield in Syria is "littered with a host of tech and weapons that range from Cold War relics to drones, sophisticated anti-tank systems, Russian jets and anti-aircraft systems — even aggressive electronic warfare tech." other lessons have to do with "camouflage and reducing electronic and observable signatures."[17] The IDF too can gain lessons for that war, including by working on this matter with the US military, as they do in other projects.

The Russian Approach to Hezbollah

Russia and Hezbollah were on the same side in the war in Syria. Despite the Russian cooperation with Hezbollah the former "repeatedly insisted that Hezbollah fighters withdraw to Lebanon." It had to do with the disagreements between Russia and Hezbollah's patron, Iran. The latter wants to "maintain a Shiite military bloc in Syria led by Hezbollah that would be subordinate to the Islamic Revolutionary Guard Corps." Russia prefers to restore the regular Syrian military, while leaving Hezbollah out of it. In addition "some Sunni militias have refused to make agreements with the Assad regime, despite Russian efforts, because local civilians are afraid of Hezbollah."[18] Israel supports taking Iran, and Hezbollah, out of

Syria. Israel opposes having in Syria another Iranian fire base, as the one Hezbollah has in Lebanon. Yet, deploying Hezbollah in Syria too, not only in Lebanon, forces the group to spread its troops on a wider front. The IDF already outnumber Hezbollah. If the latter has to protect both Syria and Lebanon its position in both countries will be less powerful, compared to concentrating its units in Lebanon solely. This advantage, for Israel, will increase its chances to defeat Hezbollah.

The Russian assistance to Hezbollah exposed the latter to methods of modern combat. The Russian aircraft provided the group with air superiority and air support, encouraging it to run large-scale operations. That group has been fighting in recent years quite a different war from the one it might have with Israel, in which Hezbollah would not enjoy the help of Russian aircraft. This huge change would make a significant impact on the ability of Hezbollah to maneuver, let alone in major formations that would be exposed to Israeli firepower, mostly from the air. In that sense Russia, by helping Hezbollah in Syria, prepared the group for the wrong war, which might turn out to have very negative ramifications for Hezbollah.

In 2020 Russia's attempted "to draw Lebanon into its sphere of influence by placing it under Moscow's air defense umbrella and selling weapons to Beirut."[19] Russia seeks to push both Iran and Hezbollah out of Syria and at the same time to get a foothold in Lebanon, Hezbollah's home base, which is therefore also under Iranian influence. Russian aircraft and air defense such as the S-300 and S-400 already have Lebanon in their range. If Russia actually sees Lebanon's skies as same as Russia considers the air space in part of Syria i.e., under Russian control, it will cause a severe problem for Israel. The IAF flies in Lebanon, collecting intelligence on Hezbollah, as part of preparing for the next war. Restrictions on the IAF let alone in a time of war between Israel and Hezbollah would be unaccepted by Israel. If Russia tries to intercept Israeli aircraft, flying over Lebanon, it will bring a serious crisis between Israel and Russia.

CONCLUSION

Israel has to avoid a friction with Russia in Syria. From the 1950s to the 1980s the Soviet Union gave massive military support and even was willing to fight for Arab states such as Egypt, against Israel. In Syria since 2015 Russia has been defending Arabs, but against other Arabs, not Israel.

Israel and Russia maintain a coordination, which makes it much easier for Israel to bomb Iranian targets inside Syria. However, another incident, as the one that happened in September 2018, when a Russian plane was shot down, can cause a major crisis between Israel and Russia. In the next time it might be even worse. A crisis let alone a fight between Russia and Israel would serve Iran. Israel has to do its best to avoid a clash with Russia and also to have an exit strategy from its Syrian campaign.

Russia and Iran are allies, but Iran and Russia have their disputes. In Syria each one of them seeks to be the dominant power. Iran and Russia also continue to support Assad, but they have disagreements regarding the future of Syria. Israel rather that Russia will leave Syria. It will help Israel in handling Iran. Since Russia would stay in Syria Israel might use Russia to its favor. Russia might restrain Iran's activity, out of concern that a war between Iran and Israel in Syria would destabilize Assad's rule. Israel and the United States can collaborate with Russia, officially or not, in limiting as much as possible the Iranian grip on Syria. Such a policy would weaken Iran's regional influence and also reduce the chances of a clash between Israel and Russia.

NOTES

1. Christopher Phillips, *The Battle for Syria: International Rivalry in the New Middle East* (Yale University Press, 2018).
2. Yosef Govrin, *Israeli–Soviet Relations, 1953–1967* (London: Routledge, 1998).
3. Efraim Karsh, *The Soviet Union and Syria: The Asad Years* (Chatham House Papers, 1988).
4. Niels Bo Poulsen and Jørgen Staun (eds.), Russia's Military Might (the Royal Danish Defence College, 2021), p. 20. https://fak.dk/en/nyheder/2021/russias-military-might/.
5. Tom O'Conner, "How Many Russian Troops in Syria? Military Reveals Full Count as U.S. Told to Leave", *Newsweek*, August 23, 2018. https://www.newsweek.com/how-many-russia-troops-syria-military-reveals-full-count-us-told-leave-1088409.
6. Lamont Colucci, "What Russia Is Up to in Syria", *The Hill*, May 4, 2020. https://thehill.com/opinion/international/495929-what-russia-is-up-to-in-syria.
7. Chris Miller, "After Five Years of Fighting in Syria, Putin Has Gotten What He Wants", *Foreign Policy*, October 8, 2020.

https://foreignpolicy.com/2020/10/08/after-five-years-of-fig hting-in-syria-putin-has-gotten-what-he-wants/.

8. Yury Barmin, "What Next for Russian–Israeli Relations?" *Aljazeera*, September 24, 2018. https://www.aljazeera.com/ind epth/opinion/russian-israeli-relations-180924164725360.html.

9. Yosi Melman, "Why Syria Isn't Firing Its S-300 Missiles at Israeli Jets", *Haaretz*, May 12, 2020. https://www.haaretz.com/isr ael-news/.premium-why-syria-isn-t-firing-its-s-300-missiles-at-isr aeli-jets-1.8841093. See also: Anat Ben Haim, "Rebuilding the Syrian Military: Significance for Israel", *INSS*, Insight No. 1519, September 15, 2021. https://www.inss.org.il/publication/syrian-army/.

10. (No Author), "Israeli Aircraft Reportedly Pound Military Outposts in Syria", *Aljazeera*, May 6, 2020. https://www.aljazeera.com/ news/2020/05/syria-israeli-jets-hit-military-outposts-aleppo-pro vince-200505022122693.html.

11. Jodah Ari Gross, "Lavrov: Israel Should Inform Moscow of Iranian Threats in Syria, Not Bomb Them", *The Times of Israel*, January 18, 2021. https://www.timesofisrael.com/lavrov-israel-should-inf orm-moscow-of-iranian-threats-in-syria-not-bomb-them/.

12. Michael Young, "Hezbollah Is Much Weaker Than It Seems", *The National*, May 25, 2020. https://www.thenationalnews.com/opi nion/hezbollah-is-much-weaker-than-it-seems-1.1028271.

13. Anat Ben Haim, "Rebuilding the Syrian…". https://www.inss. org.il/publication/syrian-army/.

14. The Nuclear Threat Initiative, September 17, 2020. https://www. nti.org/learn/treaties-and-regimes/central-asia-nuclear-weapon-free-zone-canwz/.

15. Lara Seligman, "Troops to Stay Put in Syria Even as Biden Seeks to End America's 'Forever Wars'", *Politico*, July 27, 2021. https://www.politico.com/news/2021/07/27/troops-to-stay-in-syria-biden-500848.

16. Reuters, October 10, 2021. https://www.reuters.com/world/ middle-east/arabs-ease-assads-isolation-us-looks-elsewhere-2021-10-10/.

17. Shawn Snow, "How the Syrian Battlefield Is Preparing the Corps for a Fight with Russia or China", *The Marine Corps Times*, February 7, 2019. https://www.marinecorpstimes.com/news/

your-marine-corps/2019/02/08/how-the-syrian-battlefield-is-preparing-the-corps-for-a-fight-with-russia-or-china/.

18. Grigory Melamedov, "Why Russia Wants Lebanon", *Middle East Quarterly*, Winter 2020. https://www.meforum.org/60026/why-russia-wants-lebanon#_ftn39.

19. Ibid.

CHAPTER 8

The Relations Between the United States, Israel, and Iran

There has been a long conflict between Iran and the United States, which started in 1979. The United States has been concerned about Iran's activities, including its nuclear program. The Obama and the Trump administrations, each one with its own approach, used sanctions to urge Iran to negotiate with them. The Biden administration continues more or less with the same policy. If eventually Iran obtains nuclear weapons the United States and Israel can try to contain Iran. In addition China, which has relations with Iran, also developed its relations with Israel, which concern the United States.

THE FRICTION BETWEEN THE UNITED STATES AND IRAN

In the 1970s the United States considered Iran as a powerful US ally in the Gulf.[1] Yet since 1979, the United States has been involved in a prolonged conflict with Iran.[2] The two sides clashed directly in the Gulf in the 1980s, albeit in a very limited way. Iran still has American weapon systems such as F-14 fighters and Hawk antiaircraft missiles, a reminder of the golden age between the two states, when Israel and Iran were partners too. The United States wished in the 1970s to rely on the Shah's state as a pro-American ally due to Iran's location, natural resources, size, etc. however, after the Islamic revolution Iran used its strategic strength

© The Author(s), under exclusive license to Springer Nature Switzerland AG 2022
E. Eilam, *Israeli Strategies in the Middle East*,
https://doi.org/10.1007/978-3-030-95602-8_8

against both the United States and Israel. Actually, there is a lot of similarity between the foreign policy of the Shah and the Islamic Republic of Iran, such as seeking to expand their influence in the region and to kick out world powers.[3]

For the United States, contrary to the Taliban in Afghanistan becoming an enemy in 2001, and Saddam Hussein turning into a threat after Iraq invaded Kuwait in 1990, the Iranian regime has been an enemy since it seized power in 1979. It brought Iran over and again into a collision course with the United States and with Israel too. The latter and its American patron seek to contain Iran, before it becomes too dangerous.[4]

Trita Persi claimed the feud between the United States and Iran made it more difficult for the United States to advance the negotiations between Israel and the PLO in the 1990s.[5]

Iran also opposed the United States by supporting the Palestinian Islamic Jihad and by trying to foil negotiations between Israel and the Palestinians.

Matthew Kroenig explains how the United States had to deal over the years with autocratic regimes such as the Soviet Union,[6] which was a global power. The United States is a superpower and Iran, with its autocratic regime, is a regional power solely. However, the United States has to divide its resources around the world and mostly tries to focus on areas like East Asia. Iran, with all its global activity, could concentrate its resources in the Middle East. Iran does not focus on Israel solely, since Iran has other interests in the region, which helps Israel. The United States, despite its commitments around the world, can still devote enough attention to deal with Iran and by that also to assist Israel. The latter wants that in a time of crisis with Iran let alone a war the United States will be able to have in the Middle East sufficient power, not only military one, to handle Iran.

Iran and the United States opposed the Taliban in 1998.[7] Iran benefited from the Taliban defeat in 2001. As with the fall of another Iranian adversary, Saddam Hussein, it resulted "in widespread regional perceptions of growing Iranian regional influence."[8] Iran did not want to see the Taliban return to power in Afghanistan.[9] But Iran was worried since 2003 about the deployment of US forces in its east flank, in Afghanistan and in its west flank in Iraq, and strove to drive the United States out of both of them.

In 2005 Bashar al Assad was concerned about being encircled by regimes in Jordan, Lebanon, Iraq, Turkey and Israel, all hostile toward

Syria and allied with the United States. This suspicion caused Assad to resist American moves in the Middle East.[10] No wonder insurgents in Iraq and Afghanistan got assistance from Iran and/or Syria.[11] Assad assisted the fight against the United States in Iraq without getting retribution,[12] and neither did Iran pay any penalty for its subversion against the United States. This was a concern to Israel too because if Iran can strike and provoke a world power in such a way, then Iran could do it again against the United States and its partners like Israel.

The United States has been concerned about Iran's nuclear program. Nevertheless, an American attack on Iranian nuclear facilities might have happened because of a reason which had little or even nothing to do with the nuclear issue. The ongoing sanctions caused Iran many internal hardships. This already pushed the regime to divert their public's attention to events outside the country, by creating provocations, such as in Iraq and in the Gulf. Iran would not have sought a major confrontation with the United States, but such a collision might have occurred due to escalation. A war might have led to the destruction of the Iranian unconventional project. The war in 1991 started because of an Iraqi provocation in the Gulf, the quick conquest of Kuwait, brought with it the targeting of facilities in Iraq producing unconventional weapons.

Israel experienced a kind of similar case. In 1982 the military buildup of the PLO in Lebanon worried Israel, particularly its rockets and guns that threatened those who lived in northern Israel. In 2006 Israel was concerned about the growing strength of Hezbollah, mostly because of its rockets that jeopardized Israeli civilians. In 1982 and 2006 Israel attacked those Non-State Actors after it had been provoked. In 1982 the provocation was an assassination attempt of its ambassador in London by a Palestinian group, and in 2006 it was the capturing of two Israeli troops by the Hezbollah on the border with Lebanon. Those minor assaults against Israel in 1982 and 2006 were not a threat to Israel similar to the rockets, but the provocations ignited a war in which Israel tried to destroy the menace of rockets.

Over the years Iran ran naval exercises in the Gulf, including aiming at closing the Strait of Hormuz.[13] In response, the United States, along with other states, conducted exercises in the Gulf, in case Iran blocks the Straits of Hormuz. Iran also has to be aware that "attacking U.S. allies in the Gulf and their interests would most likely prompt them to call for and finance a stronger U.S. presence in the region, making such a presence both legal and legitimate under international law."[14] If Iran had actually done that, there would have probably been an urgent international effort to reopen the Straits of Hormuz. Meanwhile the international community, including the United States, has felt the pressure if Iran had got closer to producing a nuclear weapon, creating a time bomb of sorts.

It is probable the United States would have been less reluctant to use force against Iran had the latter made obvious signs of rushing to produce a nuclear weapon than if Iran had closed the Straits of Hormuz. The American assumption might have been that Iran with a nuclear weapon could be contained, but the blockage of oil in the Gulf behind the straits of Hormuz was an immediate unacceptable crisis, and had to be dealt with quickly. Furthermore, ramifications of an American attack on Iran's nuclear sites, such as an Iranian retribution, could be more severe compared with the Iranian response to breaking its blockade on the Straits of Hormuz by force. Iran would be aware of the fact that it had started a crisis by blocking the strait, and would expect a harsh response. On the other hand, Iran might assume that producing a nuclear weapon would be seen by the international community, including the United States, as an aggressive step, but not as an actual military action like blocking the straits of Hormuz.

The Obama Administration: The Road to the JCPOA

Dennis Ross claimed that Obama, at the start of its first term, directed the Pentagon to examine the military option against Iran. Yet he did not wish that "the way we prepared that capability to leave him with no choice but to use force."[15] President Obama therefore did not rule out the military option, but he clearly preferred other ways to handle Iran.

In the unrest in Iran in 2009 the Obama administration did not support the demonstrators, out of concern that it might prevent the Iranian regime form negotiating directly with the United States about Iran's nuclear program.[16] In addition, until 2009, Western leaders failed to understand Iran during their negotiations with it, because they did not know Iranian history and culture. This caused the Iranians to look "irrational, emotional and unstable."[17] Iran on its part might not have understood Western mentality either. In late 2013 the Iranians made an effort to present a more moderate image, yet they continued to seek nuclear capability enabling them to produce a nuclear weapon in a relatively short time. Talks are no doubt a better alternative than military actions, but they might also end in a confrontation. Before the 1991 war, there were extended negotiations with Iraq, which refused to leave Kuwait and paid the price for that. Iran, insisting on obtaining a nuclear weapon, might have a similar fate. In 1991 the two sides did not necessarily desire a fight but did become entangled in it. This might have happened with Iran too.

A war game that was held in Washington in March 2012 caused concern among top American planners. They feared "that it may be impossible to preclude American involvement in any escalating confrontation with Iran." This had helped those in the Obama administration, the US military and intelligence community who warned that striking Iran "could prove perilous for the United States."[18]

Martin Indyk said on late September 2012 "given the troubled history of the Jewish people over many centuries, placing the fate of the Jewish state in the hands of foreign leaders - no matter how reliable - necessarily heightens their sense of insecurity."[19] Israel has been concerned that the Obama administration does not intend to bomb Iran because of strategic, political and economic constraints. Israel destroyed the nuclear reactor of Syria in 2007 and the one in Iraq in 1981. Israel wanted the United States to adapt this approach i.e., to attack nuclear infrastructure when there is a nuclear threat or a potential one, although the superpower did not do that with regard to the Soviet Union, China, North Korea and Pakistan. The United States might have considered a limited strike against North Korea, but it might have escalated into a full-blown war. Also unlike the Israeli strikes in 1981 and 2007, which did not bring a response, North Korea would have returned a favor.[20]

In May 2014 US Defense Secretary, Chuck Hagel, sought to assure Israel's Prime Minister, Benjamin Netanyahu, during a visit to Israel, that the United States is committed to ensuring Iran will not get a nuclear weapon.[21] Among 1200 American government officials and experts, there was an assumption that one of the issues that could concern the United States in 2014 is "renewed threat of military strikes against Iran as a result of a breakdown in nuclear negotiations and/or clear evidence of intent to develop a nuclear weapons capability."[22]

On March 2, 2015, White House press secretary Josh Earnest claimed that if there is an agreement and Iran does not comply with it, the United States might add more sanctions and "even have a military option that continues to be available to the president."[23] On March 31, 2015, US Defense Secretary Ashton Carter said that the military option remains on the table.[24] Joshua Muravchik argued in March 2015 that the United

States should attack Iran's nuclear sites, in spite of the possible risks, and that sanctions are not the solution.[25] Israel would have liked that to happen.

On April 13, 2015, Wendy Sherman, undersecretary of state for political affairs, argued that a deal with Iran is the best option, while a military strike could delay Iran's nuclear project three years at most.[26] On June 1, 2015 President Obama claimed that an attack on Iran would only slow down the Iranian nuclear project.[27] Ray Takeyh and Roger Zakheim claimed in June 2015 that "Policy makers refer to a 'credible military option,' but little has been done over the past six years to leverage a military threat to advance our diplomatic objectives."[28]

It seems that in 2015 the United States sent a mixed signal. The goal was to emphasize that negotiations are the solution, in a period when the talks with Iran reached their climax. The Obama administration, which was eager to sign an accord, was worried about any wrong move by it or by Israel that would end the political process, without a deal. However, Israel would have not dared attack Iran's nuclear sites, at least while the talks continue. The United States also wished to convince Iran that there is a creditable military option, in order to urge Iran to sign the accord and then to keep it. Therefore, for the United States to claim that Iran can rebuild its program was counterproductive. There was no guarantee Iran can accomplish that, particularly if the American attack totally annihilates Iran's nuclear sites. It took decades to create this infrastructure. The Iranian regime could run into difficulties in funding the rebuilding of its nuclear facilities.

Furthermore, if Iran had retaliated, it could have caused an escalation leading to the toppling of the Iranian regime, which would have served the interest of Israel and many other states as well. Even if Iran had restrained itself, following the American bombardments, and tried again to gain nuclear weapon capability, the US military could have hit Iran once more. There are overall all kinds of scenarios of how a war between Iran and the United States might look like.

On April 19, 2015, Mohammad Javad Zarif, Iran's foreign minister, stated that there is no military option against Iran, and the latter does not pay attention to declarations on this issue.[29] But Iran wanted the S-300, a highly sophisticated antiaircraft missile. In mid-April that year Russia announced it would give this weapon system to Iran. The Russian Foreign Minister Sergei Lavrov said this step would make those who think about attacking Iran reconsider their approach.[30] Russia claimed that the S-300 was a "purely defensive system."[31] Gen. Martin Dempsey, chairman of the Joint Chiefs of staff, said that the US military is ready for this development, as part of its planning.[32] President Obama added on 21 April that US defense budget is almost 600 billion dollars while that of Iran is about 17 billion dollars. "Even if they've got some air defense systems, if we had to, we could penetrate them."[33] Yet US budget cuts reduced the training against systems such as the S-300.[34] The US military could have still overcome the S-300 but the price might have been high. Israel could have been worried that this possible cost might bring the United States to hesitate about a mission it wishes to avoid to begin with.

On April 9, 2015, according to an NBC poll, 53% of Americans believed Iran's nuclear program is a substantial threat to the United States. 71% thought that a deal would not stop Iran from producing nuclear weapons.[35] However, the agreement about Iran's nuclear program was finally achieved on July 14, 2015, (the JCPOA). Israel opposed the JCPOA.[36] A Washington Post/ABC poll showed then that most Americans support the accord, but they have doubts it would prevent Iran from producing a nuclear weapon.[37] Defense Secretary Ash Carter added that the United States will continue to upgrade its military option, which would be used "if necessary."[38] In response Zarif criticized the "uselessness of such empty threats."[39] Nevertheless, a few days later Carter said that the military option was improved a little due to the accord since the United States has better knowledge about Iran's nuclear program that might be attacked in the future.[40] In a speech on August 5, 2015, President Obama warned that a military strike would delay the Iranian nuclear program only in a few years and it would have negative ramifications.[41] Yet it might have taken much longer to rebuild Iran's nuclear program and the implications of allowing Iran to produce a nuclear weapon are much worse, particularly for Israel. For the latter, a US attack on Iran was therefore the right move, with all its risks.

On February 9, 2016, James Clapper, Director of US National Intelligence, said that Iran preserves "some of its nuclear capabilities, as well as the option to eventually expand its nuclear infrastructure." He added the JCPOA "enhanced the transparency of Iran's nuclear activities." This allows the international community "to quickly detect changes to Iran's declared nuclear facilities designed to shorten the time Iran would need to produce fissile material."[42] Israel had doubts about that, as part of Israel's strong opposition to the JCPOA.

On June 3, 2016, Iran's supreme leader Khamenei said that the United States, Britain, and Israel are Iran's "main enemies."[43] On June 2, 2016, the US State Department said in its annual report on global terrorist activity, that Iran "remained the foremost state sponsor of terrorism in 2015, providing a range of support, including financial, training, and equipment, to groups around the world." Iran continued to provide funds and weapons to Hezbollah and Iraqi Shia groups. The department's acting coordinator for counterterrorism, Justin Siberell, said that the department was "concerned about a wide range of Iranian activities to destabilize the region."[44] Israel was worried about that too, especially in regard to the Iranian aid to Hezbollah and Palestinian groups. It has been one of Israel's major problems with the JCPOA, since this agreement did not deal with Iran's proxies.

In early July 2016, the annual report by the Federal Office for the Protection of the Constitution, the German equivalent of the FBI, claimed that Iran made at least nine attempts to develop technology, as part of building a nuclear arsenal. Germany managed to foil most of those attempts.[45] It shows the importance of international cooperation, with Israel too, in order to stop Iran from producing nuclear weapons. Overall some claimed that during the Obama administration, despite differences of opinions, there was "a steady stream of high-level coordination between Israel and the USA to diffuse the disagreement in handling" Iran.[46] Yet, there was quite a lot of tension between the Obama administration and the Israeli government, in regard to how to deal with Iran.

THE TRUMP ADMINISTRATION GETS TOUGH ON IRAN

On April 18, 2017, the Trump administration said that it extends the sanctions relief given to Iran since the latter has been complying with the JCPOA. However, the administration has been reviewing the agreement to decide if to continue with sanctions relief since Iran sponsors terrorism.[47] On May 8, 2018, President Trump announced that the United States will get out of the JCPOA.[48] On the next day US Defense Secretary Jim Mattis said that the US military has updated plans to attack Iran, in order to stop the latter if it tries to produce nuclear weapons.[49] On August 7 that year, the Trump administration imposed sanctions on Iran, aimed at putting economic pressure on the latter.[50] Israel, which called for those American steps, was obviously very pleased from the outcome. Israel hoped Iran's economy will deteriorate to such a degree it will cause a revolution or at least it will force the Iranian regime to make major concessions. The risk was that Iran will breach the JCPOA and gets closer to producing nuclear weapons, which is what eventually happened.

On November 5, 2018, the Trump administration restored the US sanctions that were lifted following the JCPOA, adding "300 new designations in Iran's oil, shipping, insurance and banking sectors." The American goal was to put pressure on Iran in order to force the latter to start negotiations that will lead to a new agreement, one which will curb Iran's missile and nuclear programs.[51] On January 8, 2019, the US Secretary of State, Mike Pompeo said that the United States is "redoubling not only our diplomatic but our commercial efforts to put real pressure on Iran."[52] The United States might have actually sought the heavy sanctions will make Iran's economy, which was already in a bad shape, deteriorate even more, hoping it will bring an uprising that will topple the Iranian regime. This would have been the best outcome for the United States, Israel, many other states, and for the Iranian people as well.

Iran's Supreme Leader Khamenei, following US sanctions, admitted on March 20, 2019, that the economy is Iran's most urgent problem, which was demonstrated for example in the devaluation of Iran's currency. According to the IMF Iran's economy was in recession in 2018.[53] It made life harder, in Iran, because of the poor shape of their economy. Israel and the United States did not want the Iranian people to suffer, but harming Iran's economy was both an alternative to war and a way to convince the Iranian regime to accept new terms about its policy, including its nuclear program.

In early 2019, the Trump administration "accelerated a secret American program to sabotage Iran's missiles and rockets." It caused failures in launching Iranian missiles.[54] On April 8, 2019, President Trump announced that since the IRGC "actively participates in, finances, and promotes terrorism as a tool of statecraft," then the United States will see the IRGC as a terrorist organization.[55] In early May, a US carrier strike group and a bomber task force were sent to the Middle East in case of an Iranian aggressive action.[56] The United States wished to deter Iran from carrying out steps such as trying to block the straits of Hormuz. There were therefore clear signs for growing tension between the two states.

In early August 2019, Israel's Foreign Minister Israel Katz said that Israel was contributing in fields like intelligence to the US-led naval effort to provide maritime security at the Strait of Hormuz, after Iran seized merchant ships there.[57] Israel could not have sent its navy because that area is too far away from Israel, and relying on Arab harbors was problematic. Arab Gulf States, in spite of their ties with Israel, still hesitated in collaborating openly with Israel, let alone militarily, against Iran.

In late August Iran revealed the "Bavar-373" system. Iran claimed that this antiaircraft missile "can reach roughly 17 miles of altitude and have a range of about 125 miles."

President Hassan Rouhani argued that the "Bavar-373" is "better than S-300 and close to S-400."[58] It was part of the attempt to deter Iran's foes, both Israel and the United States, from attacking Iran.

On September 14, 2019, cruise missiles and drones caused huge damage to Saudi oil facilities. The United States, Saudi Arabia, Britain, France and Germany have publicly blamed Iran, which denied its involvement. The United States retaliated by launching a cyber attack against Iran, without taking responsibility for that.[59] The Iranian raid demonstrated to the United States and its allies, including Israel, Iran's precision strike capabilities. Later on, in late July 2021, Iran attacked an Israeli objective with drones, by targeting a ship that was owned by an Israeli company.[60]

In early November 2019, Iran took another step to undermine the JCPOA by announcing it is about to double the number of advanced centrifuges.[61] It was an obvious provocation that was meant to put pressure on both the EU and the United States. Iran continued to take major risks, and it seemed that Iran had nothing to lose.

In mid-November there was a wave of demonstrations across Iran that was suppressed in a brutal way. About 1500 protesters were killed and the internet was blocked for several days.[62] The unrest had to do mostly with economic hardships, but some demonstrators expressed their opposition and hate to the regime itself. US sanctions had weakened the Iranian economy, which might have contributed to this outburst. There might be another wave of protests in the future and it could be strong enough to shack and even bring down the regime.

On January 3, 2020, the United States killed Qassem Soleimani, the head of Iran's Revolutionary Guards' Quds Force. The Trump administration did not want to look weak, following the latest Iranian provocations. The peak was when Iran sent its supports in Iraq to storm the American embassy in Bagdad.[63] Trump claimed he is not seeking regime change in Iran, but the latter must end its aggression in the Middle

East.[64] The killing of Soleimani, a highly influential Iranian leader, was a bold move by the Trump administration. Some welcomed it, such as Israel, while others criticized it. Israel saw Soleimani as one of its most dangerous foes due to his capabilities. Both Israel and those who were against this assassination were worried about Iranian retribution. Iran fired missiles at a US base in Iraq, causing many injuries, but without killing anyone. Iran also might have tried to assassinate the American ambassador to South Africa. There were other concerns in this matter, yet eventually there was not a major Iranian retribution.[65]

Gen. Kenneth McKenzie, head of US Central Command, claimed on June 10, 2020, that since January 2020, when the United States killed Soleimani, Iran reduced its actions aimed at challenging the US military. McKenzie said confrontations with Iran have settled into what he called a form of "contested deterrence." He argued "they have seen we have the capability and the will to respond."[66] Iran understood the United States might take drastic steps against Iran. Iran also did not strike Israel, as an indirect way to retaliate against the United States. Israel was on alert and it did absorb Iranian cyber attacks while continuing its long struggle to push Iran out of Syria, but there was no real escalation between Iran and Israel. Iran might have been concerned that Israel, with US backup, or even the United States itself will hit back hard, if Iran launches a fierce attack against Israel.

In early May 2020, President Trump "vetoed the Iran War Powers resolution, a bipartisan effort to rein in presidential authority to use military force against Iran without congressional approval." The resolution still left the US President with the right to respond in case of an "imminent attack" at the United States, without asking for congressional approval.[67] Trump sought to have freedom of action, as much as possible, against Iran, part of his strategy to put pressure on Iran. He also wanted to have the option to strike fast and hard, following Iranian attacks against US forces in Iraq and their provocations against the US navy at the Gulf. There was deep concern about that in the United States, among those who strongly oppose Trump. They were worried he might start a war. Israel wanted the Trump administration to be able to take military action in a short time, in case Iran suddenly rushes to produce a nuclear weapon.

On July 2, 2020, there was an explosion in Iran's Natanz nuclear complex, a key nuclear fuel enrichment site. This attack inflicted major damage, setting back Iran's nuclear project by months. Iran assumed

Israel and the United States are responsible for that since they sabotaged its nuclear program before.[68]

On August 14, 2020, the United Nations Security Council "resoundingly rejected a bid by the United States to extend a global arms embargo on Iran" indefinitely. "Eleven members on the 15-member body, including France, Germany and the United Kingdom, abstained. Russia and China strongly opposed extending the 13-year ban, which was due to expire on October 18 under a 2015 nuclear deal." It was a diplomatic blow to the United States, Israel, and six Gulf Arab states that supported the bid.[69] China and Russia and other states as well can use it to sell advanced weapons to Iran, which will encourage the Iranian regime to provoke and attack its foes.

In November 2020 President Trump examined a military option against Iran's main nuclear sites.[70] However, Trump, with all his opposition to Obama's policy, had the same concern. He too did not want to get involved let alone to start another war in the Middle East. Trump could have launched a limited strike against Iran, but it still could have deteriorated into war. Even a symbolic attack, on one of the Iranian sites, might have brought a showdown. During his entire presidency, Trump was quite careful about using force, despite all of his threats and warnings, such as those he expressed against North Korea and Iran. Trump has launched a few air strikes in the Middle East, in Iraq and Syria, and they were relatively minor ones, compared with war.

Trump and his staff could have tried to keep the planning of a US strike a secret. However, it was almost unavoidable that the preparations would have become public sooner or later. This would have brought enormous pressure from both American public opinion and the international community, striving to prevent the attack.

Despite those reasons, Trump could have ordered a strike in his last days in office. Trump demonstrated through his presidency his willingness to take risks and to shock the world. Furthermore Trump's "maximum pressure" did not reach its goal: to coerce Iran to negotiate on a new deal, which will include restrictions not only on its nuclear program, but also on its ballistic missile program and its regional ambitions. Another US goal, an unofficial one, was to urge the Iranian people to topple their regime. The Trump administration hoped the poor condition of Iran's economy will drive the Iranian people to turn against their ruler. However, the Iranian regime managed to survive Trump's term, without talking with him, hoping they can do better with the next administration. In addition, Trump invested significant efforts in the Middle East, mostly in regard to Israel. He gained major achievements such as the normalization between Israel and several Arab states, mostly the UAE and Bahrain. Iran's refusal to negotiate, and the fact the regime there survived, harmed Trump's foreign policy legacy in a region he was so involved. Trump might have launched a strike against Iran. The latter might have retaliated not only against the United States, but against Israel and Gulf Arab states as well. Those Arab states and Israel, officially or not, might have been willing to take this risk, out of calculation it might be their last chance to have the United States attacking Iran.

In December 2020, the US military sent into the Persian Gulf a guided missile submarine and later on two B-52 bombers. It was meant to deter Iran from attacking US forces or US allies.[71] At the same time, a diesel-powered Israeli submarine crossed the Suez Canal into the Red Sea,[72] from which it could have sailed toward Iran. It was another signal to Iran, but not a serious one. While the US submarine in the Gulf had the backup of the US military there, the Israeli submarine would have been alone there, far away from home. Maybe the US military or a friendly Arab military could have assisted the Israeli submarine.

THE BIDEN ADMINISTRATION TRIES TO GO BACK TO THE JCPOA

In early February US State Department spokesperson Ned Price said that in case of Iranian aggressions the United States will protect its troops and "vital interests," including "with appropriate force."[73] Nevertheless, the Biden administration is committed to a peaceful solution.

In late January 2021, Antony Blinken, the new US secretary of state, argued it can take time to see if the United States can rejoin the JCPOA. In response, the chief of general staff of the IDF, Lieutenant-General Aviv Kohavi claimed that if the United States returns to the JCPOA or reach "a similar accord with several improvements" it will be "bad and wrong" for Israel.[74] On February 23, 2021, Prime Minister Netanyahu said that regardless of whether Iran and the United States reach a new agreement or not, Israel will not allow Iran to produce nuclear weapons.[75]

The Director of the US national intelligence. Avril Haines, concluded in mid-April 2021 that "Iran will present a continuing threat to US and allied interests in the region as it tries to erode US influence...entrench its influence and project power in neighboring states."[76] On April 28, 2021, President Biden said that Iran's nuclear programs presents "a serious threat to America's security and world security – we will be working closely with our allies to address" this threat "through diplomacy and stern deterrence."[77] On June 7, 2021, General Kenneth McKenzie, said it is a US priority to deter "Iran's destabilizing activities, which remains the biggest threat to stability in the Middle East."[78] In August Israeli Prime Minister Naftali Bennett told CIA Director Bill Burns that the United States and Israel should prepare a joint strategy, in case there would not be a deal with Iran. It would be needed in order to prevent Iran from producing nuclear weapons.[79] In the upcoming months, the talks with Iran were not resumed. There was certain pessimism about the future of the negotiations.

On October 13, 2021, Antony Blinken, met the Israeli Foreign Minister Yair Lapid. Blinken said they "will look at every option to deal with the challenge posed by Iran. We continue to believe that diplomacy is the most effective way to do that. But it takes two to engage in diplomacy, and we have not seen, from Iran, a willingness to do that at this point."[80] This continued to be the American approach in the upcoming months. It seems the United States did not lose hope of achieving an agreement with Iran. The Biden administration assumed the alternatives, would be less effective and even counter-productive, compared to negotiations. However, an agreement with Iran would be quite limited in both its scale and its duration. Furthermore it might not last. One possibility is that Iran might breach it, if Iran has a good opportunity such as if the international community is focused on a major crisis let alone a war in another region such as in Ukraine or Taiwan.

According to a poll from early September 2021 63% of the Iranians "believed economic mismanagement had the biggest negative impact on the Iranian economy, while 34% felt foreign sanctions had the biggest negative effect."[81] It demonstrated how most Iranians blamed their government, not the United States, for their economic hardships. Such a development makes it more difficult for the Iranian regime to accuse the United States. It is clear Iran's problem, certainly in the economic level, is not the United States, but the Iranian regime itself.

COULD THERE BE REGIME CHANGE IN IRAN?

Israel might tolerate an Iran with nuclear weapons if the regime there changes. Yet there was no uprising in Iran in spite of the Arab turmoil,[82] which started in Tunisia, moved east and might have eventually arrived at the gates of Iran or returned there, assuming this entire wave of chaos started in the unrest in Iran of 2009. The Iranian supreme leader, Ali Khamenei might have refused then to accept reforms, out of concern this encouraged the opposition to demand more and more. Instead, the government adopted an aggressive approach. In 2009 its crackdown managed to break the protests. Israel could not have done much in this matter.

Following the Iranian elections in 2009, which were rigged, the Obama administration changed its approach and increased the sanctions against it.[83] Iran retaliated with cyber attacks against banks in the United States. Cyber warfare was also used against Iran, aiming to obstruct its nuclear program. In recent years Iran has improved its cyber capability. Iran could have also launched terror assaults, and like cyber ones it is often difficult to prove which states were behind them, although it is quite clear. Iran assumed that Israel and/or the United States were responsible for cyber strikes against it, just as Israel was aware that Iran conducted cyber attacks against it.

The ongoing sanctions and cyber warfare were not enough to coerce Iran to stop striving for nuclear weapons. Israel wished the sanctions be exploited to the fullest, along with imposing a real threat of direct use of force. Those actions might have convinced Iran to accept concessions that would have prevented it from having nuclear weapon capability, at least in the near future. Yet it might have also brought Iran to become more aggressive.

During 2019 there were many demonstrations, big and small, all over Iran. The peak was in November 2019. It was because of prolonged political suppression and public resentment, due to corruption and ongoing economic hardships. This instability undermined the Iranian regime. Instead of investing more in its urgent social-economic needs, Iran spent vast budgets on its foreign adventures like in Syria and Lebanon. All that had created in Iran severe unrest. It made Iran vulnerable. There has been a debate if an economic low point could bring regime change in Iran, as it did with the Soviet Union at the time. However, the circumstances in Iran might be different than those that existed in the late 1980s.[84]

Western states could have encouraged and assisted the Iranian opposition, yet it would have given the Iranian regime an excuse to expand its crackdown. Overall it seems that a US attempt to topple the regime in Iran from within would have been risky, complicated, and with low chances of reaching the goal. Therefore the United States focused on sanctions.

Groups from the Kurdish, Baloch, and Ahvazi Arab minorities in Iran sometimes conduct attacks against the Iranian regime. Those insurgencies lacked a vast base of support so they are not capable of bringing down the regime. The United States, Arab states, and Israel could be among those that could assist Iranians who wish to fight the regime there, not necessarily by providing them with military aid. This struggle must not cause harm to civilians. Helping insurgents might not be able to topple the Iranian regime, but it could be part of the overall strategy against Iran, inside and outside that country.

CONTAINING AND WEAKENING IRAN IF IT GETS A NUCLEAR WEAPON

Despite US efforts eventually, Iran might produce nuclear weapons. Iran with such an arsenal would be emboldened,[85] which could mean a serious challenge to the United States in the Middle East, since Iran might then undermine the fragile stability in many parts of the region, along with American's position.

The United States might respond by increasing its efforts, including approaching allies like Israel, in order to contain Iran and strive for an Iranian regime change, by using sanctions and an arms race. If Iran has to spend too much on its military instead of its economy and society, it might cause the people to revolt. On the other hand the United States might reduce its engagement in the Middle East, at least as far as dealing with Iran and its nuclear weapons, leading from behind or at most from the flank, and practically leaving states like Israel to handle Iran on their own.

The United States' ability to project power and support Israel was for the latter a backup, saving it from a precarious situation of exclusive self-reliance. Over the years knowing that the US stands for Israel did not deter Iran or its proxies from conducting many hostile operations against the Jewish state, calling for its downfall. This anti-Israeli activity might increase if Iran has nuclear weapons. Without substantial

American support, Israel would have to look for other allies in the region and outside it, possibly also changing its policy about nuclear weapons. As strong as Israel's conventional forces are, they would not be enough to deter an Iran with nuclear weapons, particularly if Israel is alone. Without The United States, Israel would have to mobilize all its resources including its nuclear arsenal, to face Iran.

One of Saddam Hussein's goals, when he invaded Iran in 1980, was to replace the rulers there.[86] He failed and Iran tried to return the favor but did not succeed either. Eventually in 2003 the United States deposed Iran's old adversary. Through this regime change, the United States aimed to use Iraq to help bring about a regime change in Iran. Yet Iraq, at least a large part of it, in the Shiite one, ended up being pro-Iranian. Afghanistan felt to the Taliban in August 2021. It was devastating for the United States after booting out two bitter enemies of Iran: the Taliban in Afghanistan and Saddam Hussein in Iraq, to see Iran turning those countries or part of them into its sphere of influence. The United States paid an enormous price in blood and treasure, but Iran might be the beneficiary, securing two of its flanks, in the east in Afghanistan and in the west in Iraq.

Nevertheless, there are concerns in Iran that the Taliban can harm Afghan Shiite Hazaras, "which could trigger unwelcome regional instability and have pronounced effects on Iran's ailing economy."[87]

Russia benefitted from sanctions on Iran since the latter had to avoid challenging Russia in several areas. There is a rivalry between Iran and Russia for example they compete on gaining influence in the Caucasus and Central Asia. It's possible that in the future the struggle between those two states would resume. In addition, Iran might challenge India and/or Pakistan over Afghanistan. "Iran and Pakistan have a long history of conflict with regard to Afghanistan."[88] Russia, India, and Pakistan possess nuclear weapons, but if Iran gets hold of it too, it will boost its leadership to compete with those countries. The United States, fearing a major war and regional instability, would seek to stop Iran from causing dangerous friction with other states, let alone nuclear ones, including rivals of the US, like Russia. Israel would not like Iran to spread its influence in Muslim countries in the Caucasus and Central Asia, but it might be the lesser of two evils if Iran focuses more on those regions and less on the Middle East and Israel in particular.

In the past Israel's enemies found themselves diverted to adventures against other foes. In the early and mid-1960s Egypt, under the leadership of Gamal Abdel Nasser, invested heavily in a war in Yemen, almost 2000 km south of Israel, instead of challenging the Jewish state. Israel sent some supplies to Egypt's foes in Yemen, in order to keep Egypt occupied there as much as possible. In 1976 Syria's military got deeply involved in Lebanon. Israel allowed that, since it served its interest, despite some risks involved in Syrian deployment in Lebanon. In the 1980s, Saddam Hussein collided with Iran, instead of moving in the other direction i.e., toward Israel. The latter used it to attack the PLO and Syrian forces in Lebanon in 1982. The PLO was not that important for Iraq, and Syria supported Iran. However, Israel was careful not to expand the war into Syria, and its gamble paid off since Egypt and Jordan did not intervene. If they had, it might have increased the probability of bringing Iraq too into the war, in the name of Arab solidarity. In 1990 Iraq headed south to conquer Kuwait, and once again avoided focusing on Israel. In recent years Hezbollah got entangled in the Syrian civil war, which reduced the chances of Hezbollah striking Israel. By refraining from attacking Iran, Israel also avoided having Hezbollah's attention turns back to it.

In all those cases Israel did not coerce its rivals to attack or be involved in wars in other countries. Israel's foes did it because of their priorities and the same might be with Iran if it increases its involvement outside the Levant. Israel could contribute to such a shift in Iran's strategy. Israel's attempts in stopping and even pushing back Iran as much as possible from the Levant could persuade Iran to focus on other regions such as the Caucasus and Central Asia. Iran already had made some steps in that direction. Iran for example signed "a Free Trade Agreement (FTA) with the Eurasian Economic Union (EAEU)." It causes competition between Iran and Turkey, which Israel might use to its benefit.[89]

Iran, after it produces nuclear weapons, might conclude that continuing its struggle against Israel might not be worth it. Iran does not seek to make Israel a protégé as it does with other countries, but to wipe it out. Striving for such a goal might cost Iran so dearly in a nuclear war that it might cease to exist, due to a massive Israeli nuclear attack as part of a preventive war, preemptive strike, or retribution for an Iranian nuclear offensive. Moving away from Israel would affect Iran's prestige in the Arab world, particularly in the Levant, but Iran might not care so much about that, if Iran turns its attention to other regions, where the

Israeli issue is not important at all, like the Caucasus and Central Asia. Iran would not be committed to destroying its strategic rivals there, as Iran does with Israel, a conflict that might bring a catastrophe for Iran. From Iran's perspective, the mostly non-Muslim Russia or the mostly Sunni Pakistan is not much better than Israel, but Iran could tolerate their existence, without risking a nuclear showdown.

ISRAEL, IRAN, AND US–CHINA RELATIONS

China sees Israel as a safe investment since the latter is stable and well developed. Israel's access to both the Mediterranean Sea and the Red Sea is another advantage, including as an alternative route to the Suez Canal. On the other hand, Israel's conflict with the Arabs is a downside for China that needs "international connectivity and Israel is limited in this regard." As to China and the United States in spite of some differences in their approach toward the Middle East, "their interests are largely compatible. Both want a stable Middle East with strong states that have the capacity to contribute to a regional status quo that supports their strategic and economic concerns."[90] Israel too wants to have stability in the region, particularly in Arab states that signed a peace treaty with Israel. If any of the regimes in Egypt, Jordan or the UAE will be toppled it will be quite bad for Israel. It will be even worse for Israel if the new regimes in those Arab states will be an Iranian ally.

The United States seeks to make a shift in its national priorities, moving from the Middle East to East Asia, in order to focus on China. However, US allies, those near China, depend on importing oil from the Middle East. They are worried they will be vulnerable to China, if the United States gets out of the Middle East and China would replace her, as the dominant force there.[91] It does not seem likely in the near future. However, the United States should not neglect the Middle East, a policy which serves Israel too, including in dealing with Iran's nuclear program.

In late March 2021, Iran and China signed a 25-year strategic agreement. Iran is important for China since the former serves as a bridge "from world seas to the landlocked Central Asian states (a market of about 65 million people) and the three states of the South Caucasus." China and Iran are expected to develop their economic ties. China will be careful not to get involved with Iran's aggressive policy in the Middle East. However, Both China and Iran oppose the United States and the agreement between China and Iran can assist the latter in handling US sanctions.[92] Israel might not be able to convince China that Israel is more vital to China than Iran. Nevertheless Israel, after coordinating its steps with its American patron, has to urge China to reduce its security cooperation with Iran to a minimum and particularly not to allow Iran to produce nuclear weapons. If Iran has this arsenal this development might urge other states to do the same, such as in central Asia, which does not serve China's interest.

The Biden administration puts pressure on Israel "to weaken China's access to sensitive Israeli technologies and infrastructure."[93] Israel seeks to develop its ties with China, but it is obvious for Israel it needs the United States much more, including against Iran. Stopping Iran from producing nuclear weapons is so crucial that Israel could reach an understanding with the Biden administration, accepting US restrictions on Israel's relations with China. In return, the Biden administration will be tough on Iran, particularly in regard to its nuclear program.

Pakistan and Radical Sunni Groups

Israel might bear an Iran which is similar to Pakistan, a Muslim country with nuclear weapons, not involved in the Arab–Israeli conflict, and not challenging Israel. But this does not seem practical, certainly not with the current regime in Iran. Besides, Pakistan is not very stable, and if it collapsed, there would be a race between several players to gain its nuclear weapons. Israel could not do much there, due to its distance from Pakistan. Israel can only hope the United States and its allies beat their rivals, including Iran, which is close to Pakistan. Iran would probably take part in this nuclear competition whether it has nuclear weapons or not.

Israel, the United States and Iran could have a common interest: to prevent radical Sunni groups like the Taliban, Al-Qaida or ISIS from capturing nuclear weapons in a crumbling Pakistan. From the Israeli and American perspective, Iran is a danger to many countries, yet Iran is aware that its regime would be fully responsible for using a nuclear weapon, while a terrorist group does not have such severe constraints. On the other hand radical Sunni groups might obtain only part of a nuclear weapon, but even if it has nuclear weapons, it might not have a plane or a missile to deliver it to the target. Iran has much more capability to exploit whatever nuclear material it grabs from Pakistan, if the latter falls apart.

Al-Qaida did not focus on Israel due to other priorities, but political pressure might have "forced premature and doomed involvement" in the Gaza Strip and Lebanon.[94] There Israel has been dealing with guerrilla and terror organizations (mostly with Hamas). The latter has not been as bad as Al-Qaida/ISIS, because Hamas and Hezbollah for that matter had to consider consequences to their community due to Israeli retaliation. This was one of the reasons why Hezbollah restrained itself, and Hamas sometimes made an effort to limit the clashes and the launching of rockets at Israel. If Al-Qaida/ISIS had a strong grip in Lebanon and the Gaza Strip, it would have probably continued the fight with Israel regardless of the negative ramifications to the local Arab population. ISIS already carried out attacks in the Gaza Strip, which shows the growing influence of ISIS there.[95]

CONCLUSION

Overall US policy that relied on heavy sanctions was not enough to convince Iran to accept new constraints on its nuclear program. For Israel Iran and particularly its nuclear program has been a top priority. For the United States, it is an important issue yet the United States, a world power, seeks to focus on China and Russia, not on the Middle East. Israel also supported a US attack on Iran, as a last resort, even if it brings war. The Obama, Trump, and the Biden administrations sought to avoid war, almost at all cost. It meant a conflict of interests between the global power and a local one like Israel, in spite of their strong ties.

The destruction of nuclear reactors in Iraq in 1981 and in Syria in 2007 was an independent Israeli operation, but it served Israel's American patron. A successful Israeli raid on Iran's nuclear infrastructure would have also solved the United States a major problem. However, much would have depended on the Iranian response. In 1981 and 2007 the Arabs did nothing, but Iran might not adopt such a policy, and it's not clear how strong its retaliation would be. The United States did not want to gamble i.e., let Israel attack Iran's nuclear sites alone, hoping it would not cause an Israeli–Iranian war, let alone such that would have damaged and dragged Israel's American patron into it. The United States tried to stop Iran's nuclear program in other ways, non-military ones, taking the risk that Iran would ultimately obtain nuclear weapon capability.

Notes

1. Andrew Bacevich, *America's War for the Greater Middle East: A Military History* (Random House, 2016, p. 12).
2. David Crist, *The Twilight War: The Secret History of America's Thirty-Year Conflict with Iran* (Penguin Press, 2012). Christian Emery, *US Foreign Policy and the Iranian Revolution: The Cold War Dynamics of Engagement and Strategic Alliance* (New York: Palgrave Macmillan, 2013). James Bill, *The Eagle and the Lion: The Tragedy of American–Iranian Relations* (Yale University Press, 1988).
3. James Bryant, "You Know, Mr. Khomeini, You and I Aren't So Different", *The Strategy Bridge*, October 14, 2017. https://the strategybridge.org/the-bridge/2017/10/14/you-know-mr-kho meini-you-and-i-arent-so-different.
4. On containing Iran see: Seth Jones, "Containing Tehran: Understanding Iran's Power and Exploiting Its Vulnerabilities", *CSIS*, January 6, 2020. https://www.csis.org/analysis/containing-teh ran-understanding-irans-power-and-exploiting-its-vulnerabilities.
5. Trita Parsi, *A Single Roll of the Dice* (Yale University Press, 2012), p. 6.
6. Matthew Kroenig, *The Return of Great Power Rivalry: Democracy Versus Autocracy from the Ancient World to the U.S. and China* (Oxford University Press, 2020).
7. Roger Howard, *Iran in Crisis? Nuclear Ambitions and the American Response* (New York: Zed Books, 2004), p. 70.
8. Dalia Dassa Kaye, Alireza Nader, and Parisa Roshan, *Israel and Iran—A Dangerous Rivalry* (Santa Monica, CA: Rand, 2011), p. 17.
9. Ali L. Jalali, "Winning in Afghanistan", *Parameters* (Spring 2009), p. 19.
10. Flynt leveret, *Inheriting Syria: Bashar's Trial by Fire* (The Brookings institute, 2005), pp. 6–7.
11. On Iraq see: Jubin M. Goodarzi, *Syria and Iran* (New York: Tauris Academic Studies, 2007), p. 293.
12. Barry Rubin, *The Truth About Syria* (New York: Palgrave-Macmillan, 2007), p. 5.

13. Yossi Melman and Meir Javedanfar, *The Sphinx Ahmadinejad and the Key for the Iranian Bomb* (Tel Aviv: Ma'ariv Book Guild, 2007), p. 185.

Alexandra Ma, "How the Strait of Hormuz, a Narrow Stretch of Water Where Ships Carry $1.2 Billion of Oil Every Day, Is at the Heart of Spiraling Tensions with Iran", *Business Insider*, January 13, 2020. https://www.businessinsider.com/strait-of-hormuz-explainer-oil-us-iran-tensions-2019-7.

14. Amin Mohseni-Cheraghlou, "Iran's 'Harsh Revenge': Is Blocking the Strait of Hormuzreally a Plausible Option?" *The Middle East Institute*, January 23, 2020. https://www.mei.edu/publications/irans-harsh-revenge-blocking-strait-hormuz-really-plausible-option.

15. Dennis Ross, "How Obama Got to 'Yes' on Iran: The Inside Story", *Politico*, October 8, 2015. http://www.politico.com/magazine/story/2015/10/iran-deal-susan-rice-israel-213227.

16. Jay Solomo, *The Iran Wars: Spy Games, Bank Battles, and the Secret Deals That Reshaped the Middle East* (New York: Random House, 2016), p. 9.

17. John W. Limbert, *Negotiating with Iran* (Washington, DC: United States Institute of Peace, 2009), p. 17.

18. Mark Mazzetti and Thom Shanker, "U.S. War Game Sees Perils of Israeli Strike Against Iran", *The New York Times*, March 20, 2012. http://www.nytimes.com/2012/03/20/world/middleeast/united-states-war-game-sees-dire-results-of-an-israeli-attack-on-iran.html?_r=0.

19. Testimony before the House Foreign Affairs Committee Sub-Committee on the Middle East and South Asia on "Safeguarding Israel's Security in a Volatile Environment" by Martin Indyk, Vice President and Director of the Foreign Policy Program at The Brookings Institution, September 20, 2012.

20. On Korea see: Van Jackson, "Want to Strike North Korea? It's Not Going to Go the Way You Think", *Politico*, January 12, 2018. https://www.politico.com/magazine/story/2018/01/12/north-korea-strike-nuclear-strategist-216306/.

21. Reuters, May 16, 2014. http://www.reuters.com/article/us-iran-nuclear-missiles-idUSBREA4E11V20140516.

22. On the opinion of 1200 see: Micah Zenko, "Cloudy with a Chance of Conflict", *Foreign Policy*, December 24, 2013.
23. Ben Kamisar, "White House: Iran Deal Would Not Preclude Sanctions, Military Action", *The Hill*, March 2, 2015. http://the hill.com/policy/international/234323-white-house-sanctions-mil itary-action-an-option-even-with-iran-deal.
24. Richard Sisk, "Carter Says Iran Nuclear Deal Would Not Limit US Military Options", *Military.com*, March 31, 2015. http:// www.military.com/daily-news/2015/03/31/carter-says-iran-nuc lear-deal-would-not-limit-us-military-option.html.
25. Joshua Muravchik, "War with Iran Is Probably Our Best Option", *The Washington Post*, March 13, 2015. http://www.washingto npost.com/opinions/war-with-iran-is-probably-our-best-option/ 2015/03/13/fb112eb0-c725-11e4-a199-6cb5e63819d2_story. html.
26. Stuart Winner and Joshua Davidovich, "US Negotiator: Israel's Security Concerns Legitimate, but Nuke Deal Best Option", *The Times of Israel*, April 13, 2015. http://www.timesofisrael.com/ us-negotiator-israels-security-concerns-legitimate-but-nuke-deal-best-option/.
27. Tamar Pileggi, "Obama: There Is No Military Option to Stop Iran", *The Times of Israel*, June 1, 2015. http://www.timesofis rael.com/obama-a-deal-only-way-stop-iran-no-military-option/.
28. Ray Takeyh and Roger Zakheim, "How the Threat of a Military Option Against Iran Lost Its Coercive Power", *The Wall Street Journal*, June 11, 2015. http://blogs.wsj.com/washwire/2015/ 06/11/how-the-threat-of-a-military-option-against-iran-lost-its-coercive-power/.
29. Times of Israel staff, "Iran FM: US Military Option 'Old Habit That Dies Hard'", *The Times of Israel*, April 18, 2015. http://www.timesofisrael.com/iran-fm-us-military-option-old-habit-that-dies-hard/.
30. Tovah Lazaroff, "Russia Won't Supply S-300 Missile to Iran Soon, Minister", *Jerusalem Post*, April 23, 2015. http://www.jpost. com/International/Report-Russia-says-it-wont-supply-S-300-mis sile-to-Iran-soon-399000.
31. Lynn Barry, "Iran Expects: Delivery of Russian Missiles by End of the Year", *The Washington Times*, April 14,

2015. http://www.washingtontimes.com/news/2015/apr/14/ iran-expects-delivery-of-russian-missiles-by-end-o/print/.

32. Andrew Tilghman, "Dempsey: Military Plans for Iran Remain 'Intact'", *Military Times*, April 16, 2015. http://www.milita rytimes.com/story/military/capitol-hill/2015/04/16/iran-mis sles/25895133/.

33. MSNBC, April 21, 2015. http://www.msnbc.com/msnbc/ obama-warns-iran-aiding-yemeni-rebels.

34. Clint Hinote, "Russia's Sale of the S-300 to Iran Will Shift Military Balance", *Newsweek*, April 23, 2015. http://www.newsweek.com/ russias-sale-s-300-iran-will-shift-military-balance-324341.

35. Carrie Dann, "Poll: 71% Say Iran Deal Won't Make a Real Difference in Preventing Bomb", *NBC News*, March 9, 2015. http:// www.nbcnews.com/storyline/iran-nuclear-talks/poll-71-say-iran- deal-wont-make-real-difference-preventing-n319976.

36. Trita Parsi, *Losing an Enemy* (Yale University Press, 2017), pp. 319–320. Michael Oren, *Ally* (New York: Random House, 2016), pp. 384–387.

37. Scott Clement, "56 Percent of People Support Obama's Iran Deal: But They Don't Think It Will Work", *The Washington Post*, July 20, 2015. http://www.washingtonpost.com/blogs/the-fix/wp/ 2015/07/20/56-percent-of-people-support-obamas-iran-deal- but-they-dont-think-it-will-work/.

38. *CBS News*, July 19, 2015. http://www.cbsnews.com/news/ash- carter-says-iran-deal-doesnt-bar-military-options/.

39. Times of Israel staff, "Iran Says US Threat of Military Action 'Empty, Useless'", *The Times of Israel*, July 25, 2015. http:// www.timesofisrael.com/iran-says-us-threat-of-military-action- empty-useless/.

40. Joe Gould, "DoD to Congress: Iran Deal or No, Military Options Open", *Defensenews*, July 29, 2015. http://www.defensenews. com/story/defense/policy-budget/congress/2015/07/29/ dod--congress-iran-deal--no-military-options-open/30843573/.

41. The White House (official site) August 5, 2015. https://www.whi tehouse.gov/the-press-office/2015/08/05/remarks-president- iran-nuclear-deal.

42. Statement for the Record, Worldwide Threat Assessment of the US Intelligence Community, Senate Armed Services Committee, James R. Clapper, Director of National Intelligence, February 9,

2016. http://www.armed-services.senate.gov/imo/media/doc/Clapper_02-09-16.pdf.

43. AFP, "Khamenei: US, Britain, Israel Still Iran's 'Main Enemies'", *The Times of Israel*, June 3, 2016. http://www.timesofisrael.com/us-britain-israel-still-irans-main-enemies-supreme-leader-says/.

44. CNN, June 2, 2016. http://www.cnn.com/2016/06/02/politics/state-department-report-terrorism/.

45. Times of Israel staff, "Iran Seeking Illegal Nuke, Missile Technology: German Intelligence", *Times of Israel*, July 8, 2016. http://www.timesofisrael.com/iran-seeking-illegal-nuke-missile-technology-says-german-intel-report/.

46. Nora Maher, "Balancing Deterrence: Iran–Israel Relations in a Turbulent Middle East", *Review of Economics and Political Science*, March 2020, p. 16.

47. Times of Israel staff, "Trump Administration Says Iran Complying with Nuclear Deal", *Times of Israel*, April 19, 2017. http://www.timesofisrael.com/trump-administration-says-iran-complying-with-nuclear-deal/.

48. NBC News, May 10, 2018. https://www.nbcnews.com/news/world/iranians-fear-future-after-trump-exits-iran-nuclear-deal-n872931.

49. Richard Sisk, "Military Options Ready to Stop Iran Developing Nuclear Weapons: Mattis", *Military.com*, May 9, 2018. https://www.military.com/daily-news/2018/05/09/military-options-ready-stop-iran-developing-nuclear-weapons-mattis.html.

50. ABC News, August 7, 2018. https://abcnews.go.com/Politics/trump-admin-snaps-nuclear-deal-sanctions-back-iran/story?id=57058540.

51. (No Author), "US Reinstates Tough Iran Sanctions Amid Anger in Tehran", *Aljazeera*, November 5, 2018. https://www.aljazeera.com/news/2018/11/trump-administration-reinstates-iran-sanctions-181105051328043.html.

52. Reuters, January 8, 2019. https://uk.reuters.com/article/uk-usa-pompeo-iran/u-s-pompeo-says-redoubling-efforts-to-put-pressure-on-iran-idUKKCN1P21DS.

53. France24, March 21, 2019. https://www.france24.com/en/20190321-iran-leader-calls-economy-urgent-problem.

54. David Sanger and William Broad, "U.S. Revives Secret Program to Sabotage Iranian Missiles and Rocket", *The New York Times*,

February 13, 2019. https://www.nytimes.com/2019/02/13/us/politics/iran-missile-launch-failures.html?emc=edit_na_2 0190213&nl=breaking-news&nlid=46504935ing-news&ref=headline&utm_source=CSIS+All&utm_campaign=b5e00e5c0b-EMAIL_CAMPAIGN_2019_02_13_08_54&utm_medium=email&utm.

55. CNN, April 8, 2019, https://www.cnn.com/2019/04/08/politics/iran-us-irgc-designation/index.html.

56. Reuters, May 6, 2019, https://www.reuters.com/article/us-usa-iran-idUSKCN1SC01B.

57. (No Author), "Israel Involved in US-Led Naval Mission in Strait of Hormuz—Foreign Minister", *The Times of Israel*, August 6, 2019. https://www.timesofisrael.com/israel-involved-in-us-led-naval-mission-in-strait-of-hormuz-foreign-minister/.

58. Guy Taylor, "Iran Rolls Out Homemade Missile Defense System", *The Washington Times*, August 22, 2019. https://www.washingtontimes.com/news/2019/aug/22/iran-rolls-out-homemade-missile-defense-system/?fbclid=IwAR0qUImS6w-J3xw1OgY_OEgCwd6pYiTCWfNVZXWUQWThBWA4UIOEPj-WYWU.

59. Reuters, September 17, 2019, https://www.reuters.com/article/us-saudi-aramco-security/costly-saudi-defenses-prove-no-match-for-drones-cruise-missiles-idUSKBN1W22FR.

Reuters, October 16, 2019, https://www.reuters.com/article/us-usa-iran-military-cyber-exclusive/exclusive-u-s-carried-out-secret-cyber-strike-on-iran-in-wake-of-saudi-oil-attack-officials-idUSKBN1WV0EK.

60. Times of Israel staff, "Multiple Iranian Drones Used in Deadly Attack on Israeli-Operated Ship—Report", *The Times of Israel*, July 31, 2021. https://www.timesofisrael.com/multiple-iranian-drones-used-in-deadly-attack-on-israeli-operated-ship-report/.

61. (No Author), "Iran Breaks Further Away from Crumbling Nuclear Deal", *Aljazeera*, November 4, 2019. https://www.aljazeera.com/news/2019/11/iran-breaks-crumbling-nuclear-deal-191104110945872.html.

62. Reuters, December 23, 2019. https://www.reuters.com/article/us-iran-protests-specialreport-idUSKBN1YR0QR.

63. Ewan Palmer, "Trump Decided to Kill Iran General Soleimani in Part to Appear Stronger Than Obama Was on Benghazi: Report",

Newsweek, January 4, 2019. https://www.newsweek.com/trump-general-soleimani-obama-benghazi-iran-1480389.

64. Reuters, January 3, 2019. https://www.reuters.com/article/us-iraq-security-blast/us-says-terminated-top-iran-general-to-thwart-attack-on-americans-idUSKBN1Z11K8.

65. Nahal Toosi, "Officials: Iran Weighing Plot to Kill U.S. Ambassador to South Africa", *Politico*, September 13, 2020. https://www.politico.com/news/2020/09/13/iran-south-africa-ambassador-assassination-plot-413831.

66. Richard Sisk, "Iran Has Backed Off of Challenging US Since Soleimani Killing, General Says", *Military.com*, June 10, 2020. https://www.military.com/daily-news/2020/06/10/iran-has-backed-off-of-challenging-us-soleimani-killing-general-says.html.

67. Nikki Carvajal, "Trump Vetoes Iran War Powers Resolution", *CNN*, May 6, 2020. https://www.cnn.com/2020/05/06/politics/trump-veto-iran-war-powers/index.html.

68. Farnaz Fassihi, Richard Perez-Pena, and Ronen Bergman, "Iran Admits Serious Damage to Natanz Nuclear Site, Setting Back Program", *The New York Times*, July 5, 2020. https://www.nytimes.com/2020/07/05/world/middleeast/iran-Natanz-nuclear-damage.html.

69. (No Author), "UN Security Council Rejects US Bid to Extend Iran Arms Embargo", *Aljazeera*, August 15, 2020. https://www.aljazeera.com/news/2020/08/fail-loses-bid-extend-arms-embargo-iran-200815010505938.html.

70. Patrick Wintour, "Iran Warns of 'Crushing Response' if Trump Targets Nuclear Site", *The Guardian*, November 17, 2020. https://www.theguardian.com/us-news/2020/nov/17/trump-considered-striking-iran-nuclear-sites-after-election-loss.

71. From AP, "U.S. Bomber Mission Over Persian Gulf Aimed at Cautioning Iran", *Politico*, December 30, 2020. https://www.politico.com/news/2020/12/30/bomber-mission-persian-gulf-iran-452349.

72. Ben Caspit, "Israeli, American Submarine Activity Suggests Show of Force Against Iran", *Al Monitor*, December 29, 2020. https://www.al-monitor.com/pulse/originals/2020/12/israel-us-iran-yemen-egypt-suez-canal-donald-trump-submarine.html#ixzz6i8bNSnb6.

73. Tom O'Connor, "U.S., Like Iran, Says Ready for Conflict if Diplomacy Fails", *Newsweek*, February 3, 2021. https://www.new sweek.com/iran-ready-respond-us-aggression-diplomacy-fails-156 6681.

74. Reuters, January 26, 2021. https://www.reuters.com/article/ us-nuclear-iran-israel/israels-top-general-says-its-military-is-refres hing-operational-plans-against-iran-idUSKBN29V2EX.

75. David Brennan, "Israel Will Stop Iran Nuclear Program 'With or Without' Joe Biden Deal, Benjamin Netanyahu Warns", *Newsweek*, February 23, 2021. https://www.newsweek.com/israel-stop-iran-nuclear-program-without-joe-biden-deal-benjamin-netanyahu-warns-1571301.

76. Director of national intelligence, "2021 Annual Threat Assessment of the U.S. Intelligence Community", April 13, 2021. https://www.dni.gov/index.php/newsroom/reports-publicati ons/reports-publications-2021/item/2204-2021-annual-threat-assessment-of-the-u-s-intelligence-community.

77. "Remarks as Prepared for Delivery by President Biden—Address to a Joint Session of Congress", *The White House*, April 28, 2021. https://www.whitehouse.gov/briefing-room/speeches-remarks/2021/04/28/remarks-as-prepared-for-delivery-by-pre sident-biden-address-to-a-joint-session-of-congress/.

78. "Special Briefing with General Kenneth McKenzie, Commander of the U.S. Central Command", US Department of State, June 7, 2021. https://www.state.gov/special-briefing-with-general-ken neth-mckenzie-commander-of-the-u-s-central-command/.

79. Barak Ravid, "Israel Seeks to Coordinate 'Plan B' with U.S. on Iran if Nuclear Talks Fail", *Axios*, August 12, 2021. https:// www.axios.com/iran-nuclear-deal-israel-cia-bill-burns-unlikely-c0e 2a8d7-8e65-4faf-a978-8f72f0eaf1a1.html.

80. Laura Kelly, "US, Israel, UAE Discussing 'Other Options' if Diplomacy Fails with Iran", *The Hill*, October 13, 2021. https:// thehill.com/policy/international/576571-us-israel-uae-discus sing-other-options-if-diplomacy-fails-with-iran.

81. Al Monitor Staff, "Poll: Iranians Blame Economic Woes on Corruption, Not Sanctions", October 18, 2021. https://www.al-monitor.com/originals/2021/10/poll-iranians-blame-economic-woes-corruption-not-sanctions#ixzz7A4hdcpaX.

82. On lack of uprising in Iran see: Brendan Daly, "Regime Change in Iran?" *Middle East Quarterly*, Spring 2012. http://www.mef orum.org/3225/iran-regime-change.

83. Michael O'Hanlon, "Obama's Middle East Policy in Perspective", *Brookings*, September 14, 2012. http://www.brookings.edu/ blogs/up-front/posts/2012/09/14-obama-middle-east-ohanlon.

84. Barbara Slavin, "US Policy Hinders Positive 'Regime Change' in Iran", *The Atlantic Council*, December 9, 2019. https://www.atl anticcouncil.org/blogs/iransource/us-policy-hinders-positive-reg ime-change-in-iran/.

85. Michael R. Eastman, "American Landpower and the Middle East of 2030", *Parameters* (autumn 2012), p. 11.

86. Anthony H. Cordesman and Abraham R. Wagner, *The Iran—Iraq War* (Tel Aviv: Ministry of Defense 1998), pp. 50–51.

87. Candace Rondeaux, Amir Toumaj, and Arif Ammar, "Iran's Tricky Balancing Act in Afghanistan", War on the Rock, July 28, 2021. https://warontherocks.com/2021/07/irans-tricky-bal ancing-act-in-afghanistan/.

88. On Iran and Pakistan see: Christopher Tuck, "Afghanistan: Strategy and War Termination", *Parameters* (Autumn 2012), p. 55.

89. Omid Rahimi and Ali Heydar, "How Iran and Turkey Compete in Central Asian Trade", *The Diplomat*, February 25, 2020. https://thediplomat.com/2020/02/how-iran-and-turkey-complete-in-central-asian-trade/.

90. Jhontan Fulton, "China's Changing Role in the Middle East", *The Atlantic Council*, 2019, p. 17. https://www.atlanticcoun cil.org/images/publications/Chinas_Changing_Role_in_the_Mid dle_East.pdf.

91. Jon Alterman, "Pivoting to Asia Doesn't Get You Out of the Middle East", *CSIS*, October 19, 2020. https://www.csis.org/ana lysis/pivoting-asia-doesnt-get-you-out-middle-east.

92. Alex Vatanka, "Making Sense of the Iran–China Strategic Agree-ment", *Middle East Institute*, April 26, 2021. https://www.mei. edu/publications/making-sense-iran-china-strategic-agreement.

93. Danny Zaken, "US Pressures Israel on Trade with China", *Al Monitor*, October 29, 2021. https://www.al-monitor.com/origin als/2021/10/us-pressures-israel-trade-china#ixzz7Auv9EdZK.

94. Norman Cigar, "Al Qaida Theater Strategy: Waging a World War", Norman Cigar and Stephanie E. Kramer (eds.), *Al Qaida—After Ten Years of War* (Quantico, VA: Marine Corps University Press, 2011), pp. 44–45.
95. Khaled Abu Toameh, "Gaza Resort Bombed for Holding Mixed-Gender Concert", *The Jerusalem Post*, August 8, 2021. https://www.jpost.com/middle-east/gaza-resort-bombed-for-holding-mixed-gender-concert-676168.

CHAPTER 9

How the United States Can Help Israel to Bomb Iran's Nuclear Sites

The United States is committed to Israel's national security, which sometimes requires creative solutions. The United States can deliver Israel huge bunker buster bombs, to crack the fortifications of Iranian nuclear sites. In another scenario, if the United States and Gulf Arab states were involved in a war against Iran, the latter might have tried to drag Israel into it, in order to urge the Gulf Arab states to abandon the anti-Iranian coalition. The United States and its Arab allies would have had to distinguish between their fight against Iran and the confrontation between Israel and Iran/Hezbollah.

US Commitment to Israel

During the Cold War one of the US goals was to preserve "the independence and territorial integrity" of Israel.[1] The ties between Israel and the United States, which have developed over the years,[2] were tested for example in the 1973 war.[3] According to Ephraim Inbar, Yitzhak Rabin "was one of the chief builders of the American—Israeli alliance" although he "was averse to transforming the relationship into a formal alliance."[4] In 2005, Syria's ruler Bashar al Assad claimed that during most of the last thirty five years the United States has been trying to consolidate Israel's "hegemonic position in the region."[5] Some assumed the United States wished to protect Israel while outside the latter's borders oil was the main American consideration.[6]

Michael Oren, Israel's ambassador to the United States in 2009–2013, praised the cooperation between the two states at the time, which boosted Israel's military strength.[7] The resolution by the US Senate from 22 May 2013 declared "that the United States has a vital national interest in, and unbreakable commitment to, ensuring the existence, survival, and security of the State of Israel."[8] Susan Rice said in May 2014 that "it's clear that the strength and depth of the security cooperation between Israel and the United States has never been greater" and that the United States remains "deeply committed to Israel's qualitative military edge."[9]

Following the disputes between Israel and its American patron regarding an agreement about Iran's nuclear program, Israel's Defense Minister Moshe Ya'alon emphasized, on April 8, 2015, that "no disagreement, not even about this critical issue, can diminish our enduring, profound gratitude to the president and his administration, to the Congress and the American people, for all the United States has done to enhance the security of the Jewish state."[10] On September 22, 2020 US Defense Secretary Mark Esper said "The defense relationship between the US and Israel has never been stronger. And we intend to keep it that way."[11] On April 10, 2021 US Defense Secretary Lloyd Austin reaffirmed that US commitment to Israel is "ironclad."[12]

US Military Aid to Israel and Security Cooperation

US military aid has helped transform Israel's armed forces into one of the most technologically sophisticated militaries in the world.[13] On September 14, 2016 the two states signed an agreement regarding the US military aid. Israel would receive "$3.8 billion a year over 10 years, beginning in 2019. It amounts to more than half of all direct military aid the United States provides worldwide. The funds will be disbursed in equal amounts of $3.3 million to purchase goods and services, and $500 million a year dedicated to Israel's missile defense systems."[14]

Arnon Gutfeld argued that US funds had strengthened Israel, which saved the need to send US troops to protect Israel.[15] Some, also inside Israel, called to reduce and /or to abolish the American aid.[16] Israel is about 22,000 sq. km. (like the size of New Jersey, the 5th smallest state in the US). However Israel's economy is quite developed, due to its sectors such as high-technology and industrial manufacturing. Therefore Israel might not need some of the US aid since Israel can pay for US arsenal it receives, although then Israel might consider acquiring in countries where the weapons cost less than the US ones. Israel can also rely more on its own military industry, which is quite developed. It already produced aircraft, tanks and many advanced sub systems.

On February 10, 2018 Iran sent a drone from Syria into Jordan and from there it penetrated into Israel, where it was shot down. The Iranian drone was a copy of an American one, which was captured by Iran in early December 2011. Israel monitored the drone in both Syria and in Jordan and then intercepted it inside Israel. One of the reasons for that was so Israel and the United States can learn how Iran used American technology to its favor.

The IDF and the U.S military ran joint exercises such as "Jenifer Cobra," an antimissile drill that was conducted several times since 2001.[17] In early March 2019 the THAAD system, which shoots down ballistic missiles, was deployed in Israel, "as a demonstration of the United States' continued commitment to Israel's regional security," according to the US military.[18] In early February 2021 "Juniper Falcon" took place.[19] In August that year the Israeli and US air forces trained together. It was "a first-of-a-kind aerial exercise...simulating various operational scenarios in Israel's skies."[20]

In 2020 the US military was considering how to coordinate between Israel's air defense system, Iron Dome, and other US air defense systems. There was previous successful experience with Israel's air defense Arrow system and its American counterparts. Furthermore at the time the Iron Dome was needed, by working alone, to intercept rockets that were fired by pro-Iranian militias at US troops and diplomats stationed in Iraq.[21]

US MILITARY OPTIONS AGAINST IRAN

Since 2003 the United States could have attacked Iran by exploiting a rare opportunity for a pincer movement from Iraq and Afghanistan, not including American bases in the Gulf. The American advance might have been quite fast, like in 2003, due to air supremacy and the weakness of Iranian conventional forces. However, following the cost and the hardships of the United States in the wars in Iraq and Afghanistan, a ground offensive, let alone a major one against Iran, was very unlikely.

"At least 500 U.S. military deaths in Iraq and Afghanistan were directly linked to Iran and its support for anti-American militants." This data is from "a ballpark figure based on intelligence assessments."[22] In a way the fight in Iraq and Afghanistan, where Iran helped the insurgents, was the first stage of the ground campaign against Iran, at least from the latter's perspective. It seemed as though the United States tried to reach Iran from Iraq and Afghanistan, but got bogged down there. At no point, during the long wars within those two countries, the insurgents could have stopped a massive American movement toward Iran, but the ongoing combat in Iraq and Afghanistan demonstrated the possible price of capturing and holding Iran or part of it. It would not have been easy. Although the United States has a clear military edge "even adversaries that are inferior in terms of conventional military capabilities may have numerous options to wage asymmetric warfare."[23]

The United States might have tried an air campaign against Iran, aiming at objectives such as its nuclear sites, and even trying to topple the regime. An air attack, compared with a land offensive, would have significantly reduced the American casualties, and avoided using American ground troops exhausted from the prolonged low intensity war in Iraq and Afghanistan. American aircraft contributed their share in those wars, although those battles were conducted mostly on the ground. Israel too, in its low intensity war against the Palestinians in 2000–2005, fought on the ground while a confrontation with Iran would have been based on the IAF.

Many rejected the idea of any American bombardment on Iran.[24] The ramifications of such an attack might have been an all-out war, terror attacks around the world and dragging the region and at least the Gulf into turmoil. An attack on Iran might have also increased the assaults against American objectives in Afghanistan. In Afghanistan it might have delayed or expedited the American withdrawal from that country. The United States sought to continue the retreat from Afghanistan while striving to end the war there, but in reality it could face one long front from Afghanistan through Iran and into the Gulf and Iraq. American delegations stationed there could be attacked too. The clashes could spread west to the Levant to a war in Lebanon between Israel and Hezbollah and possibly to the Gaza Strip and Syria. Yet, for Israel such a war might have worth the cost since allowing Iran to have a nuclear weapon was unbearable for Israel. Iran with a nuclear weapon will impose a much greater danger to Israel and the United States as well.

The United States and an Israeli Attack on Iran

In 1991 the United States did a huge favor to Israel by crushing Iraq's unconventional and conventional military might. Iran's conventional power is much less than the one Iraq had, so Israel does not worry too much about that. Israel wanted the United States to destroy Iran's nuclear sites or at least to help Israel in accomplishing this task.

In 2007–2008 an Israeli strike on the Iranian nuclear infrastructure might have started a war that would have destabilized the Middle East.[25]

There was a debate in the Obama administration about if and when Israel might attack Iran, with the impact it would have on Israel's relations with the United States. In 2012 "U.S. spy agencies stepped up satellite surveillance of Israeli aircraft movements. They detected when Israeli pilots were put on alert and identified moonless nights, which would give the Israelis better cover for an attack. They watched the Israelis practice strike missions and learned they were probing Iran's air defenses, looking for ways to fly in undetected." Many in the United States "jumped to the mistaken conclusion that the Israelis had made a dry run. At the time, concern and confusion over Israel's intentions added to the sense of urgency inside the White House for a diplomatic solution." In the summer of 2012 Israel wanted to obtain "military hardware useful for a strike."[26]

The military option continued to rise again and again under all kinds of circumstances. One of them was on January 22, 2013 when there were general elections in Israel, which was a reason to postpone a raid on the Iranian nuclear sites. Yet, in 1981 Israel destroyed the Iraqi nuclear reactor three weeks before general elections.

US secretary of state John Kerry argued on May 3, 2015 that his country keeps the military option against Iran. He also added that he assumes Israel would not attack Iran without first talking with the United States about that "at considerable length, because we would be deeply involved in what would happen as an aftermath, and there are huge implications to that."[27] The United States, as much as it is opposed to Iran having a nuclear weapon, was paramount in resisting a strike against Iran, including by Israel. The latter might have hoped its American patron would join it in deterring Iran from igniting a war, after an Israeli raid.

In recent years Iran had breached the 2015 nuclear agreement, which could have brought Israel to consider striking Iran. Iran and the United States have been concerned about an Israeli strike. Both Iran and the

United States would have wanted to know when this sudden attack occurred, since the targets were already familiar to everyone, unless Israel would have surprised and had bombed other targets like Iran's oil industry. Israel would obviously like Iran to find out about the attack when the bombs had already smashed their targets. The United States wanted to hear about that before the raid. It would have depended on several key aspects like field security. As soon as the United States had learned about the upcoming raid, the administration would have probably immediately put its forces, particularly those around Iran, on high alert, in case Iran retaliated against them, or against American allies in the Gulf. This alone might would have warned the Iranians that Israel, or the United States for that matter, was about to strike them. After so many years of dreading this moment, Iran had enough time to prepare, scramble fighters, get its men in nuclear sites to be ready to absorb bombardments, etc. Iran would have also considered a preemptive strike like hitting Israeli airfields with every missile and rocket Iran and Hezbollah could launch at them. Those steps might have disrupted the Israeli raid.

Iran would have probably blamed both Israel and the United States, regardless of which had bombed Iran. For the latter it might have been enough that its two sworn foes collaborated against it by various means such as sharing intelligence on its nuclear program, years before the raid. Iran would have accused the United States and Israel for committing an aggressive act against a Muslim country, since they are both non-Muslim states clashing with Muslims. This might have served Iran in gaining support of public opinion at least in the Muslim world.

In a war against Iran the Hezbollah might have been involved by initiating assaults on American and/or Israeli objectives around the world. From its base in Lebanon Hezbollah could have targeted Israel. The United States could have assisted Israel by sending military supply such as precision-guided munitions, without intervening directly in the battles between the IDF and Hezbollah. American forces might have contributed their part in striking Hezbollah in Lebanon. However, this was not essential, for apart from coordination problems, Israel should handle its own fights, particularly campaigns against non-state actors such as the Hezbollah, where the IDF enjoys overwhelming military superiority.

Following the destruction of the Iraqi nuclear reactor in 1981 by Israeli F-16, the United States delayed the delivery of more F-16 to Israel.[28] At the time that aircraft was the IAF's new fighter-bomber. Since 2016 the IAF has been assimilating the F-35 to keep its edge in air to air combat and long range strikes. However, until then, following an Israeli strike in Iran, the United States might have postponed the delivery of the F-35. Israel might not have cared that much, assuming it would take a few years for all those planes to arrive anyway, and during which time, as it was with the F-16 in 1981, the United States might again forgive Israel. Yet, in 1981, Iraq did not retaliate against Israel or against the United States that had provided Israel with the F-16 that bombed the Iraqi reactor. Iran might have reacted differently after being attacked. If the ramifications of an Israeli raid would have been quite harsh to the United States and/or its allies, the United States might have taken severe steps against Israel, not just postponing the sending of weapon systems.

Eventually, after Israel's many warnings, the IDF might have struck Iran. There were other occasions when Israel threatened to take military action against other foes, like after its retreat from Lebanon in 2000 and from the Gaza Strip in 2005. Israel warned publicly that in case of hostilities from Lebanon and/or the Gaza Strip against Israel, the IDF would strike back hard. Yet, when assaults were launched from those territories, Israel hesitated, and usually acted in a limited way. It took six years in Lebanon and four years in the Gaza Strip for Israel to start a major offensive on those fronts. The process of producing an Iranian nuclear Bomb has not been an actual attack on Israel, yet it has been a much bigger threat than any assault Israel absorbed from Lebanon or the Gaza Strip. Therefore Israel might have attacked Iran, before the latter produces nuclear weapons.

John Hannah argued in October 2021 that if there is no US military option against Iran, the United States can try "diplomacy, sanctions, and covert action", but they might "fail to halt Iran's relentless nuclear advances." In such a case the "remaining option is to make sure that Israel has the military assets it needs to, first, inflict maximum damage on Iran's nuclear infrastructure and, second, prevail as quickly as possible in the devastating war that Iran and its regional proxies would likely impose on the Jewish state in response."[29]

GIVING ISRAEL THE B-52 AND AT LEAST THE RIGHT BOMB

In late November 2014 according to Efraim Halevy, a former head of the Mossad intelligence agency, "Israel has the means to attack and cause severe damage to Iran."[30] Yet, according to Kenneth Pollack in 2013 "Israel's ability to cause meaningful damage to the Iranian nuclear program has now diminished to the point" where it should not affect American decision making about Iran.[31] Brig. Gen. (Ret.) Michael Herzog mentioned in late November 2014 that the credibility of Israel's "military option (which still exists) has decreased in the eyes of the United States and Iran."[32] "Part of the problem is that the window of opportunity for an effective Israeli airstrike closed" after Iran had opened the Fordow enrichment facility deep inside a mountain, which made that site immune to Israel's bunker buster bombs.[33] "The enrichment facility in Natanz is also heavily fortified. The complex is underground, covered by layers of concrete and metal."[34] The IAF therefore has to blast its way through the fortifications of some Iranian nuclear sites.

Maj. Gen. Tal Kalman, who heads the IDF's Iran Directorate, argued in late March 2021 that Israel can destroy Iran's nuclear program.[35] In August 5 that year Israeli Defense Minister Benny Gantz argued that Israel is ready to attack Iran.[36] The IAF has bunker buster bombs such as the GBU-28, but a much bigger bunker buster bomb is required.

The US MOP (Massive Ordnance Penetrator) is a huge bomb that can crack very thick Iranian fortifications, such as the one in Fordow.[37] The IAF needs it to guarantee the accomplishment of its mission in Iran. Israel's F-15 or F-16 could not carry this giant bomb. Israel requires a strategic bomber like the B-52. Another option for the IAF might have been its C-130J, a transport plane, yet one that might have been able to carry and drop the MOP in Iran. The US military managed to conduct such a mission in Afghanistan in 2017. Using the C-130 to drop the MOP in Iran would be a very risky operation, but it might have to be done, if is there is no better option to prevent Iran from having nuclear weapons.

In October 2020, a bill in the US Congress asked the Department of Defense to "consider selling Israel bunker-buster bombs capable of penetrating heavily fortified underground facilities."[38] Dennis Ross suggested in July 2021 that the Biden administration would give Israel the MOP.[39] Delivering Israel the B-52 and at least the MOP would have proved US commitment to the security of Israel. This move would have bolstered Israel's confidence, reducing the pressure; some in Israel feel, about the need to attack Iran's nuclear sites. Israel might have been convinced to postpone its raid since the IAF would have required time to assimilate the B-52 and the MOP. Once this process ended, Iran's nuclear infrastructure would not be impregnable any more. This upgrading of the IAF might have deterred the Iranians from proceeding to build a nuclear weapon, but had they not; Israel could strike Iran's nuclear sites, as a last resort.

In the 1948–1949 war Israel got its first American planes including a few B-17, the mythological bomber from the Second World War. Since the late 1960s Israel started to assimilate hundreds of American aircraft like the A-4 attack plane and the F-4 fighter-bomber. In the 1970s Israel received the F-15 and F-16. Israel became well familiar with American aircraft, but not with US strategic bombers. In recent years Israel could have sent air and ground crews to the United States to study the B-52 and to prepare its infrastructure for those huge planes. The IAF already had gained vast experience with other big planes, Boeing 707 that serve for air refueling.

The IAF had learned how to operate new planes in a short period of time. The IAF got the French Md.452 Mystere a few months before the 1956 war, and managed to operate this plane in that confrontation. During the war of attrition against Egypt in 1967–1970, the IAF received the F-4 that was quickly thrown into combat. In 1981, the IAF bombed the Iraqi nuclear reactor with its new F-16, a plane that was not very familiar to the IAF at the time. Despite this experience the IAF should have assimilated the B-52 as soon as possible, so the IAF will have the time to study it.

In the 1956 war, French jets that were deployed in Israel launched dozens of sorties inside Sinai, including bombardments, as part of the secret pact between Israel, France and Britain.[40] Instead of giving Israel the B-52, the United States might agree to place in Israel B-52 with American crews. The aim would have been to deter Iran. Israel and its American patron would have formed procedures to use those bombers, based on their experience from joint exercises and cooperation, including in combat. In the 1991 war American Patriot missile batteries were deployed in Israel to defend it from Iraqi long range missiles. The risk to the American troops in Israel was relatively low then, since Iraq launched a few dozen missiles solely. However, in dispatching B-52 to Iran the stakes would have been higher, if it had come to that. Israel should have considered suggesting a similar assistance, like dispatching Israeli infantry troops to South Korea, where there might be war. The number of the Israeli troops stationed in South Korea would have been according to the amount of American troops who would have served with their B-52 in Israel. The IDF did not have to send to South Korea ground and air crews, like those of the B-52 in Israel. The Israeli concept might have been based on the logic that ground and air crews have different tasks and risks, like in an infantry unit where some take care of logistic issues and others storm the enemy.

To sum it up, the United States and Israel could deal with common strategic challenges by helping each other.

The B-52 let alone the C-130J would have been at risk from Iranian antiaircraft fire, due to their relative vulnerability. As old as the Iranian air force is, its fighters could jeopardize the B-52 / C-130J. Therefore the B-52 / C-130J should have been heavily escorted by Israeli F-15 and F-16 to suppress Iranian air defense and intercept Iranian fighters. Electronic and cyber warfare would have assisted too in jamming and confusing Iran, for enough time to allow the B-52 / C-130 get in and out safely.

The IAF did not have to handle the entire Iranian air defense, only the Iranian forces that might have jeopardized Israeli planes, particularly the B-52 / C-130J. The IAF conducted hundreds of sorties against a strong air defense since 2012, inside Syria, without absorbing almost any loses. Only one time, on February 10, 2018, an Israeli F-16 was shot down. Israel and Syria gained combat experience in this prolong aerial camping. Syria and Iran are partners so they share information, including about Israel. Therefore both Israel and Iran could learn from the lessons of the fight in Syria, to be better prepared in case Israel strikes Iran.

The IDF, with or without the B-52, could have used long range surface to surface missiles to neutralize some Iranian targets, instead of sending Israeli planes to accomplish that task. This would have enabled the IAF to allocate more planes to other missions, and by that to drop more bombs on a certain target, which would have increased the chances of success. However, although Israel's surface to surface missiles could have attacked not only targets like air defense, but also nuclear sites, the well-protected facilities could only be destroyed by the B-52 and the MOP.

Saving Israeli Air Crews During a Raid on Iran

In 1990, before the war against Iraq, the latter might have attacked Israel. The IDF might have retaliated, which required coordination with the United States, since its forces were deployed in the Gulf. Israel's planes might have run into an American aircraft on their way to Iraq and the two parties might have opened fire on each other.[41] In recent years the United States opposed an Israeli strike on Iran, yet as in 1990 some coordination was needed if Israeli aircraft had struck Iran by flying over the Gulf, where

American aircraft were deployed. The United States and Israel also had to reach an understanding about saving Israeli air crews if they had to jump from their planes, after being hit by an Iranian missile, or because of other problems. In such a situation Israelis might have landed near American troops stationed around Iran.

The IAF had to improve the survival training of its air crews,[42] knowing full well that rescuing them when they were hundreds or more than a thousand km from Israel, would have been a tall order. Israeli helicopters might not have been able to reach all of them because of the distance. The IAF's transport helicopter with the longest range, about a 1000 km, is the CH-53. It could refuel in the air but Israel's tankers would have served many other aircraft as well, during the attack on Iran. Israel's transport aircraft, the C-130, has much more range than the CH-53 yet unlike a helicopter it could not land anywhere or hover over its destination, which could be crucial during a rescue.

During a raid on Iran, Israeli air crews abandoning their planes would have had to do it mostly over Iran, Iraq, Syria, Jordan, Gulf Arab states, and the Gulf itself. Israeli air crews would have avoided parachuting into Iran and also into its allies' countries: Iraq and Syria, where they might have been killed, in the worst case, or be turned over to Iran. In Syria both Assad's forces and the various armed groups and militias there, particularly Islamic extremists are enemies of Israel. It's possible that some groups would have considered exchanging captured Israeli air crews for weapons, money, etc. Israel proved in the past that it was willing to pay a lot to get back its captive troops. Israel's air crews' best chances in Syria and Iraq might have been with the Kurds, like those in north Iraq, due to ties between Israel and some of the Kurds. Yet, there would have been no guarantee of Kurds helping Israel, for fear of an Iranian retribution.

The United States was left with limited leverage in Iraq in recent years. The United States did not have much of a chance to help Israel, if the Iraqi government had taken Israeli air crews as prisoners. It is doubtful whether Iraq cared much about an American request to reach an unofficial deal with Israel about Israel's air crews. Maybe Israel's strongest argument in both Iraq and Syria would have been an Israeli threat to bomb targets there, and/or go after anyone involved in surrendering captured Israeli air crews to Iran, let alone killing them.

Compared with Iraq and Syria, Jordan would have probably been relatively less hostile to Israeli air crews, due to its prolonged cooperation with Israel in security affairs that go back several decades before their

1994 peace treaty. However, in spite of the Hashemite kingdom's worry about the Iranian nuclear project, Jordan would not have wished to be seen in any way as assisting Israel in a raid against Iran. Nevertheless, Jordan might have allowed the IAF to pick up its air crews from its territory, or turn them over to Israel if they fell into Jordanian hands. The United States might have helped in this matter, by relying on its ties and support of Jordan.

Israeli air crews might have jumped from their planes over Iran's Muslim neighbors in the north, east or south. In the north there are states like Turkmenistan, which has diplomatic relationships with both Israel and the United States, and Azerbaijan that has developed productive ties with Israel. Israel could perhaps have hope of bringing its air crews home safely, from those two Muslim countries.

Some Israeli air crews could be forced to bail out over the gulf, where they would have striven to parachute near United States' ship or base, such as in Bahrain or Qatar. The Israelis could be caught by Gulf Arab states. Some governments there share with Israel a mutual concern about Iran and the UAE and Bahrain normalized their relations with Israel on September 15, 2020. Yet those Arab states would have been worried about Iran's retribution for hiding Israeli air crews, or for allowing American forces to do that in bases on Arab soil. Therefore Israeli air crews would have had to leave those states immediately.

A more complicated and dangerous challenge for the United States would have been if Israeli air crews had landed a few kilometers away from an American ship or harbor in the Gulf. If the American unit there had spotted the Israelis, it might have sent a boat or a helicopter to save them, but the Iranians too might have been on their way to capture the helpless Israelis. The American dilemma would have been whether to go on with the rescue, risking a clash with the Iranians. Besides endangering American troops, such a skirmish might have escalated into a major crisis, which was against American interests. The United States had to decide in advance what its military should do under such sensitive circumstances. Much would depend on how clear the administration's orders would be. In case of ambiguity the US military would have interpreted them according to the views of its top brass, or that of the senior officer in the field. It could even be the decision of an officer in charge of a vessel, or a base close to where an Israeli air crew hit the water. This man could give an order, or pass on this hot potato to his superiors. Many factors might have impacted this officer's decision, his willing to take risks, his opinion about the IAF, Israel, perhaps Jews in general.

ISRAEL, THE UNITED STATES, AND GULF ARAB STATES, IN A WAR AGAINST IRAN

The United States put its troops in harm's way in order to protect Gulf Arab states through the war against Iraq in 1990–1991,[43] during which the United States deterred Iraq from dropping its CW on American forces or on their allies, including Arab ones.

By early 2021 US partners in the Middle East "had good reason to become more uncertain about the continuing level of U.S. commitment to strategic partnerships in the region."[44] If Gulf Arab states are under threat by a nuclear Iran they might consider relying on the United States, as states in Western Europe did in the Cold War. As long as Iran does not possess ICBM (intercontinental ballistic missile) that could reach the United States, the latter could hit Iran without facing much danger to its mainland. Iran might attack the Continental United States but mostly with cyber warfare and terror attacks. However, American forces in bases in the Middle East, mostly in the Gulf, are in danger of Iranian nuclear strikes, and while the United States accepted this risk in a possible fight for Christian Europe, during the Cold War, they might not necessarily have the same approach protecting Arab Muslims i.e., Gulf Arab states. Therefore Gulf Arab states must make a very serious effort to prevent Iran from having nuclear weapons to begin with.

If Iran wants to hit Israel, it has to rely on its protégés due to the distance between Iran and Israel, and the limited capability of Iran in striking that far. If the United States had attacked Iran, Israel would have probably not been asked to join its patron, particularly if the US offensive was based on a coalition with Gulf Arab states. As much as some Gulf Arab states are against Iran, collaborating openly with Israel is politically too problematic for them. For the United States keeping the Arabs in the anti-Iranian coalition would have been one of its main constraints during a fight against Iran. It would have been essential for the United States to prevent Arab departure from the coalition, mostly because of the need of Muslim countries from the Middle East in fighting another Muslim country from that region. There would have been also a military necessity, the naval and air bases in Arab countries, mostly those near Iran in the Gulf.

In a war between a coalition with Arab members and Iran, the latter might have tried to drag Israel into that confrontation by firing missiles at it, forcing Israel to strike Iran. Iran's aim would have been to present the alliance against it as an axis between Israel and Arabs, assuming the latter would have then been forced to abandon the coalition. Iraq did the same in the 1991 war[45] for similar reasons. In contrast to 1991 Israel might have absorbed rockets from the Hezbollah in Lebanon too. In response Israel might have avoided striking Iran, and would have attacked only Iran's Lebanese protégés, which is Arab, a fact that Iran would have exploited to put pressure on Arab states to leave the alliance against it. Arab states like those in the Gulf, would have opposed the bombing of Lebanon by Israel, but would have welcomed the destruction of the Hezbollah, which is their enemy, although it is Arab. When Israel clashed with the Hezbollah in 2006, Gulf Arab states hoped for its defeat. Therefore Israel might have targeted Hezbollah solely, avoiding bombing objectives that belong to the Lebanese state such as infrastructure. Israel has to be careful in this matter, in order not to disrupt its own plans. Israel can reach its goals by launching a limited strike.

Gulf Arab states as well as the United States would have claimed their fight against Iran and the clash between Israel and the Hezbollah are two separate wars, due to the giant distance between the fronts, one in the Gulf and the other in Lebanon. Although Iran would have supported the Hezbollah, the United States, let alone Arab states, would have emphasized that there is no coordination or mutual assistance between them and Israel. This argument would have required some political acrobatics, using a certain precedent. In the war of 1991, Iraq and the Palestinians were partners, the latter conducting their uprising against Israel. Iraq faced its foes on its own land and in Kuwait. The Palestinians in the West Bank and the Gaza Strip were several hundred kilometers west of Iraq and Kuwait. Seemingly, Iraq and the Palestinians were together, on two different fronts, against Israel and the United States. During the crisis and the war against Iraq in 1990–1991, the Palestinian uprising seemed like it was losing steam, although there were some deadly collisions between the two sides. In the 1991 war the PLO launched at one time a few rockets from south Lebanon to Israel.[46] It was a symbolic act of solidarity with Iraq. In a war with Iran, the Hezbollah might have started a second front against Israel by launching thousands of rockets. In response Israel should have attacked Hezbollah, while restraining itself from bombing Iran, in order to destroy any linkage between the Arab American coalition against

Iran and the war in Lebanon, even if Iran had fired its missiles on both Gulf Arab states and Israel, as Iraq did in 1991.

The United States would have focused on Iran, as it did with Iraq in 1991, allocating many sorties to suppress Iran's firing long range missiles at Israel. In 1991 the United States also sent Israel military aid, defensive one, since the aim was to help protect Israel but not encourage it to initiate offensive operations in Iraq. During a war against Iran and the Hezbollah, the United States would probably allow Israel to conduct a massive attack, against the Hezbollah in Lebanon, as air defense would not be sufficient to stop a barrage of thousands of rockets from Lebanon.

The development of Iranian missiles[47] causes concern in both Israel and Gulf Arab states. Iran could have fired its long range missiles at Israel while shooting its drones and short-range missiles at Gulf Arab states. Iran might have attacked Arab targets such as oil and natural gas infrastructure, as Iran already did in 2019. Gulf Arab states and the United States could have hit back against Iran's oil and natural gas sites, which are within reach from airfields in Gulf Arab states. The Iranian air force is not that powerful to begin with. Iran had upgraded its air defense by assimilating systems such as the S-300 but it might not be enough to stop a massive air attack. Arab and American planes could have inflicted heavy damages to Iranian oil and gas infrastructure. The exchange of punches might have caused enormous destruction of oil and/or gas industries in both Iran and Gulf Arab states.

CONCLUSION

During the prolonged struggle over Iran's nuclear program, the United States have preferred not to attack Iran. If Israel had bombed Iran, the United States might have supported it, or not. Israel might have attacked even without US backup and assistance. However, it might not have prevented an Iranian retribution against US forces in the region. Therefore Israel had to consider when to notify its American patron about the raid, in order to allow US troops to be ready to absorb a possible Iranian retribution.

Also the United States might have been asked by Israel to assist in rescuing Israeli air crews, who would have had to eject from their aircraft, and then landing near American forces in the Gulf. This might have caused a collision between Iranian and American units.

The United States could have given Israel the huge bunker buster bomb, the MOP, to crack the fortifications of Iranian nuclear sites. It would have also required delivering Israel the B-52 to carry that giant bomb. The IAF might have managed to drop the MOP even without the B-52. Providing Israel with the B-52 and at least the MOP would have deterred Iran from producing a nuclear weapon, because if Iran had tried to do that, Israel could have destroyed Iran's nuclear sites. This outcome would have served all those including the United States that seek to stop Iran from having nuclear weapons.

If the United States had collaborated with Gulf Arab states in an offensive against Iran, Israel would have probably been asked to stay out of it. Gulf Arab states might have had to leave the anti-Iranian coalition, not to seem fighting with Israel against Muslims. If subsequently the pro-Iranian Hezbollah had confronted Israel, Iran might have tried to connect that clash with the war against Iran, to create the impression that Israel fights Muslims, including Arabs i.e., Hezbollah. Gulf Arab states like Saudi Arabia oppose the Hezbollah, and they would have wanted Israel to destroy this Shiite group. However, the United States and its Arab allies might have tried to show they distinguish between their fight against Iran and the one between Israel and the Hezbollah.

NOTES

1. James L. Gelvin, *The New Middle East: What Everyone Needs to Know* (Oxford University Press, 2018), p. 17.
2. Abraham Ben Zvi, *The United States and Israel—The Limits of the Special Relationship* (Columbia University Press, 1993). Steven L. Spiegel, *The Other Arab—Israeli Conflict* (The University of Chicago, 1985). Robert Friedman, *Israel and the United States: Six Decades of US-Israeli Relations* (New York: Routledge, 2012).
3. Edward C. Keefer (general editor), *Arab—Israeli Crisis and War 1973* (Washington, Department of State, United States Government Printing Office, 2011). https://history.state.gov/historicaldocuments/frus1969-76v25.
4. Ephraim Inbar, *Yitzhak Rabin and Israel's National Security* (Washington: Wilson Center and Johns Hopkins University Press, 1999), p. 168.
5. Flynt leveret, *Inheriting Syria: Bashar's Trial by Fire* (The Brookings Institute, 2005), p. 6.

6. Lin Noueihed, *The Battle for the Arab Spring: Revolution, Counter-Revolution and the Making of a New Era* (Yale University Press, 2012), p. 17.
7. Michael Oren, *Ally* (New York: Random House, 2016), p. 88.
8. US Congress, (official site), February 28, 2013. https://www.congress.gov/bill/113th-congress/senate-resolution/65/text.
9. "Remarks by National Security Advisor Susan E. Rice at Palmachim Air Force Base," *The White House* (official site) May 9, 2014. http://www.whitehouse.gov/the-press-office/2014/05/09/remarks-national-security-advisor-susan-e-rice-palmachim-air-force-base.
10. Mose Ya'alon, "Current Iran Framework Will Make War More Likely", *The Washington Post*, April 8, 2015. http://www.washingtonpost.com/opinions/israels-defense-minister-the-risky-nuclear-framework-with-iran/2015/04/08/292a9cd2-de05-11e4-be40-566e2653afe5_story.html.
11. Al Monitor Staff, "Esper, Meeting with Gantz, Reaffirms Commitment to Israel's Regional Military Edge", *Al Monitor*, September 22, 2020. https://www.al-monitor.com/pulse/originals/2020/09/israel-us-pentagon-f35-uae-edge.html#ixzz6YycuKim4.
12. *Reuters*, April 11, 2021. https://www.reuters.com/article/us-usa-israel-austin/israel-pledges-to-work-with-u-s-on-iran-idUSKBN2BY05X.
13. Jeremy Sharp, "U.S. Foreign Aid to Israel", *The Congressional Research Service (CRS)*, June 10, 2015. http://www.fas.org/sgp/crs/mideast/RL33222.pdf.
14. Carol Marello and William Booth, "Israel, U.S. Sign Massive Military Aid Package, in Low-Key Ceremony at the State Department", *The Washington Post*, September 14, 2016. https://www.washingtonpost.com/world/national-security/israel-us-sign-massive-military-aid-package-in-low-key-ceremony-at-the-state-department/2016/09/14/23035db6-7abd-11e6-ac8e-cf8e0dd91dc7_story.html?postshare=8241473894193205&tid=ss_fb.
15. Arnon Gutfeld, "From 'Star Wars' to 'Iron Dome': US Support of Israel's Missile Defense Systems", *Middle Eastern Studies* (Vol. 53, No. 6, 2017), p. 944.
16. Eli Lake, "Some of Israel's Top Defenders Say It's Time to End U.S. Aid", *The Daily Beast*, July 18, 2014. http://www.thedailyb

east.com/articles/2014/07/18/some-of-israel-s-top-defenders-say-it-s-time-to-end-u-s-aid.html.

17. Yaakov Lapin, "Army Set to Start Joint 'Juniper Cobra 16' Drill", *The Jerusalem Post*, February 6, 2016. http://www.jpost.com/Israel-News/Army-set-to-start-joint-Jupiter-Cobra-16-drill-444062. Aron Donzis, "Israel and US Conduct Joint Missile Defense Drill", *The Times of Israel*, May 18, 2014. http://www.timesofisrael.com/israel-and-us-conduct-joint-missile-defense-drill/.
18. *Reuters*, March 4, 2019. https://www.reuters.com/article/us-usa-israel-military/u-s-says-deployed-thaad-missile-defense-system-to-israel-idUSKCN1QL1B8.
19. Judea Ari Gross, "Israel, US Launch Joint Juniper Falcon Air Defense Drill, Possibly for Last Time", *The Times of Israel*, February 4, 2021. https://www.timesofisrael.com/israel-us-launch-joint-juniper-falcon-air-defense-drill-possibly-for-last-time/.
20. Emanuel Fabian, "Israeli, US Air Forces Complete First-of-a-Kind Joint Drill in Southern Israel", *The Times of Israel*, August 10, 2021. https://www.timesofisrael.com/israeli-us-air-forces-complete-first-of-a-kind-joint-drill-in-southern-israel/.
21. Ibid.
22. Andrew Tilghman and Andrew deGrandpre, "Iran Linked to Deaths of 500 U.S. Troops in Iraq, Afghanistan", *Military Times*, July 14, 2015. http://www.militarytimes.com/story/military/capitol-hill/2015/07/14/iran-linked-to-deaths-of-500-us-troops-in-iraq-afghanistan/30131097/.
23. Ted Galen Carpenter, "What Would a U.S.-Iran War Look Like? One Word: Bloody", *Cato*, November 3, 2020. https://www.cato.org/commentary/what-would-us-iran-war-look-one-word-bloody.
24. Kori Schake, "The Disastrous Idea That Won't Go Away", *The Atlantic*, November 19, 2020. https://www.theatlantic.com/ideas/archive/2020/11/attacking-iran-would-be-disastrous-parting-move/617145/.
25. Gawdat Bahgat, "Iran and the United States: The Emerging Security Paradigm in the Middle East", *Parameters* (Summer 2007), p. 12. Yair Evron, "An Israel—Iran Balance of Nuclear Deterrence: Seeds of Instability", Ephraim Kam (ed.), Israel and a Nuclear Iran: Implications for Arms Control, Deterrence and Defense, INSS, (July 2008), p. 57.

26. Tom Burton, "Spy vs. Spy: Inside the Fraying U.S.-Israel Ties", *The Wall Street Journal*, October 22, 2015. http://www.wsj.com/article_email/spy-vs-spy-inside-the-fraying-u-s-israel-ties-1445562074-lMyQjAxMTI1MzI1NDcyNTQ0Wj.

27. On Kerry: Times of Israel staff, "Kerry: I Don't Believe Israel Would Hit Iran Without Consulting Us First", *The Times of Israel*, May 3, 2015. http://www.timesofisrael.com/kerry-i-dont-believe-israel-would-hit-iran-without-consulting-us-first/.

28. Yossi Melman and Dan Raviv, *Friends in Deed: Inside the U.S—Israel Alliance* (Jerusalem: Ma'ariv Book Guild, 1994), p. 178.

29. John Hannah, "Israel Needs Weapons to Stop Iran's Bomb", *Foreign Policy*, October 15, 2021.

30. Jean-Luc Renaudie, "Israeli Strike Threat Only a 'Diplomatic Card' Against Iran", *The Times of Israel*, November 23, 2014. http://www.timesofisrael.com/israeli-strike-threat-only-a-diplomatic-card-against-iran/.

31. Kenneth M. Pollack, *Unthinkable: Iran, the Bomb, and American Strategy* (NY: Simon & Schuster, 2013), p. 394.

32. Michael Herzog, "Israel Views Extension of Iran Talks as Lesser of Two Evils", *Al Monitor*, November 25, 2014. http://www.al-monitor.com/pulse/originals/2014/11/iran-nuclear-talks-agreement-israel-influence-attack.html.

33. Karl Vick and Aaron Klein, "Israel and U.S. to Hold Military Exercises When Iran Deal Ends", *Time*, November 27, 2013. http://world.time.com/2013/11/27/israel-and-u-s-to-hold-military-exercises-when-iran-deal-ends/.

34. Thomas Saether, "Bombing Iran: Tough Tasks for Israeli Intelligence", *The National Interest*, January 30, 2014. http://nationalinterest.org/commentary/bombing-iran-tough-tasks-israeli-intelligence-9789?page=1.

35. Yoav Limor, "'Israel Has the Ability to Completely Destroy Iran's Nuclear Program", *Israel Hayom*, March 30, 2021. https://www.israelhayom.com/2021/03/29/israel-has-the-ability-to-completely-destroy-irans-nuclear-program/.

36. Brendon Cole, "Israel 'Ready to Attack Iran' as Defense Minister Says 'We Need to Take Military Action'", *Newsweek*, August 5, 2021. https://www.newsweek.com/israel-iran-benny-gantz-nuclear-military-action-act-1616434.

37. Michael Crowley, "Plan B for Iran", *Politicio*, June 24, 2015. http://www.politico.com/magazine/story/2015/06/plan-b-for-iran-119344.html#.VYsxbOnbKpo.

38. On Congress see: (no Author) "US Senators Push to Sell Bunker-Busting Bombs to Israel", *Aljazeera*, October 29, 2020. https://www.aljazeera.com/news/2020/10/29/us-senators-to-introduce-bill-on-sale-of-bunker-bombs-to-israel.

39. Dennis Ross, "To Deter Iran, Give Israel a Big Bomb", *The Washington Institute for Near East Policy*, July 23, 2021. https://www.washingtoninstitute.org/policy-analysis/deter-iran-give-israel-big-bomb.

40. Israel Defence Forces—Air Force History Branch, From the War of Independence to Operation Kadesh (Tel Aviv: Ministry of Defence, 1990), pp. 257–258.

41. Moshe Arens, *Broken Covenant* (Israel: Yedioth Ahronoth, 1993), p. 177.

42. Yoaz Hendel, "Iran's Nukes and Israel's Dilemma", *Middle East Quarterly* (Winter 2012). http://www.meforum.org/3139/iran-nuclear-weapons-israel.

43. Barry Rubin, *The Tragedy of the Middle East* (University of Cambridge, 2002), p. 233.

44. Anthony H. Cordesman with the assistance of Grace Hwang, The Changing Security Dynamics of the MENA Region, Center for Strategic International Studies (CSIS), March 22, 2021. https://csis-website-prod.s3.amazonaws.com/s3fs-public/publication/210302_Cordesman_Military_Dynamics.pdf?aFbaUdiB0knUgNbAmZ_SEJOABTSDemZ7.

45. On 1991 see: Arens, *Broken Covenant*, pp. 162, 174.

46. Arens, *Broken Covenant*, pp. 171–174, 181, 213.

47. On Iran's Missiles see: Arms Control Association, March 2020. https://www.armscontrol.org/act/2020-03/news/iran-displays-new-solid-fuel-missile.

CHAPTER 10

Historical Perspective of the Iranian Challenge

Key security aspects of the Israeli perspective on Iran can be examined in several ways. Lessons can be drawn from the Cold War between the United States and the Soviet Union. There is also a resemblance between Israel's wars in 1956 and 1967 and a possible Israeli confrontation with Iran. One can also compare Iran to the Third Reich.

THE SIMILARITY BETWEEN IRAN AND THE SOVIET UNION

There is a certain resemblance between Iran and the Soviet Union. Similar to what the latter used to do, Iran too looks for traditional spheres of influence such as the Middle East. Iran strives to spread its version of Islam, as the Soviet Union did with its version of communism. Iran's desire is to expand and create a security belt around it, such as in Iraq, parallel to the Soviet Union using Eastern Europe as a forward defense area. This was a lesson Iran learned from the Iraqi invasion, and the long and costly war that followed it, in the 1980s. The Soviet Union had traumatic memory from the German invasion in 1941 and from its extremely brutal showdown in the 1940s. Furthermore, Iran and the Soviet Union, as Russia before it, had suffered other invasions in the past, which increased their fear of absorbing another massive penetration. Hence, the Iranian leadership, as that of the Soviet Union, might be quite paranoid, assuming the next threat is right around the corner, whether it is a real one or not.

Israel's nuclear weapons are its main military advantage over Iran, similar to the edge the United States had over the Soviet Union in the late 1940s. Iran, as the Soviet Union did, is striving to close this gap. The global Cold War between the United States and the Soviet Union, due to its length and scale, provides many valuable lessons. It could help to predict the nature of the Iranian-Israeli conflict, if Iran has nuclear weapons.[1]

Avner Golov and Uri Sadot assume that containment, as the one the United States implemented against the Soviet Union, would not succeed in the case of Israel and Iran. It might even increase the probability of war.[2] Mutual deterrence might work.

The huge and unprecedented cost both Israel and Iran would pay for annihilating each other would be unbearable, and risk the survival of both states. Iran is much bigger than Israel in its size, just as the Soviet Union was bigger than the United States. Yet Iran, like the Soviet Union, has similar drawbacks in a nuclear war, such as centers of population and industry that would be the main targets.

In a time of war, as the two superpowers planned to do during the Cold War, Iran and Israel would strive to destroy the other's nuclear weapons. They might use their nuclear weapons for that task, assuming it would crack nuclear silos. If their enemy's launcher was in open area, hitting near it could neutralize the launcher because of the blast. As to aircraft and ships, the relatively small number of airfields and few harbors Israel has would narrow down the number of targets Iran would have to hit in order to cripple Israel's capability to hit back with nuclear weapons. Such drawbacks might increase the chances of an Israeli first strike.

Israel, as the two sides did during the Cold War, developed second strike capability with its submarines that are supposed to obtain cruise missiles with nuclear warheads.[3] Lunching them would require solving several problems, such as overcoming the range to the targets in Iran. Robert Farley said this nuclear option is for Israel "an exceedingly tenuous bluff, more of a last, desperate gamble for revenge than a cold, calculating mechanism for destruction."[4] Furthermore Israel has six conventional submarines.[5] It could be estimated that Israel would have to have at least one submarine on high alert around the clock, in case of a sudden Iranian nuclear attack. The same would be with Israel's surface to surface missiles and aircraft that could deliver nuclear bombs. But in contrast to the

United States in the Cold War, Israel—and Iran for that matter—might not afford keeping similar readiness around the clock i.e., enough aircraft, submarines, and missiles, with nuclear weapons, ready to fire immediately at any time. The reason for this is that for every weapon system such as a submarine that would be on high alert, with nuclear weapons, there would be other submarines in training, maintenance, other missions, etc.

If Iran puts some of its nuclear weapons in Lebanon or Syria i.e., near the border with Israel, the latter would have almost no warning. Israel might not tolerate such a dangerous development, just as the United States did not accept a similar situation in Cuba in 1962. In addition, during the Cold War the Soviet Union might have launched ICBM from its mainland at the United States, which would have given the latter very short notice, to get ready to absorb a nuclear strike and to decide how to retaliate. Iran and Israel, which are much closer to each other than the two superpowers are, would have much less time in a similar scenario. Another option for both the Soviet Union and the United States was to penetrate with strategic bombers or to send submarines to sneak in and hit major targets. Iran and Israel, due to the relatively short distance between them, could use a fighter-bomber, long range attack plane, cruise missile, or a drone for that task. The smaller size of those weapon systems compared with a strategic bomber, would allow more flexibility in infiltrating secretly into enemy territory, with a nuclear cargo.

An Israeli fighter-bomber like F-15I and F-35 could refuel in the air on the way to Iran. The latter might dispatch its planes with enough fuel to reach their objective in Israel, without returning to Iran. The Iranian air crews might sacrifice themselves in a kind of nuclear kamikaze like attack, or drop their bombs and then parachute over a friendly territory nearby Israel, such as Lebanon. An air strike might be sudden so antiaircraft batteries and fighters on both sides must be all year long on high alert, ready to intercept an aircraft carrying a nuclear weapon. For Israel shooting down Iranian missiles that might have nuclear warheads would depend solely on its antimissile system, the Arrow. Iran has no antimissile system. The difficulties for both sides in stopping an aircraft and/or a missile with a nuclear cargo emphasize the crucial importance of deterrence, as it was in the Cold War. The lessons from that conflict could be very important, mostly in a crisis situation that might occur following an escalation. Learning from past experience would be essential, even if it would not be exactly the same case as in the Cold War.[6]

If there had been a conventional war between the United States and the Soviet Union, they would have had time for negotiations to end the battles, before escalating into exchange of punches with nuclear weapons. Yet such a conventional war might have also led to a nuclear showdown if western forces were not able to stop a Soviet land invasion deep into West Germany. Israel and Iran could not invade each other, and this removes a cause for use of nuclear weapons. At most, Iranian forces might openly join their partners in Lebanon and/or Syria in confronting the IDF. This would increase the tension between Israel and Iran, but probably not up to a level that might ignite a nuclear war.

The United States and the Soviet Union had diplomatic relationships and the Moscow–Washington hotline, which gave them direct communication, a crucial component in preventing miscalculations in a time of severe crisis. Israel and Iran don't have those ways to talk with each other. Israel and Iran might reach a third party that has ties with both of them like Russia, India, etc. It would be essential for Iran and Israel to agree in advance on such a broker, and not wait to look for one during a major crisis. Israel and Iran should have a strong trust in this mediator, considering the huge stakes. Still, conflicts of interests, misunderstandings, delays, etc. due to delivering messages through a third party, might cause a disaster neither side would want.

Before the 1991 war against Iraq, Israel was concerned about Iraqi long range missiles, while Iraq might have been worried about an Israeli attack. Moshe Arens, Israel's Defense Minister at the time, did not want hostilities to break out due to misunderstanding by one of the sides. He approached the French ambassador in Israel, since France had relatively good ties with Iraq, more than any other western state, and could serve as a broker between Israel and Iraq. France, however, avoided taking on this task.[7] In the case of Israel and Iran, a potential mediator might also refuse to play this role, fearing the complexity and the responsibility of such a commitment.

For the United States the Soviet Union was a very substantial threat since a barrage of hundreds of ICBM with nuclear warheads would have devastated the American mainland. If Iran launches a massive nuclear strike at Israel, the tiny state would suffer a similar fate. Recovering from such a catastrophe would have taken the United States many years, even decades, and the same could be said about Israel. The two neighbors of the United States, Mexico and particularly Canada, would probably assist the rebuilding of the United States, without exploiting its vulnerability by seizing lands, for example.

In contrast, Israel would face a serious threat if it is too weak and helpless, since some Arabs who are near Israel could exploit it. Ironically, not only Iran's allies among the Arabs, but also Arabs who oppose Iran might assume Iran had won and rush to join it. Either way, many Arabs might conclude they have a rare opportunity to force Israel to either make major concessions, or better still to capture vast parts of it, and even wipe it out completely.

Eventually, as it was with the Soviet Union, the Iranian regime might fall, because of internal reasons like a crippling economy. Both Iran and the Soviet Union had spent too much in areas such as assistance to other states and protégés. Israel and the United States could impose a highly expensive arms race, vis-a-vis Iran that might contribute to the collapse of the Iranian regime, as the United States did with the Soviet Union. Another tactic of weakening the Soviet Union—causing inner instability by exploiting tension between the rulers and its minorities—could also be used with Iran.

Ever since the late 1970s, Israel and the United States have been hoping for another revolution in Iran, which would overthrow the current regime. Iranians, during the unrest in the summer of 2009 and maybe also in 2019–2020, did not necessarily want to bring down the regime, just to reform it and mostly to improve the economic situation. In addition, some in Iran's leadership might seek to create an "Iranian Glasnost." Iranian people can ask for that, following their economic hardships and the failure of the current leadership to fix those problems. Yet the regime might refuse to change, fearing—perhaps justly—the same outcome as in the Soviet Union.

A new regime in Iran might not be an ally of Israel but it might not be a threat either, as it was with the post-Soviet Russia and the United States in the 1990s. A new regime in Iran might also be less stable and the economy would deteriorate, as it happened in Russia in the 1990s. Such a situation might increase the probability that—as with Russia—nuclear experts, knowledge and materials within Iran would find their way into the wrong hands. However, in 1991 the Cold War was over and with it the nightmare of a nuclear showdown. This might occur with Iran as well, which would remove the danger of a possible nuclear war in the Middle East.

In 853 BC there was a Battle of Qarqar, in the north—west of today's Syria. Ancient Israel and twelve other kingdoms, which often fought against each other, joined forces against Assyria, a growing power in the region that wished to spread out at their expense. This ad-hoc coalition managed to hold it back. NATO was established to confront the Soviet Union. Israel and some Arab states, with US support, might not be able to build a kind of NATO against Iran that seeks to gain hegemony in the region. Yet, they could create a Semitic alliance against Iran, for a specific and limited campaign. If no other means prevent Iran's striving for nuclear weapons, Israel and Gulf Arab states could turn to a military option.

The 1956 War and Israeli Exercises/Possibility of a Raid Against Iran

Nasser was a powerful leader, who controlled Egypt from 1954 to 1970. He sought to have a military that can match the IDF, in case of a war against Israel.[8] The 1956 war was Israel's first major challenge after the 1948–1949 war. Israel initiated the 1956 war as a preventive war, fearing the growing strength of Egypt. Israel, in the last decade, has deep concerns about Iran's growing power.

There is a certain linkage between the 1956 war and drills that the United States and Israel had conducted in the last decade. The American aim was to defend Israel's skies, as in the 1956 war, when two European powers, Britain and mostly France, assisted Israel to protect its rear from air bombardments. It was needed since the IAF struggled to do it by itself.[9] In 1956, Israel's enemy was Egypt while in the exercises in the last decade there was no official foe, but it was clear they were aimed against Iran and its proxies, such as the Hezbollah.

In 1956 the IAF was not well prepared to shoot down Egyptian bombers, due to shortage of weapon systems like fighters. In the last decade the IAF has been dealing with the challenge of intercepting rockets and missiles.

Western powers helped Israel in both 1956 and in the last decade. In the war of 1956 two French squadrons, with their ground crews, were dispatched to Israel, and French warships with antiaircraft guns were stationed near Israel's shores. In the last decade, during drills, United States' AEGIS, an antimissile ship together with antimissile batteries, were sent to Israel.

During the 1956 war Egyptian planes penetrated only twice into Israel, without causing any casualties or serious damages. In this sense the Israeli–French cooperation then, as far as defending Israel's skies, was actually like an exercise. In the last decade American–Israeli drills were suspected by some to be a cover for a raid on Iran, which did not happen.

There was a similarity between the 1956 war and a possible Israeli raid on Iran. In 1956 Israel attacked Egypt, aiming at slowing down Egypt's massive conventional build up, before it becomes a major danger to Israel. In recent decades Israel has been planning to attack Iran, if the latter tries to produce a nuclear weapon, which might be a mortal threat to Israel.

In the 1956 war, France and Britain destroyed Egypt's air force in its airfields.[10] The two western powers accomplished this offensive instead of the IAF, which had less capability and no such experience. Its troops had never carried out such an attack. In the last two decades Israel has hoped the United States attacks Iranian nuclear sites, since the American military force is much more powerful than the IAF.

In July 1956, the nationalization of the Suez Canal by Nasser was the main reason France and Britain attacked Egypt. If Iran had closed the Straits of Hormuz, a vital naval route in its area, Western powers and mostly the United States would have confronted Iran. In 1956 France and Britain had another goal: to topple Nasser's regime. The United States too might have aimed to bring down the enemy's regime during a war against Iran.

In the 1956 war, in spite of the cooperation between Israel and two European powers, the latter fought in the Suez Canal while Israel attacked on a separate front, in Sinai. The United States might have confronted Iran in the Gulf, while Israel fought on another front, against Iranian proxies, mostly the Hezbollah in Lebanon.

THE 1967 WAR AND AN ISRAELI ATTACK ON IRAN

In early 1960, about three Egyptian divisions were secretly sent to Sinai, surprised the IDF although they did not invade Israel.[11] The latter was quite lucky. A sudden and massive Egyptian offensive might have cost Israel dearly. If Iran has nuclear weapons it might try to launch a sudden nuclear attack. If Israel received no warning it would pay an enormous price.

In mid-May 1967, Egypt openly sent seven divisions into Sinai. They did not invade Israel, but Egypt's massive military presence in Sinai, and the blocking of the Tiran Straits—i.e., closing the naval route to the Israeli city of Eilat—later on, meant crossing red lines for Israel.[12] This led to an Israeli offensive. As to Iran, according to Kenneth Pollack, by 2013 Iran has crossed Israel's red lines six times, but the IDF did not attack.[13] It should be emphasized that until 1967 Israel accepted the presence of Egyptian forces in Sinai, as long as it was a minor one. It stands to reason that if Egypt had pulled back most of its troops from Sinai, and had removed the blockade on Eilat, in 1967, a war would have been avoided. Israel, for lack of better options, might eventually tolerate an Iranian nuclear program, if it is limited to such an extent that it does not pose a threat to Israel in the near future.

At the eve of the 1967 war, many in Israel felt their state is facing a possible national catastrophe, following declarations from several Arab states that called for the destruction of Israel.[14] Simultaneously there was an Arab military deployment around Israel, especially Egyptian forces in Sinai. In recent years, many in Israel have deep concerns due to announcements by Iranian leaders who threaten Israel. Iran also builds its nuclear capability, thus providing Iran the means of implementing its intentions.

There could be a debate whether Egypt and its Arab allies in 1967, or Iran during the last decades, meant what they said about their desire to do away with Israel. As to their capability to actually put Israel at risk, the 1967 war proved that Arab militaries were no match to the Israeli forces. Since its previous war with Israel in 1956, Egypt in 1967 had eleven years to get its troops ready for combat, but apparently it was not enough. Iran has been working for several decades on its nuclear program, and still does not produce a nuclear weapon. Nevertheless, as in 1967, Israel could assume it is better to be safe than sorry, which in Iran's case may mean attacking its nuclear infrastructure, if all other options fail.

In the three weeks before the 1967 war, Israel gave western powers, including the United States, an opportunity to resolve the crisis peacefully. The United States, which was then entangled in Vietnam, sought to prevent war in the Middle East that might have forced the superpower to intervene there as well. Yet, the diplomatic efforts reached a dead end. Although the United States warned Israel that if the latter strikes alone it would remain alone,[15] eventually the superpower backed Israel. In the last decade the United States and other powers negotiated with Iran. As in 1967, the United States was once again involved in a war in Asia, this time in Afghanistan, and once more opposed a confrontation in the Middle East that might drag it into it. The United States therefore tried to convince Israel not to take matters into its own hands. Israel might have concluded, as in 1967, that talks and in Iran's case even an agreement, don't bring the right results, and Israel's only option is to attack, even if American support comes later, or not at all.

In 1967 Israel focused on Arab militaries, although as with Iran's nuclear program, the problem for Israel was not only its rival's military capabilities, but its leadership as well. In 1967 Israel hoped an Egyptian defeat would shake and topple their leader Nasser, but this goal which was not realized. A successful Israeli attack on Iran would have probably also failed to bring down its dictatorial regime.

On June 5, 1967 Israel launched a massive air attack on Egyptian airfields.[16] Iran, like Egypt in 1967, had years to prepare for the absorption of an air offensive. Yet, as in 1967, Israel might have managed to gain a total surprise, since Iran's military could not have been on full alert all the time. Therefore it was possible to capture Iran off guard, as it was proven with Egypt in 1967.

The 1967 showdown was part of a prolonged conflict between Israel and the Arabs. The Israeli victory in 1967 did not end the conflict, only changed it and made it more complicated, because of the territories Israel captured.[17] The fight on Iran's nuclear project is part of the long struggle between Israel and Iran. The latter, as Egypt in 1967, is a regional power that strives to dominate the Middle East, or at least increase its influence as much as possible. Iran seeks to play the role of the "revolutionary patron," the one Egypt had in 1966.[18] Iran could have tried to achieve this goal the hard way, helping people in the region by gradually improving their economic conditions. Iran does give economic aid to its supporters, such as those in Lebanon. Yet, as Egypt in the 1960s, Iran invests a major effort in acts of subversion in Arab states, and in diverting Arab frustration toward Israel and Western powers, instead of taking care of the Arabs' real problems.

THE CERTAIN SIMILARITY BETWEEN IRAN AND THE THIRD REICH

Iran is not a new version of Nazi Germany—the Third Reich, but there is some resemblance between the two.

The Third Reich was controlled by a dictator, the Fuhrer. In Iran there is the supreme leader in this role. Within the Third Reich there were internal power struggles, sometimes that regime looked even chaotic.

In Iran there has been often a fierce power struggle inside the government. Yet, the loyalists of the rulers of both countries kept a firm hold over their people. The resistance movement inside the Third Reich failed to bring down the regime. Neither did the opposition in Iran. The best chances for an internal regime change in the Third Reich probably lay in the hands of the German military. Its top brass had to gather enough support from the troops while avoiding the watching eyes of those who followed and obeyed the regime, including its military units, which were well equipped. In Iran all those factors exist as well.

The Third Reich suppressed its people, monitoring, imprisoning, torturing and killing those who oppose it or were suspect of that. The Iranian regime does the same. The Third Reich also locked 50,000 gay men in concentration camps. They suffered terrible abuse and some died there.[19] The Iranian regime executed up to 6000 gays since the 1979 revolution.[20]

In late March 2015 former CIA Director James Woolsey claimed Iran strives to expand as the Third Reich did.[21] The Third Reich presented a clear and present danger to the world, particularly to European states, most of which came under its rule or influence. Iran also wishes to expand and exercise its authority, at least in the Middle East. Iran's ambitions are based on having—as the Third Reich—more than seventy million people, a vast territory, military strength, and strategic location, all of which makes them a regional power at the very least.

Bret Stephens claimed the nuclear agreement with Iran from late November 2013 had "many of the flaws" of the agreement with Germany in 1938.[22] In addition, the Third Reich prepared its military for war during the 1930s. This military was quite effective, particularly in the early years of the Second World War. Hitler's forces were conventional ones, nevertheless in terms of their effect, they could be classified as equal to weapons of mass destruction, since they killed millions and caused huge damages to numerous cities, towns, villages, etc. Iran's conventional military has not been a war machine as the German one in the early 1940s. Yet, if Iran produces weapons of mass destruction, a nuclear arsenal, Iran could rely on it to expand its influence across its region and/or to conduct massive deadly attacks like Germany did with its conventional forces.

Leaders of the Third Reich remembered Germany's former showdown—the First World War—as a long, costly and exhausting fight, they should avoid. Nevertheless, they found themselves in the thick of such a conflict in the Second World War. Iran had its extended and brutal show-down with Iraq in 1980–1988 that often looked like the First World War because of trench warfare, CW, vast artillery barrages, etc. This grim and possibly traumatic memory could cause Iran to avoid being entangled in another such difficult confrontation.

Before the Second World War the Third Reich spread to territories the Nazis considered should be under German rule, particularly areas populated with people whose ethnic origin was German. Iran strives to increase its influence in countries that had once been part of the ancient Persian Empire and/or presently populated by Shiites.

The Third Reich gained control over territories in the 1930s without clashing in the battlefield, since western powers were not determined enough to oppose the Germans, let alone by force. Iran has been increasing its grip in countries across the Middle East like in Syria, Iraq, Lebanon, and Yemen, while avoiding an official invasion. No western power has been willing to block Iran with military measures, if necessary.

The United States did not strive for a military confrontation with the Third Reich in the 1930s or with Iran in recent years. The physical distance between Iran and the United States, as it was between the latter and the Third Reich, gave the United States a sense of security. Yet Iran has been a growing challenge to American vital interests, just as the Third Reich was some eighty years ago. At that time, the Third Reich might have eventually confronted the United States' mainland, as Iran might do with cyber warfare, terror assaults and in the future maybe with ICBM carrying unconventional weapons.

The war in Afghanistan in 2001 started because of the surprise attack on 9/11 that year, which was compared to the strike on Pearl Harbor on December 7, 1941[23] that brought the United States into the Second World War. On both occasions, the United States was determined to destroy a driven and brutal foe, Japan in 1941 and Al-Qaeda in 2001, by transferring the fight into the enemy's territory. In 1941 the Third Reich and Japan, in spite of the differences between them, were two states that shared a radical fascist ideology and the same foe, Western states such as the United States. Iran and Al-Qaeda, with all the disputes between them, adhere to an extreme doctrine, and face the same enemy, Western states led by the United States.

One of the decisions of the NATO summit, from November 20, 2010 was to protect Europe from long range surface to surface missiles.[24]

Those kinds of missiles were first launched by the Third Reich from continental Europe in 1944–1945 to the North West, and toward Britain. NATO takes into consideration that similar missiles might be fired again, only from the Middle East to mainland Europe. As with the Third Reich, it could be a vengeance weapon of a retaliating Iran, following an attack on it. As long as those missiles, like the German ones from 1944 to 1945, are with conventional warheads, they would not pose an existential threat, but they could cause casualties and damages.

Iran as the Third Reich, in Connection to Israel

On December 3, 2017 the Israeli Prime Minister, Benjamin Netanyahu, compared Iran to the Third Reich because of Iran's hate to Jews.[25] US Vice President Mike Pence accused Iran on February 14, 2019 of being the "greatest threat to peace and security in the Middle East," claiming that Iran's regional goals can cause a "new Holocaust."[26] The "final solution" was the Nazi effort to exterminate the Jewish people. Iran's supreme leader Ayatollah Ali Khamenei referred in late May 2020 to the "final solution" in regard to Israel. Following the criticism about that Khamenei claimed that he did not call to kill Jews, only to destroy Israel.[27]

During the Second World War, the United States focused on the bigger picture, beating the Third Reich, and not on disturbing Nazi efforts to kill Jews. When victory was achieved, it stopped the suffering of tens of millions of people, including many Jews, but for six million Jews it came too late. In recent years Israel did not want the United States to conquer Iran like the allies did with Germany in 1945, which ended Nazi rule. Israel has been seeking to get rid of the Iranian regime, but the challenge has not been to force unconditional surrender on Iran, as with the Third Reich. Israel's problem is preventing Iran from producing nuclear weapons. The United States' overall goal may only be to contain and deter Iran if it ultimately gets nuclear weapons. The US strategy might defeat Iran, but it might not prevent Iran from throwing nuclear weapon on Israel. There might not be another Jewish Holocaust, but as with the Third Reich an American victory might be too late to avoid a heavy price Jews in Israel would have to pay.

If western states had insisted in the 1930s on enforcing restrictions on the German military, the Third Reich would not have become such a threat to the world, and particularly to the Jews. Most of the Jews who were killed in the Holocaust were in Poland and the Soviet Union, countries Nazi Germany could not have invaded without the military created after 1933. Iran without a military edge, a nuclear weapon, also could not put at risk Jews in its region i.e., the state of Israel. Yet, if Iran produces nuclear weapons, it would be more powerful than the Third Reich, a fact which requires stopping its nuclear program in time.

In late September 2013 the Iranian president, Hassan Rouhani, denounced the crimes the Nazis had committed against the Jews. Yet it was not clear if and how he actually referred to the Holocaust.[28] Its predecessor, Mahmoud Ahmadinejad, has over and over denied the Holocaust.[29] For many in Israel it was an amazing lie of Iran, same as claiming it does not seek a nuclear weapon, which could inflict on Israel a terrible disaster, and in the worst case cause another Holocaust.

There is a resemblance between the anti-Semitism of the Third Reich and that of Iran.[30] According to Jeffrey Herf, a Professor in the department of history at the University of Maryland, "we must remember that the Islamic Republic of Iran is the first government since Hitler's in which anti-Semitism constitutes a central element of its identity. An Iran with nuclear weapons would thus be the first government since Hitler's to be both willing and able to threaten a second Holocaust."[31] Now there are more than six million Jews in Israel, which brings to mind the same amount of Jews who were murdered by the Third Reich.

The Third Reich argued the Germans are an Aryan race and therefore superior to all other races. The word Iran comes from Aryan. Iran sees its people as being on a higher level compared with other populations and nations such as the Jews. Furthermore, the Third Reich was willing to absorb millions of casualties in the Second World War rather than give up power in order to end the war. Iran lost hundreds of thousands of its people in a war that had dragged on for eight years with Iraq, although Iran had opportunities to end the war before that. Regimes like those of the Third Reich and Iran, demanding such a high cost from their own people—considered by them to be superior to others—don't care much about the lives of others considered to be inferior.

German Jews accepted the rise of Hitler to power in 1933, thinking they could live with him in the same country. Israel was willing to tolerate the Iranian revolution in 1979, based on the assumption the two states could coexist together in the Middle East. The Third Reich demonized the Jews, described them as enemy of the state and acted against them. It served not only Nazi ideological goals, but political purposes as well such as gathering public support. Iran has been operating against Israel, presenting it as the devil, and as the enemy of the region. As the Third Reich did with the Jews, Iran has been going after Israel not only because of ideological belief, but also because of political reasons like promoting Iran's position in the Arab world. Iran has been pushing its people to believe it is their duty to fight Israel, like the Third Reich did against the Jews.

The Third Reich took away from Jews their basic rights as citizens. Iran opposes the national right of Jews to have Israel as their state. Iran talks about destroying Israel, not the Jews, but Israel is a Jewish state where Jews fight for their country, so an Iranian struggle against Israel is also against Jews. At first, the Third Reich wanted to drive out the Jews from the teritory it controlled. Iran seeks to throw Israel out of the Middle East, an area it wishes to control. Iran might allow Israeli Jews to stay, as obedient residents under an Arab pro-Iranian rule, but find it best to exile them from their country, which Iran sees as its land or at least a Muslim one.

The Third Reich concluded that ideologically it must wipe out the European Jews. For the Third Reich the best way to do that turned out to be by using gas. Iran too might decide that an unconventional weapon, nuclear in this case, is the most efficient method to solve its Israeli, i.e., Jewish problem.

Israel is a Jewish state, with various minorities, mostly Arab. Israel's Jewish government is aware of its historical responsibility not only with regard to its Jewish citizens, but toward all the Jews. Following the Holocaust, Israel is supposed to be a safe place for every Jew, a country the gates of which will never close to Jewish refugees. This means dealing with the Iranian threat.

Many Jewish people in Israel, are descendent of those who were killed, or survived the Holocaust. They hesitate between supporting a strike against Iran, and containing Iran. One of the arguments against attacking Iran maintains that an Iranian nuclear strike at Israel does not make sense because it might generate such a retribution that would devastate Iran completely. Before the 1940s, genocides such as the Holocaust were not considered possible, let alone in a civilized country like Germany. Yet, the latter committed this historical crime, as part of the war they had started, and for which they paid a huge price. Iran might not learn from this German experience.

Strategically, it was a terrible mistake by the Third Reich to force Jews out of Germany, because they could have helped the regime win the showdown Hitler had planned, but instead they contributed to his enemies' military machines. The Third Reich could have used the Jews during the war, and dealt with them after the victory. However, as a result of the deep hatred and twisted logic of Hitler's regime, they continued slaughtering Jews during the Second World War, although it was at the expense of the German war effort. The Iranian regime has a similar approach toward Israel. Iran could have enjoyed a vast cooperation with Israel, and only after profiting from it act against the Jewish state, instead of driving Israel against Iran to begin with.

Jews in mainland Europe in the era of the Second World War had ties with Britain and the United States, partly through the Jewish communities in those countries. However, this contact with rivals of the Third Reich did not save most of the European Jews. Israel has relations, some of them are quite tight, with states that oppose Iran such as the United States, although Israel's patron might not come in time to help it against Iran. Furthermore, the Third Reich massacred the Jews because they were defenseless, and Israel can protect itself. The IDF, mostly its nuclear weapons, could destroy Iran in a very short time.

Following the agreement about Iran's nuclear project on July 14, 2015 former Israeli Prime Minister Ehud Barak said that Israel is a powerful state and it is "not (helpless) Europe in the 1930s."[32] He implied that Iran is like the Third Reich but Israel could defend itself, unlike Europe i.e., states like France that were defeated by Nazi Germany in 1940.

The commander of the IAF in 2013 was Maj. Gen. Amir Eshel. On September 4, 2003 he was in one of the three Israeli F-15 aircraft flying over the Auschwitz-Birkenau extermination camp.[33] It was a symbolic act implying the IAF could bomb Iran's nuclear sites. The F-15 is an American plane like those that did not bomb extermination camps in the Second World War. At that time American Jews who served in bombers attacking inside the Third Reich were not sent to bomb extermination camps, although some of those Jews went over Auschwitz-Birkenau.[34] Israeli Jews, with all their constraints, including those concerning the United States, could bomb Iran's nuclear sites with their American aircraft.

Britain, while participating in the American project to develop the Bomb, launched assaults against facilities in occupied Norway, in order to disrupt the production of a German nuclear weapon. Israel, possessing nuclear weapons and striving to prevent Iran from obtaining them, could do it by attacking Iran's nuclear sites.

The Third Reich had chemical weapons, and so did its enemies, like Britain. The mutual deterrence kept this unconventional arsenal out of the fight. It might be the same with Israel and Iran, if the latter holds nuclear weapons.

Conclusion

If Iran produces a nuclear weapon, there will be key security aspects that resemble relations between the United States and the Soviet Union during the Cold War. Iran, as the Soviet Union was, is vulnerable since both countries have concentrations of population and infrastructure, which will be a major target. Israel also has been developing second strike capability, as the United States did, although Israel's capabilities are much more limited. The relatively short distance between Israel and Iran expose both of them to a surprise attack by aircraft or missiles, armed with a nuclear weapon, as Soviet and American submarines could have done. It shows the importance of deterrence.

A conventional war between Israel and Iran might buy time for talks, aiming at stopping a nuclear showdown, as it might have happened with the superpowers in the Cold War. However Israel and Iran don't have diplomatic ties, not even a hotline. Israel and Iran might accept the service of a broker such as a state that has relationships with both of them; Russia or India, but this might not work and in some cases make the situation worse.

In the 1956 war Israel needed Western military assistance, from France and Britain, to defend its cities from Egyptian bombers. In the last decade US forces trained with the IDF in protecting the Israeli rear from a possible missile attack, including from Iran. In addition in 1956 Israel launched a preventive war in order to disrupt the Egyptian military buildup. In the last two decades Israel might have conducted a raid aiming to slow down the Iranian nuclear program, before it produces a nuclear weapon.

In the early and mid-1960s Nasser was expected to lead the fight against Israel, based on the might of the Egyptian military. Iran with nuclear weapons, like Nasser with his conventional power, might not wish to confront Israel. In May 1967 Nasser was pushed to provoke

Israel by sending massive reinforcements to Sinai, a process that ended in his defeat. Iran would not want to repeat that mistake.

Iran would probably assume that some of those Arabs urging it to clash with Israel actually wish for both Iran and Israel to annihilate each other in a showdown. Therefore, as Nasser in the years before the 1967 war, Iran might claim it requires more time to be fully ready, which indeed might be true.

NOTES

1. John Gaddis, *We Now Know: Rethinking Cold War History* (Oxford University Press, 1997). Jonathan House, *A Military History of the Cold War, 1944–1962* (University of Oklahoma Press, 2012).
2. Avner Golov and Uri Sadot, "Why Israel Fears Containment of Nuclear Iran", *The National Interest*, May 21, 2014. http://nationalinterest.org/feature/why-israel-fears-contai nment-nuclear-iran-10507.
3. On Israel's second strike capability see: Gabe Fisher, "Israel's German-Built Submarines Are Equipped with Nuclear Weapons, Der Spiegel Reports", *The Times of Israel*, June 3, 2012. https:// www.timesofisrael.com/new-submarines-will-have-second-strike-nuclear-capability/. David Rodman, "'If I Am Not for Myself...' Methods and Motives Behind Israel's Quest for Military Self-Reliance", *The Israel Journal of Foreign Affairs* (Vol. 4, No. 1, 2010), p. 58.
4. Robert Farley, "Nukes on the High Seas: Israel's Underwater Atomic Arsenal", *The National Interest*, October 9, 2014. http://nationalinterest.org/feature/nukes-the-high-seas-isr aels-underwater-atomic-arsenal-11434.
5. On the Israeli navy see: Ehud Eiran, "The Israeli Navy in a Changing Security Environment", CIMSEC, September 16, 2020. https://cimsec.org/the-israeli-navy-in-a-changing-security-environment/.
6. Keith B. Payne, *The Great American Gamble: Deterrence Theory and Practice from the Cold War to the Twenty-First Century* (National Institute Press, 2008).
7. Moshe Arens, *Broken Covenant* (Israel: Yedioth Ahronoth, 1993), pp. 155–156.

8. Saïd K. Aburish, *Nasser—The Last Arab* (Thomas Dunne Books, 2004).

9. Israel Defence Forces—*Air Force History Branch, from the War of Independence to Operation Kadesh* (Tel Aviv: Ministry of Defence, 1990).

10. Neville Brown, *The Future of Air Power* (London: Croom Helm, 1986), p. 29. The Israel Defense Forces and Defense Establishment Archives (IDFA) 59/172/100.

11. Uri Bar-Joseph, "Rotem: The Forgotten Crisis on the Road to the 1967 War", *Journal of Contemporary History* (Vol. 31, No. 3, 1996), pp. 547–566.

12. On Israel's red lines in 1967 see: Micha Bar, *Red Lines in Israel's Deterrence Strategy* (Tel Aviv: Ministry of Defense, 1990), pp. 77–103.

13. On red lines about Iran see: Kenneth M. Pollack, *Unthinkable: Iran, the Bomb, and American Strategy* (New York: Simon & Schuster, 2013), p. 394.

14. Israel Defense Force Archive (IDFA) 77/717/86. Simeon Peres, *David's Sling* (Jerusalem: Weidenfeld and Nicolson, 1970), p. 201.

15. Michael Oren, *Six Days of War* (Tel Aviv: Dvir, 2004), pp. 177–186.

16. IDFA 83/1210/147.

17. Oren, *Six Days of War*.

18. On the role of "revolutionary patron" see: Barry Rubin, *The Truth About Syria* (New York: Palgrave Macmillan, 2007), p. 10.

19. On The Third Reich and Gay men see: United States holocaust memorial museum. https://www.ushmm.org/information/exhibitions/online-exhibitions/special-focus/nazi-persecution-of-homosexuals.

20. Benjamin Weinthal, "Iran Executes 'High Number' of Gays, Says German Intelligence", *The Jerusalem Post*, June 9, 2020. https://www.jpost.com/middle-east/iran-executes-high-number-of-gays-says-german-intelligence-630751..

21. Matthew Belvedere, "Iran Like a Modern Day Nazi Germany: Ex-CIA Chief", CNBC, March 30, 2015. https://www.cnbc.com/2015/03/30/iran-like-a-modern-day-nazi-germany-ex-cia-chief.html.

22. Bret Stephens, "Worse Than Munich", *The Wall Street Journal*, November 25, 2013. http://online.wsj.com/news/articles/SB1 0001424052702303281504579219931479934854.
23. Petula Deveroak, "Historians Fear Attack Date's Significance Could Fade", *The Washington Post*, September 10, 2015. http://www.washingtonpost.com/wp-dyn/content/article/2005/09/10/AR2005091001188.html.
24. "Lisbon Summit Declaration", NATO (official site), July 31, 2012. http://www.nato.int/cps/en/natolive/official_texts_68828.htm?mode=pressreleas.
25. Amir Tibon, "Netanyahu at Saban Forum: Iran, Like Nazi Germany, Has 'Ruthless Commitment to Murdering Jews'", *Haaretz*, December 3, 2017. https://www.haaretz.com/us-news/netanyahu-iran-like-nazi-germany-has-commitment-to-kill-jews-1.5627565.
26. Times of Israel staff, "Pence Urges EU to Pull Out of Nuclear Deal, Says Iran Planning 'New Holocaust'", *The Times of Israel*, February 14, 2019. https://www.timesofisrael.com/pence-urges-eu-to-pull-out-of-nuclear-deal-says-iran-planning-new-holocaust/.
27. Times of Israel staff, "Iran FM: 'Disgusting' for Israel to Object to 'Final Solution' Poster", *The Times of Israel*, May 21, 2020. https://www.timesofisrael.com/iran-fm-disgusting-for-israel-to-object-to-final-solution-poster/.
28. Reuters, September 25, 2013. http://www.reuters.com/article/2013/09/25/us-un-assembly-rouhani-holocaust-idUSBRE98O00H20130925.
29. "Mahmoud Ahmadinejad Refuses to Acknowledge Holocaust on 'Piers Morgan Tonight' (VIDEO)", *The Huffington Post*, September 25, 2012. http://www.huffingtonpost.com/2012/09/25/mahmoud-ahmadinejad-piers-morgan-interview_n_1911613.html.
30. Matthias Kuntzel, "Iranian Anti-Semitism: Stepchild of German National Socialism", *The Israel Journal of Foreign Affairs* (Vol. 4, No. 1, 2010), pp. 43–49.
31. Jeffrey Herf, "Taking Iran's Anti-Semitism Seriously", *The American Interest*, June 2, 2014. http://www.the-american-interest.com/articles/2014/06/02/taking-irans-anti-semitism-seriously/.

32. Daniel Bernstein, "Ehud Barak: Iran Likely to Go Nuclear Within Decade", *The Times of Israel*, July 14, 2015. http://www.timeso fisrael.com/barak-iran-likely-to-become-nuclear-within-decade/.
33. Ari Shavit, "Fighter Jets Over Auschwitz—IAF Commander Talks About a Mission That Shaped Israel's Future Decision", *Haaretz*, September 10, 2013. http://www.haaretz.com/weekend/mag azine/.premium-1.546270.
34. On those who went over Auschwitz—Birkenau see: (No Author) "Jewish WWII Veterans Remember Fight Against Nazis", *Chicago Tribune*, November 9, 2010. http://articles.chicagotribune.com/ 2010-11-09/news/ct-x-n-jewish-vets-20101109_1_auschwitz-ger man-war-machine-missions.

CHAPTER 11

Conclusion

This book examines several key national security aspects of the Israeli perspective on Iran and its proxies, mostly Iran's nuclear program and Hezbollah's missiles and rockets.

Iran opposes any peace between Israel and Arabs, since Iran seeks to destroy Israel while the latter wants to topple the Iranian regime. The balance of power such as in the size of population and natural resources clearly favors Iran, yet Israel has significant power, including military one. Furthermore Israel has nuclear weapons, while Iran does not. Iran strives to produce nuclear weapons, so it could both put pressure on Israel and have the option to annihilate its nemesis. Iran might be willing to pay a high price, including if many Arabs are harmed too during such a war.

Iran considers itself superior to Israel, and might have convinced itself it could do better than the Arabs, who failed to beat Israel. The latter and some Arab states, mostly those near Iran, are concerned about Iran's regional ambitions and its nuclear program.

Israel could have bombed Iran's nuclear sites, as the IAF did in Iraq in 1981 and in Syria in 2007, hoping to wipe out and at least to delay Iran's nuclear program as much as possible. Israel avoided such a move, due to its risks. Gulf Arab states prefer that Israel will strike Iran's nuclear sites before it is too late. Arabs might allow Israeli aircraft to fly over their territory in order to accomplish this mission, accepting there might be an Iranian retribution against them. If eventually Iran produces nuclear

E. Eilam, *Israeli Strategies in the Middle East*, https://doi.org/10.1007/978-3-030-95602-8_11

weapons there will be many negative ramifications for Israel and other states as well. Arab states such as Saudi Arabia might try to gain a nuclear weapon or at least to get a nuclear umbrella from the United States.

The Syrian civil war caused a rift between Hamas and Iran, after Hamas refused to fight for Assad, unlike another Iranian protégé, Hezbollah. The latter paid a heavy price in Syria and it also has to struggle to keep its domination in Lebanon. Assad managed to stay in power, but he lost much of his military strength and has been busy getting back control of Syria. He has not been able to contribute much in case of a war between Iran and Israel.

Israel does not seek another war with Hezbollah, due to its high cost. Hezbollah also does not want war right now, but if Israel strikes Iran the latter might order Hezbollah to confront Israel. It is not clear to what extent Hezbollah will obey. Hezbollah is a loyal Iranian protégée that fought for its interests not only in Lebanon, but in other Arab states as well, mostly in Syria. Nevertheless, Hezbollah has been well aware of the enormous price its home state and Shiite community will pay in a war with Israel. Hezbollah's combatants gained vast experience in Syria. However, there they enjoyed air support from both the Syrian and the Russian air forces, which will not assist them against the IDF. Hezbollah also absorbed heavy casualties in Syria; this deters the group from getting involved in a war with Israel that might be much more costly for Hezbollah than the Syrian war. The deep economic crisis in Lebanon is another important reason why Hezbollah might hesitate in confronting Israel, let alone in conducting a full scale war.

The IDF outnumbers Hezbollah, let alone in the number of weapon systems such as armored vehicles. However, Hezbollah is elusive and have an impressive arsenal of rockets and missiles that can hit almost every place in Israel. The IDF has highly advanced air defense, but it will not be enough to shoot down most of the missiles and rockets.

During a war against Hezbollah the IDF seeks to gain decisive and quick victory, relying mostly on air power. Yet, the IAF might not be able to do it by itself. Its air bases might also come under attack, because Hezbollah can hit them with its missiles. A large-scale ground offensive might be needed, penetrating deep into Lebanon. The IDF will not conquer land, due to the negative ramifications of such a strategy. The IDF will only stay inside Lebanon in order to destroy targets and then it will retreat.

The IDF's new multi-year plan, "Momentum" for 2020–2024 is supposed to make the IDF more lethal and effective. The plan is based on new units that combine troops from several corps and state of the art technology for finding and destroying targets. Yet, budget constraints and/or an outburst in the West Bank might cripple "Momentum."

The decline of the Syrian military, during the Syrian civil war, was a significant development in favor of Israel. After several decades of preparing to fight its strongest rival, Assad's forces, the latter had a melt-down, with no cost to Israel. The downside was that Iran exploited the Syrian civil war to deliver weapons to Hezbollah in Lebanon and to estab-lish a base in Syria, aimed against Israel. The IAF has been bombing inside Syria since 2012, in an effort to stop and at least to limit the Iranian pres-ence in Syria. Israel had some achievements, yet it needs an exit strategy in this matter.

The coordination mechanism between Israel and Russia has been working quite well, allowing Israel to bomb Iranian objectives inside Syria. However, in late September 2018 a crisis occurred between Russia and Israel, after a Russian reconnaissance plane was shot down by Syrian air defense, following an Israeli air attack in western Syria. Such an inci-dent might happen again and if it is not contained it might escalate. A collision between Israel and Russia would serve Iran that seeks to end the Russian–Israeli cooperation and to case a rift between Russia and Israel.

Russia and Iran fought their mutual enemies in Syria. In recent years, following Assad's victory, Russia does not need Iran that much. Further-more, Iran and Russia, which already have disputes in other matters, become rivals in Syria as well. Each one of them wants to call the shots in Syria. They both support Assad, but Iran's presence in Syria brings Israel to bomb there, which can undermine Assad. Israel can use it to mobilize Russia against Iran.

The Assad regime survived the Syrian civil war, but it remained too weak to provide substantial help to Iran against Israel. Iran might still try to attack Israel from Syria. In response Israel can inflict a major blow to Assad, which might undermine its rule. Russia would strongly oppose it, after all its effort to save Assad. Israel can use its ability to harm Assad as leverage, in order to convince Russia to help in reducing the Iranian presence in Syria.

Iran invested heavily in Syria, which was at the expense of taking care of the Iranian people. It causes frustration in Iran against the government. Israel seeks to get rid of the Iranian presence in Syria. However, in a way

Israel wants Iran to pour money into Syria, if eventually it undermines the Iranian regime. Toppling the Iranian regime would be a much better outcome than forcing Iran to leave Syria.

The United States and Iran have been foes since 1979. Iran supported insurgents who fight against the United States in both Iraq and Afghanistan. Both Israel and the United States are deeply concerned about Iran's nuclear ambitions. The United States could have inflicted a devastating blow to Iran's nuclear program. Both the Obama and the Trump administrations avoided taking a military action against Iran's nuclear sites. They preferred diplomacy and used sanctions to force Iran to negotiate. The Obama administration ended up with the JCPOA, which put some restraints on Iran's nuclear program, but limited ones both in their scale and their time period. The Trump administration focused on imposing heavy sanctions, which did not bring the required results.

The United States can deliver the IAF the suitable arsenal to crack the Iranian nuclear sites that are well fortified. The huge bunker buster bomb, the MOP, can do the job. The IAF can use also a heavy bomber, the B-52 to carry the MOP. If not maybe a C-130 can carry the MOP to the target, although it will face Iran's air defense, including the S-300, which will have to be suppressed. It will be a very dangerous task, but it will have to be done, due to the importance of the mission, preventing Iran from having a nuclear weapon. The IAF already took enormous risks in the past. Furthermore, Israel might not have to attack at all. Having the MOP and the B-52 will buy Israel time, even years, because it might deter Iran from producing a nuclear weapon. It would help the United States too, by allowing it to wait and not bombing Iran or allowing Israel to do that. Right now, if there are signs Iran gets too close to having a nuclear weapon, the Israeli government will be under enormous pressure to attack.

If Israel had attacked Iran, the United States might have been asked by Israel to assist in rescuing Israeli air crews, those who would have had to eject from their damaged aircraft. Some of them might have landed near American forces in Iraq or in the Gulf, which might have caused a fight between Iranian and American units, if there had been a race between them to get to the Israelis first.

There could have been a war between Iran and a US–Arab coalition. In such a case Iran might have tried to drag Israel into this war, in order to force the Arabs to leave the coalition.

Iran's protégé, Hezbollah in Lebanon, is situated near the northern border of Israel while the other, Assad, rules Syria that lies in the north east. Israel's American patron is present in proximity of Iran, but following retreats from its neighboring countries the American position diminished. Iran might have not completely trusted its protégés to be fully committed in a time of war against Israel, and the latter might have not relied too much on American support during a war against Iran. It depended among others on who would had started the war, and whether American objectives were targeted by Iran.

The United States and its allies such as Israel strive to contain Iran and to weaken it. Iran's economy is in bad shape, but it manages to function somehow. The Iranian regime also survived waves of civil unrest. Sill, ongoing and well-coordinated international effort, including economic one, might eventually bring down the Iranian regime. It has to be done before Iran produces nuclear weapons.

Iran, despite all the efforts to prevent it from producing nuclear weapons, might eventually reach its goal. In such a case, in a moment of truth, if Iran threatens or actually launches its nuclear missiles at Gulf Arab states, the United States might hesitate in using its nuclear weapons against Iran, in order not to jeopardize thousands of American troops who are deployed in the Gulf.

If Iran gets nuclear weapons, Israel will have to adjust to a new scary reality. It will not be easy. The conflict between them might have a certain resemble to the conflict between the United States and the Soviet Union during the Cold War. Iran is much bigger than Israel, but Iran's population centers and key infrastructure are vulnerable, as it was with the Soviet Union at the time. Israel and Iran will develop second strike capability, yet a much more limited one compared to the Cold War. Israel and/or Iran might be both striking and absorbing a nuclear attack at a very short notice. There are also major differences between the two conflicts such as lack of a hotline for direct communication between Israel and Iran. Using a broker will take time and it might cause misunderstanding that will end in a huge tragedy. Furthermore the United States had better chances to recover than Israel after a nuclear war. The Soviet Union could not have invaded American mainland. Iran could not invade Israel too, but Arabs might exploit Israel's low point to force it to make painful concessions and even to try to destroy it.

All in all, from Israel's perspective, it has to defeat and at least to contain Iran and its allies. Iran has a partnership with Russia, since they both help Assad. Yet, there are severe disagreements between Iran and Russia. Israel can use it against Iran. The Iranian–Israeli conflict involves other Arab states mostly those that are near Iran such as Saudi Arabia and the UAE. They can join forces with Israel, against Iran. If Israel attacks Iran's nuclear sites, Israeli planes might have to cross Gulf Arab states. In the last decade there were signs Israel and Gulf Arab states could agree to create an unofficial, limited, and temporary coalition against Iran. Yet, there are also signs the chances of such an alliance might be fading. It depends among others on how much US support they will receive.

Israel might fight Iran's most powerful protégé, Hezbollah that holds up to 150,000 missiles and rockets. However, Israel's biggest challenge is Iran's nuclear program. The United States could have assisted Israel in this matter, by providing it with the right arsenal, yet the Obama and the Trump administrations had other ideas how to handle Iran. The Biden administration will try to stop Iran from producing a nuclear weapon, by relying on diplomacy and sanctions. If this policy fails, and the United States decides not to take military action, then Israel might do that, even without US support. It will be done only as a last resort, if Iran tries to produce nuclear weapons.

Appendix: North Korea Compared with Iran and Hezbollah

There is a certain resemblance between North Korea and both Iran and Hezbollah.

Iran Compared with North Korea

There are differences but also some similarity between Iran and North Korea on the nuclear issue. Iran with a nuclear weapon would pose a danger at least to US allies and to American forces near Iran, as it has been with North Korea. The latter is kind of a model for Iran, since its nuclear capability might deter the United States from any direct attack on it. Since Iran does not possess a powerful conventional military its asymmetric warfare approach would not be sufficient to stop a possible US attack. It means that Iran might use or warn it might fire its nuclear weapon in the early stages of a war in which the Iranian regime would feel threatened.

Iran, as North Korea, sees that the process of producing a nuclear weapon comes with a substantial price, like isolation and a crippling economy due to sanctions. Yet, Iran might manage to do better. In comparison to North Korea, Iran has many advantages: vaster natural resources like oil, natural gas, vital strategic location, for example dominating part of a major and narrow international sea route, very experienced top leadership, and long history as an empire. Furthermore, Iran's

E. Eilam, *Israeli Strategies in the Middle East*, https://doi.org/10.1007/978-3-030-95602-8

territory and population are bigger than North Korea, and it has stronger international ties and carries more influence in its region than North Korea does in its part of the world. Nevertheless, just like North Korea, Iran is busy trying to stay on its feet.

Similarity Between Hezbollah and North Korea

There is a certain similarity between Hezbollah and North Korea, particularly if there was a war that would have involved one of them. There was already a war between Hezbollah and Israel, in 2006, and a war between North Korea and other states, including the United States, in 1950–1953. A second round, in each case, might have occurred.

North Korea is a state but quite a weak one, following its policy and its isolation. Hezbollah is a non-state actor, yet a powerful one and it is part of the government in Lebanon, where Hezbollah actually acts as it wishes. Furthermore the leaders of both North Korea and Hezbollah are very dominant in the decision making process that regard their people and they have gained influence and had worried their foes.

In both Lebanon and Korea a war might have started since any of sides there could have launched a preventive war/preemptive strike, particularly if it had suspected its rival is about to attack. The border between North Korea and South Korea and the border between Israel and Lebanon has been quiet, but the mutual tension there was clear. Each side closely monitored its foe, in an attempt to spot in advance any sign of aggressiveness let alone an upcoming offensive against it. Each side got ready for war while trying to deter its rivals by boosting its military buildup, and also by demonstrating its military might by publically showing its weapons and troops in exercises, war games, parades, etc. In spite of the preparations for war, both sides, in both cases, did not seek war but a war might have happened due to miscalculations, an incident on the border that would have deteriorated fast, etc.

The United States, together with other states, tried to contain North Korea, as an alternative to war. Yet this policy brought ongoing friction, sometimes even a crisis, with North Korea, which increased the chances of a confrontation. Israel strove to contain Hezbollah, including by force. Since 2012 Israel launched hundreds of air bombardments, aiming at destroying advanced weapons, before they had reached Hezbollah in Lebanon. This approach reduced Hezbollah's ability to hit Israel during a possible war. Yet each Israeli air raid raised the probability of an escalation that might have ignited a war, from which both sides wish to avoid.

China is in a way the patron of North Korea. Iran is the patron of Hezbollah. Both Hezbollah and North Korea might not be able to function for long without their patrons. China does not want North Korea to crumble, but China would have hesitated to join North Korea if the latter had confronted the United States. Iran would have probably remained out of a war between Hezbollah and Israel, as Iran did in 2006.

Sunni led Arab states like those in the Gulf, particularly Saudi Arabia; are against Hezbollah, since the latter is both pro-Iranian and Shi'ite. Those Arab states have disputes with Israel but they indirectly endorse Israel if the latter confronts Hezbollah. States near North Korea particularly Japan have deep concerns about North Korea. The neighbors of North Korea also have disagreements with the United States but they all oppose North Korea.

In late November 2017 the Trump administration returned North Korea to the list of state sponsors of terrorism. The United States, Israel and other states as well, including Arab ones, consider Hezbollah to be a terror organization. Although Hezbollah's Islamic ideology is far different from the dogma of North Korea, both of them are a destabilizing factor in their region, following their radical approach. Hezbollah, with Iranian support, carried out terror attacks across the Middle East. The group also helped other pro-Iranian groups that conducted such assaults as well. Those operations undermine states such as Yemen and Iraq.[1]

Hezbollah fought for keeping Assad in office. North Korea's nuclear capability is supposed to secure the regime there i.e., to guarantee that it will not be toppled by outside forces. The same could have happened if Assad had produced a nuclear arsenal, after building a nuclear reactor by cooperating with North Korea. With such an edge Assad would have become a much bigger threat to Israel. The latter therefore bombed that Syrian reactor in 2007.

Hezbollah/the North Korean military possess an impressive firepower, which is based on artillery and/or rockets that could have inflicted substantial casualties and heavy damages. This fire could have been suppressed, at least partly, due to the air superiority of their foes. Hezbollah/the North Korean military might also have conducted land attacks near the border such as infiltrating by tunnels or by exploiting the terrain. They might have been able to gain surprise and to capture some territory but not for long. Sooner or later their forces would have been annihilated or pushed back since the South Korean military, with the close support of the US military, is more powerful than their North Korean counterpart. The IDF has overwhelming superiority over Hezbollah.

Both Hezbollah and North Korea are aware that a full scale war might bring their downfall. Yet Hezbollah and the regime of North Korea had assumed that they can survive even a destructive war. Hezbollah was willing that Lebanon, including its population, will pay dearly during a war, and the same was with the regime of North Korea in regard to its country. The United States would have tried to limit collateral damage while seizing part and even all of North Korea. Israel too would have made an effort to minimize the civilian losses in Lebanon during the capturing of territory there. Furthermore the goal of such offensives, in both wars, would not have been to conquer land for a long period but to defeat the enemy, hopefully to get rid of it, and then to withdraw. In the bottom line North Korea and Hezbollah pose a major challenge to their rivals.

NOTE

1. Ashley Lane, "Iran's Islamist Proxies in the Middle East", *The Wilson Center*, May 20, 2021. https://www.wilsoncenter.org/article/irans-islamist-proxies.

Glossary

APC Armored personnel carrier
CW Chemical weapons
Gulf The Persian/Arab Gulf
IAEA International Atomic Energy Agency
IAF Israeli air force
ICBM intercontinental ballistic missile
IDF Israel defense forces
IED Improvised explosive device
IRGC Islamic Revolutionary Guard Corps
JCPOA The Joint Comprehensive Plan of Action
MOP Massive Ordnance Penetrator
NSA Non-State Actor
PA Palestinian authority
PIJ Palestinian Islamic Jihad
PLO Palestine liberation organization
UAE United Arab Emirates
UAV Unmanned air vehicle

BIBLIOGRAPHY

BOOKS

Ajami Fouad, *The Syrian Rebellion* (Stanford University Press, 2012).

Arens Moshe, *Broken Covenant* (Israel: Yedioth Ahronoth, 1993).

Aronson Shlaomo, *Nuclear Weapons in the Middle East* (Jerusalem: Akademon, 1995).

Bacevich Andrew, *America's War for the Greater Middle East: A Military History* (Random House, 2016).

Baconi Tareq, *Hamas Contained: The Rise and Pacification of Palestinian Resistance* (Stanford University Press, 2018).

Ben Gurion David, *Uniqueness and Destiny* (Tel Aviv: Ministry of Defense, 1972).

Ben Zvi Abraham, *The United States and Israel—The Limits of the Special Relationship* (Columbia University Press, 1993).

Brown Neville, *The Future of Air Power* (London: Croom Helm, 1986).

Claire Rodger, *Raid on the Sun: Inside Israel's Secret Campaign That Denied Saddam the Bomb Paperback* (New York: Crown, 2005).

Cohen Avner, *The Last Taboo* (Or Yehuda, Israel: Kinneret, Zmora—Bitan, Dvir, 2005).

Cordesman Anthony, *Weapons of Mass Destruction in the Middle East* (London: Brassey's, 1991).

Daher Joseph, *Hezbollah: The Political Economy of Lebanon's Party of God* (London: Pluto Press, 2016).

Dupuy N. Trevor, *Elusive Victory* (London: Macdonald and Jane's, 1978).

© The Editor(s) (if applicable) and The Author(s), under exclusive license to Springer Nature Switzerland AG 2022
E. Eilam, *Israeli Strategies in the Middle East*,
https://doi.org/10.1007/978-3-030-95602-8

El Gamasy Ghani Abdel Mohamed, *The October War* (The American University in Cairo, 1993).

Eyal Zisser, *Syria at War—The Rise and Fall of the Revolution in Syria* (Maarachot—The IDF's Publishing House and the Moshe Dayan Center for Middle Eastern and African Studies, Tel Aviv University, 2020).

Freilich Charles, *Israeli National Security* (Oxford University Press, 2018).

Gelvin L. James, *The New Middle East: What Everyone Needs to Know* (Oxford University Press, 2018).

Hamzeh Nizar Ahmad, *In the Path of Hezbollah* (Syracuse University Press, 2004).

Hendel Yoaz and Katz Yaakov, *Israel vs. Iran: The Shadow War* (Dulles: Virginia Potomac Books, 2012).

Howard M. Adam (general editor). *Arab-Israeli Dispute August 1978–December 1980* (Washington, DC: Department of State, United States Government Printing Office, 2014).

Howard Roger, *Iran in Crisis? Nuclear Ambitions and the American Response* (New York: Zed Books, 2004).

Hudson Michael, *Trying Again: Power-Sharing in Post-Civil War Lebanon* (Brill, 1997).

Inbar Ephraim, *Yitzhak Rabin and Israel's National Security* (Washington, DC: Wilson Center and Johns Hopkins University Press, 1999).

Kam Ephraim, *From Terror to Nuclear Bombs: The Significance of the Iranian Threat* (Tel Aviv: Ministry of Defense, 2004).

Karsh Efraim, *The Soviet Union and Syria: The Asad Years* (Chatham House Papers, 1988).

Kaye Dassa Dalia, Alireza Nader, Parisa Roshan, *Israel and Iran—A Dangerous Rivalry* (Santa Monica, CA: Rand, 2011).

Kober Avi, *Practical Soldiers—Israel's Military Thought and Its Formative Factors* (Boston: Brill, 2015).

Kroenig Matthew, *A Time to Attack* (New York: Palgrave Macmillan, 2014).

Limbert W. John, *Negotiating with Iran* (Washington, DC: United States Institute of Peace, 2009).

Ma'oz Moshe, *Syria and Israel: From War to Peace—Making* (Tel Aviv: Ma'ariv Books, 1996).

Marcus D. Raphael, *Israel's Long War with Hezbollah: Military Innovation and Adaptation Under Fire* (Georgetown University Press, 2018).

Mayzel Matitiahu, *The Golan Heights Campaign June 1967* (Tel Aviv: Ministry of Defense, 2001).

Melman Yossi and Javedanfar Meir, *A Hostile Partnership* (Tel Aviv: Yediot Aharonot, 1987).

Melman Yossi and Javedanfar Meir, *The Sphinx: Ahmadinejad and the Key for the Iranian Bomb* (Tel Aviv: Ma'ariv Book Guild, 2007).

Melman Yossi and Raviv Dan, *Friends in Deed: Inside the U.S–Israel Alliance* (Jerusalem: Ma'ariv Book Guild, 1994).

Noueihed Lin, *The Battle for the Arab Spring: Revolution, Counter-Revolution and the Making of a New Era* (Yale University Press, 2012).

Oren Michael, *Ally* (New York: Random House, 2016).

Parsi Trita, *Losing an Enemy* (Yale University Press, 2017).

Phillips Christopher, *The Battle for Syria: International Rivalry in the New Middle East* (Yale University Press, 2016).

Pollack M. Kenneth, *Unthinkable: Iran, the Bomb, and American Strategy* (New York: Simon & Schuster, 2013).

Porter D. Bruce, *The USSR in Third World Conflicts* (Cambridge University Press, 1984).

Poulsen Bo Niels and Staun Jørgen (eds.), *Russia's Military Might* (The Royal Danish Defence College, 2021).

Rabinovich Itamar, *The Lingering Conflict: Israel, The Arabs, and the Middle East* (Brookings, 2012).

Rabinovich Itamar and Carmit Valensi, *Syrian Requiem: The Civil War and Its Aftermath* (Princeton University Press, 2021).

Rodham David, *Combined Arms Warfare in Israeli Military History: From the War of Independence to Operation Protective Edge* (Sussex Academic Press, 2019).

Rubin Barry, *The Tragedy of the Middle East* (University of Cambridge, 2002).

Rubin Barry, *The Truth About Syria* (New York: Palgrave Macmillan, 2007).

Rundell David, *Vision or Mirage: Saudi Arabia at the Crossroads* (London: I.B. Tauris, 2020).

Safran Nadav, *Israel—The Embattled Ally* (Tel Aviv: Schocken, 1979).

Schiff Zeev and Ehud Ya'ari, *A War of Deception* (Tel Aviv: Schocken, 1984).

Seliktar Ofira and Farhad Rezaei, *Iran, Israel, and the United States: The Politics of Counter-Proliferation Intelligence Hardcover* (Lanham, MD: Lexington Books, 2018).

Shireen T. Hunter, *Iran's Foreign Policy in the Post-Soviet Era* (Santa Barbara, CA: ABC—CLIO, 2010).

Shlaim Avi, *The Iron Wall* (Tel Aviv: Ydiot Ahronot, 2005).

Solomon Jay, *The Iran Wars: Spy Games, Bank Battles, and the Secret Deals That Reshaped the Middle East* (New York: Random House, 2016).

Tal Israel, *National Security* (Tel Aviv: Dvir, 1996).

Yaniv Avnr, *Politics and Strategy in Israel* (Tel Aviv: Sifriat Poalim, 1994).

Yaniv Avnr, Maoz Moshe, and Kober Avi (eds.), *Syria and Israel's National Security* (Tel Aviv: Ministry of Defense, 1991).

Yariv Aharon, *Cautious Assessment* (Tel Aviv: Ministry of Defense, 1998).

Yigal Allon, *Curtain of Sand* (Tel Aviv: Hakibbutz Hameuchad, 1960).

Zak Moshe, *King Hussein Makes Peace* (Israel: Bar Ilan University Press, 1996).

POLICY ANALYSIS

Alrifai Oula, Nakissa Jahanbani, and Mehdi Khalaji, "Iran's Long Game in Syria", The Washington Institute for Near East Policy, March 25, 2021.

Ardemagni Eleonora, "The UAE's Military Training-Focused Foreign Policy", *Carnegie Endowment for International Peace*, October 22, 2020.

Blanford Nicholas and Orion Assaf. "Counting the Cost—Avoiding Another War Between Israel and Hezbollah", *The Atlantic Council*, May 13, 2020.

Brower S. Kenneth, "Israel Versus Anyone: A Military Net Assessment of the Middle East", The Begin-Sadat Center for Strategic Studies, August 2020.

Cordesman H. Anthony with the assistance of Hwang Grace, "The Changing Security Dynamics of the MENA Region", Center for Strategic International Studies (CSIS), March 22, 2021.

Grant Rumley and Neri Zilber, "A Military Assessment of the Israel-Hamas Conflict", The Washington Institute for Near East Policy, May 25, 2021.

Hendel Yoaz, "Iran's Nukes and Israel's Dilemma", *Middle East Quarterly* (Winter 2012), pp. 31–38.

Herzog Michael, "New IDF Strategy Goes Public", The Washington Institute for Near East Policy, August 28, 2015.

Holliday Joseph, "The Syrian Army Doctrinal Order of Battle", The Institute for the Study of War, February 15, 2013.

Kenneth M. Pollack, "Sizing Up Little Sparta: Understanding UAE Military Effectiveness," American Enterprise Institute, October 27, 2020.

Lappin Yaacov, "The IDF in the Shadow of the Pandemic", *The Begin-Sadat Center for Strategic Studies*, October 22, 2020.

Maher Nora, "Balancing Deterrence: Iran-Israel Relations in a Turbulent Middle East", *Review of Economics and Political Science*, March 2020.

McVann Christine, "How to Balance Competing Priorities with an F-35 Sale to the UAE", The Washington Institute for Near East Policy, September 23, 2020.

Nerguizian Aram, "The Struggle for the Levant: Geopolitical Battles and the Quest for Stability", Center for Strategic International Studies, September 18, 2014.

Rabinovich Itamar, "A Jewish State in an Arab World", Hoover Institute, May 13, 2014.

Samaan Jean-Loup, "Nonstate Actors and Anti-Access/Area Denial Strategies: The Coming Challenge" (US Army War College Press, June 2020).

Schenker David, "Getting Tough with Egypt Won't Work", *The Institute for Near East Policy*, March 25, 2021.

Witty M. David, "Egypt's Armed Forces Today: A Comparison with Israel", *MECRA*, September 26, 2020.

Zilber Neri, "Peace for Warplanes? How Domestic and Foreign Disputes Over the Potential Sale of F-35 Jets to the UAE Could Complicate the Country's Normalization Deal with Israel," The Washington Institute for Near East Policy, August 21, 2020.

ARTICLES

Ali a. Jalali, "Afghanistan in Transition," *Parameters* (Vol. 40, No. 3, 2010), pp. 17–31.

Bahgat Gawdat, "The Brewing War Between Iran and Israel: Strategic Implications", *Middle East Policy* (Vol. 25, No. 3, 2018), pp. 67–79.

Bar-Joseph Uri, "Israel's Northern Eyes and Shield: The Strategic Value of the Golan Heights Revisited", *The Journal of Strategic Studies* (Vol. 21, No. 3, September 1998), pp. 46–66.

Berglund Christopher and Souleimanov Aslam Emil, "What Is (Not) Asymmetric Conflict? From Conceptual Stretching to Conceptual Structuring", *Dynamics of Asymmetric Conflict* (Vol. 13, No. 1, 2020), pp. 87–98.

Blanga Yehuda, "Saudi Arabia's Motives in the Syrian Civil War", *Middle East Policy* (Winter 2017, No. 4), pp. 45–62.

Bowen Wyn, Knopf Jeffery, and Moran Matthew, "The Obama Administration and Syrian Chemical Weapons: Deterrence, Compellence, and the Limits of the 'Resolve Plus Bombs' Formula", *Security Studies* (Vol. 29, No. 5, 2020), pp. 797–831.

Christian Kaunert and Ori Wertman, "The Securitisation of Hybrid Warfare Through Practices Within the Iran-Israeli Conflict: Israel's Practices for Securitizing Hezbollah's Proxy War", *Security & Defence Quarterly* (Vol. 31, No. 4, 2020), pp. 99–114.

Giovanni Coletta, "Politicising Intelligence: What Went Wrong with the UK and US Assessments on Iraqi WMD in 2002", *Journal of Intelligence History* (Vol. 17, No. 1, 2018), pp. 65–78.

Goodarzi M. Jubin, "Syria and Iran: Alliance Cooperation in a Changing Regional Environment", *Middle East Studies* (Vol. 4, No. 2, 2013), pp. 31–59.

Gutfeld Arnon, "From 'Star Wars' to 'Iron Dome': US Support of Israel's Missile Defense Systems", *Middle Eastern Studies* (Vol. 53, No. 6, 2017), pp. 934–948.

Hanna Elias, "Lessons Learned from the Recent War in Lebanon", *Military Review* (Vol. 87, No. 5, 2007), pp. 82–89.

Hecht Eado, "War on the Northern Front", *Infinity Magazine*, (Vol. 6, No. 2, 2018), pp. 23–29.

Itamar Rabinovich, "A 'Track-in-Waiting': The Prospects of New Israeli–Syrian Negotiations", *The Israel Journal of Foreign Affairs* (Vol. 3, No. 3, 2009), pp. 7–13.

Javed Ali, "Chemical Weapons and the Iran–Iraq War: A Case Study in Noncompliance," *The Nonproliferation Review* (Vol. 8, No. 1, 2001), pp. 47–48.

Ketbi Ebtesam, "Contemporary Shifts in UAE Foreign Policy: From the Liberation of Kuwait to the Abraham Accords", *Israel Journal of Foreign Affairs* (Vol. 14, No. 3, 2020), pp. 391–398.

Kuntzel Matthias, "Iranian Anti-Semitism: Stepchild of German National Socialism", *The Israel Journal of Foreign Affairs* (Vol. 4, No. 1, 2010), pp. 43–49.

Litvak Meir, "Iran and Israel—The Roots of Iran's Ideological Hate Toward Israel", *The Ben Gurion University, Iyunim Bitkumat Israel: Studies in Zionism,—The Yishuv and the State of Israel* (Vol. 14, 2004), pp. 367–392.

Olmert Joseph, "Israel and Alawite Syria: The Odd Couple of the Middle East?", *Israel Journal of Foreign Affairs* (Vol. 7, No. 1, January 2013), pp. 17–25.

Pollack Joshua, "Tracing Syria's Nuclear Ambitions", *The Journal of International Security Studies* (Vol. 19, Fall/winter, 2010), pp. 1–14.

Primor Avi, "'No Permanent Allies, No Permanent Enemies, Only Permanent Interests': Israeli–Iranian Relations", *Israel Journal of Foreign Affairs* (Vol. 8, No. 1, January 2014), pp. 33–38.

Salamey Imad, "Failing Consociationalism in Lebanon and Integrative Options", *International Journal of Peace Studies* (Vol. 14, No. 2, 2009), pp. 83–105.

INDEX

A

Afghanistan, 5, 6, 109, 138, 139, 153, 171, 172, 176, 196, 199, 212
al Assad, Bashar, 35, 98, 99, 117, 138
Alawite, 98, 129
al-Jubeir, Adel, 34
Al-Qaida, 105, 156, 157
al-Sisi, Abd al-Fatah, 48

B

The Bab al–Mendab Straits, 101, 102
Bahrain, 33, 37, 38, 43, 45, 149, 180
Beirut, 81, 133
Bennett, Naftali, 18, 19, 48, 111, 150
B-52, 6, 176–178, 184, 212
Biden administration, 40, 51, 132, 137, 149, 150, 156, 157, 176, 214
Blinken, Antony, 149, 150
Britain, 8, 144, 146, 177, 194, 195, 200, 203, 204

C

China, 51, 101, 132, 137, 141, 148, 155–157, 217
the Cold War, 7, 8, 14, 15, 60, 115, 126, 130, 132, 169, 181, 189–191, 193, 204, 213
C–130J, 176, 178
Covid–19, 85, 86, 100

E

Egypt, 1, 3, 8, 9, 12, 16–18, 21, 25, 34, 36–38, 41, 42, 48–53, 62, 101, 103, 104, 107, 115, 125, 126, 130, 154, 155, 177, 194–197, 204

F

Fatah, 61, 66
First World War, 9, 198, 199
F-35, 3, 20, 33, 39–42, 52, 86, 110, 128, 174, 175, 191
France, 8, 146, 148, 177, 192, 194, 195, 203, 204

G

Gantz, Benny, 19, 176
Gaza Strip, 3, 16, 38, 50, 59–62,
    67–72, 83, 88, 102, 106, 157,
    172, 175, 182
Germany, 144, 146, 148, 192, 197,
    198, 200–203
Golan Heights, 20, 85, 89, 98,
    103–105, 107, 109, 113,
    115–118
Gulf Arab states, 1–3, 33–35, 39,
    43–46, 52, 148, 149, 169,
    179–184, 194, 213, 214

H

Hamas, 1, 3, 14, 24, 41, 43, 50, 51,
    59–62, 66–72, 79, 83–85, 88,
    90, 102, 105, 106, 157, 210
Haniyeh, Ismail, 61, 62
Herzog, Michael, 176
Hezbollah, 1, 3–5, 7, 14, 20, 24, 35,
    36, 41, 45, 46, 51, 59–63, 65,
    66, 72, 79–91, 97–100,
    102–109, 111, 113, 115–118,
    127, 132, 133, 139, 144, 154,
    157, 169, 172, 174, 182–184,
    194, 195, 209–211, 213, 214,
    216–218
Holocaust, 10, 200–202
Houthis, 101
Hussein, Saddam, 21, 24, 43, 138,
    153, 154

I

IAF (Israeli air force), 4, 6, 19–21,
    40, 41, 44–47, 70, 71, 81,
    85–88, 102, 106, 109–112,
    127–129, 133, 172, 174,
    176–181, 184, 194, 195, 203,
    209–212

IDF (Israel Defense Forces), 3, 4, 8,
    14–16, 19, 20, 25, 33, 41, 43,
    45, 51, 60, 67–70, 72, 79–91,
    98, 104–112, 115–117, 126,
    132, 133, 149, 171, 174–178,
    192, 194–196, 203, 204, 210,
    211, 218
Iran's nuclear program, 18, 19, 21,
    33, 130, 132, 139, 140, 143,
    150, 155, 170, 176, 183, 197,
    209, 212, 214
Iraq, 2, 3, 5, 6, 9, 15–21, 23, 26, 34,
    41, 43, 45–48, 51, 52, 88, 99,
    100, 104, 106, 108, 111, 112,
    114, 118, 138, 139, 141, 144,
    146–148, 153, 154, 157,
    171–175, 177–179, 181–183,
    189, 192, 199, 201, 209, 212,
    217
IRGC (Islamic Revolutionary Guard
    Corps), 12, 14, 100, 109, 112,
    116, 132, 145
Iron Dome, 70, 80, 90, 171
ISIS, 3, 35, 45, 47, 49–51, 105, 130,
    156, 157

J

JCPOA (The Joint Comprehensive
    Plan of Action), 18, 140,
    143–146, 149, 212
Jordan, 3, 7, 16, 18, 34, 37, 38, 41,
    42, 46, 47, 52, 104, 138, 154,
    155, 171, 179, 180

K

Kalman, Tal, 16, 71, 176
Kerry, John, 173
Khamenei, Ali, 12, 13, 66, 144, 145,
    151, 200
Kohavi, Aviv, 19, 70, 111, 149
Kroenig, Matthew, 18, 138

Kurds, 3, 15, 45, 46, 179

L
Lapid, Yair, 19, 150
Lebanon, 3, 4, 8, 16, 36, 43, 44, 46,
    60, 61, 63, 65, 66, 80–83,
    85–91, 97, 98, 100, 102, 104,
    106, 108, 110, 113, 114, 117,
    118, 120, 126, 131–133, 138,
    139, 151, 154, 157, 172, 174,
    175, 182, 183, 191, 192, 195,
    197, 199, 210, 211, 213, 216,
    218
Libya, 43, 50, 51

M
Mattis, Jim, 144
MB, 50, 51, 62, 98
McKenzie, Kenneth, 65, 147, 150
Mediterranean, 52, 90, 100, 101,
    114, 118, 131, 155
"Momentum" plan, 4, 84, 85, 211
MOP (Massive Ordnance Penetrator),
    6, 176, 178, 184, 212

N
Nasser, Gamal Abdel, 12, 16, 154,
    194, 195, 197, 204, 205
NATO, 194, 199, 200
natural gas fields, 183
Netanyahu, Benjamin, 19, 108, 116,
    141, 149, 200
1956 war, 8, 25, 83, 177, 189, 194,
    195, 204
1967 war, 9, 12, 37, 49, 83, 104,
    125, 126, 189, 195–197, 205
1973 war, 12, 16, 17, 22, 45, 49,
    104, 115, 126, 169
North Korea, 141, 148, 215–218

NSAs (Non-State Actors), 3, 4, 33,
    51, 68, 79, 83, 84, 98, 102, 105

O
Obama administration, 6, 51,
    140–142, 144, 151, 173, 212

P
Pakistan, 35, 141, 153, 156
Palestinians, 13, 14, 22, 24, 38, 39,
    42, 43, 47, 59, 66–72, 85, 88,
    104, 114, 138, 139, 144, 172,
    182
PA (Palestinian authority), 3, 39, 59,
    61, 66–68, 70–72
Persi, Trita, 138
PIJ (Palestinian Islamic Jihad), 67,
    69–72, 138
PLO (Palestine liberation
    organization), 43, 66, 98, 138,
    139, 154, 182
Pompeo, Mike, 145

R
Raisi, Ebrahim, 13
Rouhani, Hassan, 38, 146, 201
Russia, 5, 8, 40, 51, 59, 63, 90, 99,
    106, 110, 117, 125–134, 142,
    148, 153, 155, 157, 189, 192,
    193, 204, 210, 211, 213, 214

S
Salman, Mohammed bin, 34
Saudi Arabia, 2, 7, 15, 33–37, 39–43,
    45, 49–52, 66, 130, 146, 184,
    210, 214, 217
Second World War, 9, 177, 198–201,
    203
Sherman, Wendy, 142

Shiite, 7, 24, 33, 37, 43, 59, 63, 79, 89, 100, 105, 109, 132, 153, 184, 199, 210

Sinai, 9, 48–50, 177, 195, 196, 205

Soleimani, Qasem, 62, 146, 147

the Soviet Union, 7, 8, 48, 104, 125–127, 130, 133, 138, 141, 151, 189–194, 201, 204, 213

S-300, 128, 130, 142, 143, 146, 183, 212

the Strait of Hormuz, 139, 140, 145

Sunni, 24, 33, 35, 37, 59, 61, 62, 69, 71, 98, 99, 101, 105, 132, 155, 156, 217

Syria, 2–6, 15–22, 24, 26, 33–37, 39, 41, 44, 46, 48, 52, 59–63, 71, 72, 86, 89, 90, 97–119, 125–134, 139, 141, 147, 148, 151, 154, 157, 169, 171, 172, 178, 179, 191, 192, 194, 199, 209–211, 213, 217

T

Taliban, 138, 153, 156

Third Reich, 9, 189, 197–204

Trump administration, 6, 33, 39, 40, 130, 137, 144–148, 212, 214, 217

Turkey, 15, 38, 39, 46, 127, 138, 154

U

UAE (United Arab Emirates), 2, 3, 33, 34, 36–45, 50, 52, 127, 149, 155, 180, 214

the United States, 1, 5–8, 14, 35, 36, 39–41, 43, 51–53, 63, 65, 67, 72, 80, 100, 103, 108, 117, 127, 128, 130–132, 134, 137–153, 155–157, 169–184, 189–196, 199, 200, 203, 204, 210, 212–218

W

the West Bank, 3, 21, 39, 43, 59, 61, 67, 68, 71, 72, 85, 88, 182, 211

Y

Yemen, 33, 49, 101, 112, 114, 154, 199, 217

Z

Zarif, Mohammad Javad, 13, 111, 142, 143

Zimmt, Raz, 13, 18

CPSIA information can be obtained
at www.ICGtesting.com
Printed in the USA
LVHW080847120522
718581LV00004B/201

9 783030 956011